MOSCOW AND THE POLISH CRISIS

Also of Interest

Poland Between the Superpowers: Security vs. Economic Recovery, Arthur R. Rachwald

Poland: Socialist State, Rebellious Nation, Ray Taras

†*The USSR: The Politics of Oligarchy*, Second Edition, Fully Revised and Updated, edited by Darrell P. Hammer

The Soviet Union and the Gulf in the 1980s, Carol R. Saivetz

†*The Soviet State: The Domestic Roots of Soviet Foreign Policy*, edited by Sir Curtis Keeble

†*Soviet-Third World Relations*, Carol R. Saivetz and Sylvia Woodby

Soviet Politics in the 1980s, edited by Helmut Sonnenfeldt

Economic Relations with the Soviet Union: American and West German Perspectives, edited by Angela E. Stent

Economics and Politics in the USSR: Problems of Interdependence, edited by Hans-Hermann Höhmann, Alec Nove, and Heinrich Vogel

†Available in hardcover and paperback.

About the Book and Author

During the Polish crisis of 1980–1981, the Western world was uncertain of the Soviet response to turmoil in Poland, and speculation about an invasion was rife. The timing of the Polish declaration of martial law came "without forewarning to the United States," according to then Secretary of State Alexander M. Haig, Jr. In retrospect, Dr. Ploss points out that it is clear the Soviet press was the best source of clues to Kremlin thinking regarding Poland. Dr. Ploss uses propaganda analysis to trace the Kremlin's policy decisions and its internal leadership debates during the crisis. The published anxieties of officials in the USSR's western borderlands were especially indicative of Soviet elite fears of political contagion from Poland, but this material had to be interpreted in the context of such basic influences as Soviet Russian history, communist doctrine, and current Moscow politics. The final warning of the imminent crackdown in Poland came when the Soviet media began to replay their 1968 pattern of action preparation for stifling democratic reforms in Czechoslovakia.

Dr. Ploss has traced extensively Soviet dynastic anomalies and propaganda fluctuations over the course of the Polish crisis. He draws on the memoirs of the U.S. president and his national security adviser to illustrate the focus of official U.S. concern in December 1980 and questions the accuracy and realistic balance of the intelligence assessment those memoirs reveal.

Sidney I. Ploss is a senior Soviet analyst at the U.S. State Department. His books include *Conflict and Decision-Making in Soviet Russia* and *The Soviet Political Process: Aims, Methods, and Examples of Analysis*. He has taught at Princeton, Harvard, Pennsylvania, and George Washington universities.

For Kaya

MOSCOW AND THE POLISH CRISIS

An Interpretation of Soviet Policies and Intentions

Sidney I. Ploss

Westview Press / Boulder and London

Westview Special Studies on the Soviet Union and Eastern Europe

This Westview softcover edition was manufactured on our own premises using equipment and methods that allow us to keep even specialized books in stock. It is printed on acid-free paper and bound in softcovers that carry the highest rating of the National Association of State Textbook Administrators, in consultation with the Association of American Publishers and the Book Manufacturers' Institute.

Published in 1986 in the United States of America by Westview Press, Inc.; Frederick A. Praeger, Publisher; 5500 Central Avenue, Boulder, Colorado 80301

Library of Congress Cataloging-in-Publication Data
Ploss, Sidney I.
  Moscow and the Polish crisis.
  (Westview special studies on the Soviet Union and
Eastern Europe)
  Includes bibliographical references and index.
  1. Poland—Foreign relations—Soviet Union. 2. Soviet
Union—Foreign relations—Poland. 3. Poland—History—
1980–   . I. Title. II. Series.
DK4185.S65P55 1986   327.438047   85-31504
ISBN 0-8133-0351-6

Composition for this book was provided by the author.
This book was produced without formal editing by the publisher.

Printed and bound in the United States of America

The paper used in this publication meets the minimum requirements of the American National Standard for Permanence of Paper for Printed Library Materials Z39.48-1984.

6   5   4   3   2   1

Contents

Acknowledgments

I thank Paul Costolanski and Werner Hahn for their assistance in the preparation of this work. I also thank Carl Linden, who kindly read these pages and commented upon them. The views expressed do not necessarily reflect the positions or policies of my employer, the U.S. Department of State.

Sidney I. Ploss

Why does the government not want to give up Poland? Because it realizes that when Poland is free Russia will be free, and that means that the government itself will be ruined. . . . It believes that, by crushing the Polish movement, it will make any movement of the kind in Russia quite impossible.

—Alexander Herzen, 1863

Introduction

The intelligence picture is never entirely clear. Any set of political or military circumstances is complex and largely unpredictable. Even after the event it is often difficult to determine the relative importance of factors that helped to shape a development. That has been true of elections, revolutions and battles throughout modern history.

Nevertheless, policymakers have an insatiable desire for information about foreign governments that are real or potential adversaries. Capabilities and calculations of an opposing elite are intelligence questions of special interest. The same is true of conflicts and rivalries within a competing power center; it is desirable to know how far the other side can be pressed in a diplomatic encounter.

Human assets and technical means of collecting data are invaluable tools for reckoning the military might of another state. But classical intelligence collection techniques sometimes cannot supply answers to questions about the opposition's estimates and intentions, as well as internal debates.

The problem was outlined concisely when Kremlin leader Yuri Andropov died and Soviet experts at the Central Intelligence Agency had to assess the latest developments in Moscow. C.I.A. officials recalled for an inquiring journalist the remark of their onetime Director Richard Helms to the effect that the Soviet leadership is "the toughest target of all" for American intelligence agencies. The reporter's story continued:

> The deliberations inside the Kremlin cannot be photographed by American satellites. Nor can the conversations and politicking in the Politburo be monitored by electronic eavesdropping equipment, intelligence officials say. . . . The C.I.A. depends on information gathered by agents and collected from sources both inside the Soviet Union and abroad. "It's old-fashioned

1

intelligence," one C.I.A. official said. "The Kremlin is one place where we can't depend on high technology to penetrate the target."[1]

Alexander L. George reviewed the performance of U.S. analysts of Nazi propaganda during the Second World War and suggested the utility of their technique as a means of making inferences about policy-relevant questions.[2] The examples of successful prediction of major Nazi actions included a limited German offensive against the Soviet Union in 1943, contrary to the Allied intelligence estimate of an attack on a "monstrous scale."[3] George emphasized that propaganda analysis is not a fool-proof intelligence method; deception and subtlety in communications can throw off the unwary analyst. But he was able to establish from historical materials on the Nazi conduct of the war that propaganda analysis is capable of more than isolated successes in trying to gauge an elite's private expectations.

The inquiry of George led him to define some of the procedures that analysts followed in making inferences. Any attempt to summarize here the modes of reasoning would be oversimplified in view of the complexities. Suffice it to say that the method of inferences was of a logic-of-the-situation variety: in the realm of prediction, for example, it was assumed that a decision maker must choose between a few alternative courses of action, and even if his final choice is kept secret, he is likely to influence the media to manage the news so that in time the public will react properly to announcement of the selected course of action; by listing the decisionmaker's probable alternatives and comparing the pertinent media content with each of the possible courses of action, the analyst would make a supposition about policy intent behind the media message. The essentials of this method of inferences have been helpful to Soviet policy analysts because of the similarity between propaganda structure and practice in Nazi Germany and the USSR. In the cases of both regimes, one sees a usual coordination of propaganda and policy, with the propaganda strategy shaped by elite aims.

A prerequisite for the unity of policy and propaganda is the existence of a national director of propaganda who has access to inside information about what is really going on. Dr. Goebbels held that post in the Nazi hierarchy while in Moscow, propaganda is usually controlled by a joint member of the Communist Party's ruling Politburo and Secretariat, or executive board. The main office for drafting propaganda directives under Goebbels was the Propaganda Ministry; in the Kremlin scheme of things it is the Secretariat's Propaganda Department, which is headed by a "chief." A Soviet monograph describes as follows the intimacy of political leaders and media experts:

Prior to each important development, whether it be a new stage in the organizing of Socialist Competition, a scheduled report-back-and-election campaign in Party organizations, discussion of one or another Party decision, preparation for a congress of anniversary, as well as before the solving of important current-day matters, *CPSU [Communist Party of the Soviet Union] Central Committee secretaries and other key Party officials regularly meet with the leaders of central newspapers, journals, publishing houses, television and radio stations, and information agencies. They discuss the urgent political and economic problems and give practical advice and instructions.* This is done without interfering into the minutia of the daily work of editorial boards and other journalistic work forces.[4]

Without getting ahead of the story, one might ask: What could be the nature of the directives that senior Party executives tender to the media specialists? The main function of Soviet opinion-makers, it is clear from educational texts, is to build confidence in the Politburo among officials and the public. So it is safe to assume that Soviet audiences must be supplied with data and commentary serving to justify policy decisions that are extant or imminent. Any information that might tend to undermine faith in the collective wisdom of the Politburo should be suppressed. Otherwise, an impression of high-level shortsightedness might be created, and the exacting of respect for authority could be hampered. The media leaders, accordingly, must be briefed on the latest thinking about important matters at the top.

In spite of the claim that Soviet leaders do not meddle into the day-to-day affairs of propagandists, that is known to have happened. The wartime editor of the Soviet military organ *Red Star* has recalled that in October 1941 Stalin telephoned him and directed that a photograph of Zhukov, commander of the western front, be run in the next day's issue. According to D.I. Ortenberg, the editor, that graphic was unusual insofar as *Red Star* had till then carried photos of unit commanders only. The purpose of Stalin's order was to remind the readers of *Red Star* that forces defending Moscow were headed by someone on whom the people and army could depend.[5] In post-Stalin Russia a continuing bond of Party and media heads can be seen from the removal of the chiefs of *Pravda*, *Izvestiya* and the State Radio Committee just after Khrushchev's ouster in 1964 or the appointment of new chief executives in the CPSU Propaganda Department, *Izvestiya* and *Sovetskaya Rossiya* after the rise of Andropov in 1982. (The Stalin example, it may be added, had a Nazi parallel: The Goebbels diary informs that Hitler personally gave orders to play up the execution of captured American airmen in Japan, making it the big spread for the Good Friday editions of German newspapers.[6])

The transfer value of Nazi propaganda analysis for the Sovietologist is maximized by the tendency of both elites to use the media to prepare the domestic audience for their intended major actions. Hitler projected his own intentions onto the British preceding the invasion of Norway. Stalin had earlier tried to give moral justification for his impending military attack on Finland, charging that shots from Finnish territory had struck a Soviet border unit. After Stalin, Soviet preparatory propaganda included the halting of internal press criticism of nuclear weapons tests in the atmosphere by France in the months prior to a resumption of such tests by the USSR (1961). The Kremlin evidently believed that Soviet audiences who got exercised over French nuclear testing would do the same if their own rulers were to follow suit.

Like the analyst of Nazi propaganda, the student of Soviet media texts can safely assume that his research materials have usually been crafted with much care, and even minor shifts in content must be taken seriously. Soviet Communists expect as much when receiving political messages in Party circles. Thus, a Moscow journalist writes from the provinces:

"Valentin Yakovlevich Pristupa went from the post of senior agronomist of the district agricultural directorate to work as chairman of the 'Friendship' collective farm and *quickly* was able to bring the average-level farm to the level of advanced ones not only in the district but in the region as well." This phrase rang out especially clearly in the report of the first secretary of the Kovelskiy city committee of the Party, V.V. Kryvtsun, speaking at a plenary meeting that was discussing the tasks of the Party organization in light of fulfillment of the Food Program. What was striking was not that someone had gone from administrative to production work (one often hears about this nowadays), but that the new chairman was able *quickly* to bring an average-level farm up to the level of an advanced one. I twice underlined this short word in my notebook because having visited many and diverse farms, learning about their development, I knew well that such a thing cannot be done at once; it takes years and years, sometimes decades. *Was it possible that the short, little word had accidentally fallen from the tongue of the rapporteur? But the subject of the speech was so critical that one had to think that each phrase, each word was regulated and weighed.*[7]

The Soviet analyst, therefore, must take for granted the purposeful and precise formulation of most propaganda texts that he examines.

One category of inferences which George did not elaborate had to do with the possibility of squabbles within the Nazi elite. But he did mention Goebbels' occasional use of his propaganda machine to champion personal policy views, including resort to pressure tactics against Hitler himself, and cited implicit speculation about a behind-the-scenes dispute between military and civilian leaders regarding the proper military strategy for Germany.[8] On the Soviet scene too, factional struggle over power and policy has given rise to tell-tale signs in the media. The devices utilized to discredit rivals and their opinions have ranged from editorial selectivity in the handling of official statements to criticism of proxies at home and abroad. This offshoot of propaganda analysis, sometimes called Kremlinology, has proven to offer more insights into Soviet political life than is often thought to be the case.[9]

The present report is an effort to employ propaganda analysis for the purpose of reconstructing the Soviet leadership's hidden policy objectives in the Polish crisis of 1980-81. During that period, history repeated itself to the extent that great uncertainty surrounded the question of how the Soviet elite would respond to a quest for genuine democracy in a neighboring Communist state. Would the Soviets risk a military invasion? President Johnson's memoir informs that as late as August 19, 1968, or one day before the Soviet assault on Czechoslovakia, the President and his national-security advisers "debated whether the Russians would move," especially in view of a planned Washington-Moscow summit, and "Opinions were divided."[10]

Speculation about a Soviet invasion of Poland was rife in December 1980. At least three schools of thought were assertive as the Soviet military was maneuvering around the Polish borders. One opinion was that Kremlin leaders were probably bluffing and with the help of the Catholic Church, then seeking compromise inside Poland, the crisis would probably pass.[11] A second view was that the Soviet Politburo had decided at its regular Thursday meeting on November 27, in principle, to intervene in Poland, leaving the date to be determined later, and the danger period for invasion was the time around Christmas, or when the Soviets had invaded Afghanistan in the previous year.[12] A third commentator ventured that it was a 50:50 proposition if the Soviet Army would overrun Poland, with events inside that country being the decisive factor.[13]

Soviet tanks did not roll, but another invasion scare erupted in April 1981 as the result of new military activities by the Kremlin. The fear of a Soviet move lingered till the special congress of the Polish Communist Party in July. One body of opinion as exemplified by the remarks of a British scholar was that there was "a 51 percent chance" that the Soviets would not invade while another was reflected in a colleague's assertion that invasion was "inevitable."[14] In the United States, few accurately forecasted that the Warsaw regime would impose martial law.[15]

Most important, an intelligence failure occurred in Washington. Alexander M. Haig, Jr., was then Secretary of State and in an account of his tenure notes that hours before the Polish martial law declaration he had "no foreknowledge of events" that soon broke in Poland. Haig elaborates on the Polish crackdown: "The timing of this action, which obviously had been meticulously prepared—and which we knew had been planned in minute detail in the USSR—came *without forewarning* to the United States. For a period of many days, Poland had been covered by thick cloud, so the movement of troops and militia and the other signs that might have been observed by space satellites were undetected."[16]

An unknown factor rarely considered was the possibility of dissension within Soviet leadership. U.S. sources later told the press that a razor-thin decision not to invade Poland was reportedly taken in Moscow in early December 1980. The Politburo vote, allegedly, was 6 to 6 until Brezhnev broke the tie with a rejection of the motion for direct intervention.[17] Was this story merely fabricated in Moscow for the purpose of unnerving indecisive Polish leaders?

Definitive answers to such questions are unlikely to be given until the Kremlin archives are opened to independent scholars. In the meantime, it may be fruitful to look back at the Polish crisis and, with the vision of hindsight, seek to improve the methods of analysis which might help to give warning of Soviet actions. If the technique is only slightly refined it could mean the difference between high- and low-grade assessment in another regional or global crisis involving the Soviet Union.

NOTES

1. "C.I.A. Seeks to Read Moscow Auguries." By Philip Taubman. *New York Times*, Feb. 13, 1984.

2. Alexander George, *Propaganda Analysis. A Study of Inferences Made from Nazi Propaganda in World War II.* (Row, Peterson and Company, Evanston, Illinois, 1959).

3. *Ibid.*, pp. 155–161.

4. Valentin Ye. Yevseyev, *Partiynoye vozdeystviye pressy. Voprosy istorii i metodologii pechati kak sredstva ideynogo i organizatsionnogo ukrepleniya KPSS* (Moscow, 1980), p. 170. Emphasis supplied.

5. *Sovetskaya Rossiya*, Oct. 20, 1981.

6. George, *op. cit.*, p. 164.

7. *Selskaya Zhizn*, Sep. 28, 1982. Emphasis supplied.

8. George *op cit.*, pp. 68–72 and 158.

9. Discussion of this topic may be found in *The Soviet Political Process. Aims, Techniques and Examples of Analysis.* Edited, with introductions by Sidney I. Ploss. (Ginn and Company, Waltham, Massachusetts, 1971). A recent application with some predictive value is my article "Soviet Succession: Signs of Struggle," *Problems of Communism* (Washington, D.C.), Sept.-Oct. 1982, pp. 41–52.

10. Lyndon Baines Johnson, *The Vantage Point. Perspectives of the Presidency 1963–1969.* (Holt, Rinehart and Winston, New York, 1971), p. 487.

11. James Reston in the *New York Times*, Dec. 3, 1980.

12. Victor Zorza in the *Washington Post*, Dec. 5, 1980.

13. Seweryn Bialer on WNET TV's "MacNeil-Lehrer Report," Dec. 3, 1980.

14. "Kremlin's maneuvering on Poland backfires." By Elizabeth Pond. *The Christian Science Monitor*, June 16, 1981. Polish expert Anthony Polonski was cited on "a 51 percent chance" and Soviet specialist Peter Reddaway on the "inevitable" invasion.

15. George F. Will did so in the *Washington Post*, Sep. 24, 1981 although he added that, "There will be disorder, followed by some sort of Soviet intervention."

16. Alexander M. Haig, Jr., *Caveat: Realism, Reagan, and Foreign Policy.* (Macmillan, New York, 1984), pp. 246–247. Emphasis supplied.

17. *Los Angeles Times*, Apr. 4, 1981. Robert Toth, who related this account, indicated that it may have reached the United States via Western Communists who attended the Soviet Party Congress in February 1981.

ONE

"A Fist . . . Is . . . Senseless"

(AUG.–SEPT., 1980)

Dreaming has long mingled with realism in the political forecasting of national leaders, including those of Soviet Russia. As early as 1918 Lenin mused that a revolutionary explosion was imminent in Germany and would serve to annul the harsh peace terms of Berlin which he had assented to in order to get the new Soviet state out of World War I and to consolidate Bolshevik power at home. Germany's defeat by the Allied powers a few months later helped to save Lenin's prestige, but even so there was no internal upheaval at the center of the European world. A little more than twenty years later, Stalin agreed to a non-aggression pact offered to him by Hitler, avowedly to gain space and time for bolstering the military strength of the Soviet regime. But the wily Georgian overrated the capacity of the French army to fight a mutually exhaustive struggle with the Germans in Western Europe after Hitler had struck at France's client, Poland. And in 1962, Khrushchev no less calmly sent missiles to Cuba in hope of redressing the balance of strategic power with the United States and maybe too as a diplomatic bargaining counter. He too misjudged the real state of affairs in the outer world.

A similar lack of prescience can be found in Soviet reflections on the cohesiveness of Moscow-allied regimes in eastern Europe at the height of the Brezhnev era. Spokesmen of the Soviet governing class repeatedly professed confidence in the stability of those regimes, even though not required to do so in the circumstances. A USSR deputy defense minister in 1978 relegated to oblivion the idea of social protest movements bursting out as they once did in East Germany (1953), Hungary (1956) and Czechoslovakia (1968). Army Gen. Ivan Pavlovskiy, commander-in-chief of ground forces, remarked that, "Relying on the aid of our troops, the socialist peoples and governments have foiled *once and for all* the schemes of the counterrevolutionary coups organizers."[1] A Soviet political theorist in 1979 would not go so far as to exclude a future challenge to political authority in countries of the Eastern bloc. But he made it appear to be a fairly remote possibility, and one that could be dealt with handily:

> A counterrevolutionary situation is not a product of historical necessity. On the contrary, it is a rare occurrence that is usually due to mistakes and lack of vision in politics. It is less and less probable the further a country has progressed along the path of socialist development. And it is overcome by socialist forces in a relatively easy and dependable manner. The sooner a correct policy line is formulated and is implemented energetically, and the masses brought into action (their basic interests are safeguarded only by a consistently socialist policy), the system of unfavorable factors is eliminated (the system which created the crisis situation), and there remain just certain unfavorable factors which do not threaten the very existence of the socialist state.[2]

The "masses" of Poland were about to be "brought into action" against their political guardians in accordance with an improvised plan that not even the most farsighted student of communism could have envisaged.

As of 1980, Poland was the most important alliance partner of the USSR in terms of the size of its population, gross national product, and regular military forces. The country had 35.7 million people; a GNP estimated at $146.1 billion; and regular military forces numbering 317,500 (185,000 conscripts).[3] Even so, Poland was dwarfed by the Soviet colossus: the USSR's population was about seven and a half times larger and its military ranks over ten times more numerous; the Soviet Union's territory could contain over 50 countries the size of Poland; and its resources far excelled those of its immediate neighbor to the west.[4]

Nevertheless, Poland's geographical location and natural wealth made it strategically and economically important for the Soviet Union. An extension of the north German plain, the land was a corridor through which Germany had invaded Russia during the First and Second World Wars. Since then, Poland's railway system was a vital cog in the Soviet military-industrial machine stretching from Asia to middle Europe. That rail line was a main artery for the flow of manpower and supplies to the 20 or so Soviet Army divisions in East Germany, and it was used to ship sizable amounts of coal, sulphur and copper from Poland to Soviet firms.

What John King Fairbank has said of the Chinese and Russian peoples after 1949 was equally true of Poles and Russians after World War II: "Behind the facade of communist rhetoric, history provided few bonds of mutual admiration or successful cooperation." In fact, antipathy of the deepest sort had existed between Russia and Poland for centuries. The antagonism was fueled by rival territorial claims and the competing dogmas of Polish Roman Catholicism and Russian Greek Orthodoxy. The Poles had besieged Moscow in the seventeenth century; tsarist Russia had joined Prussia and Austria in partitions of Poland that deprived it of independence during the eighteenth century. A scholar has compared the policies pursued by Russia, Austria and Prussia in their Polish territories in the second half of the nineteenth and in the early twentieth century and observed that in the Russian part of Poland "there had been less law and order, the welfare functions of the state were more limited, and officials were less competent and more corrupt. At various times the area was either ruled by martial law or at least was under a military administration. Considerable contingents of troops were required to keep internal peace."[5] Russian troops put down the nationalist uprisings of Poles in 1830 and 1863. A full-scale guerrilla war was fought between Russian troops and Polish irregulars in the years just following the Russian Revolution of 1905. The historic bitterness carried over into the period of Russia under Leninist rule and renewed Polish sovereignty. Highlighting the ethnic and political feud was the Soviet-Polish War (1920); Nazi-Soviet agreement to partition Poland (1939); Soviet massacre of thousands of Polish officers taken captive by the invading Red Army (1940); and Stalin's refusal to cooperate with his Grand Alliance partners for the regular airdropping of supplies to Poles who had risen against German occupiers in Warsaw (1944).

The vast majority of Poles doubtless viewed as a Soviet puppet the Communist-led government which Moscow set up in their country at the close of World War II. Although Poland made remarkable economic and social progress in the Stalinist years 1946–53 the cost was a major loss of national pride and human dignity. The Poles after Stalin benefited from a looser dictatorship and more contacts with the West than enjoyed by other nations in eastern Europe. Private farming regained predominance over the socialized variety in the countryside. The Catholic Church was less restricted and its vast moral authority had to be recognized by the regime if only tacitly. Unregulated structures—"flying universities" and dissident groups—were tolerated on a scale unmatched elsewhere in the Soviet orbit. The lure of freedom from political interference and material scarcity was enlarged by countless ties with millions of emigre Poles in western countries.

All of these decentralizing tendencies had an impact on relations between most ordinary Polish citizens and the Soviet-oriented core of the ruling Polish United Workers (Communist) Party, which in 1970 had only slightly more than three million members. The divergent interests of society and regime sparked a number of momentous clashes between workers and students, on the one hand, and police, on the other, from the mid-fifties through the mid-seventies. Communist Party leaders rose and fell in the wake of bloody street fights, with the incoming chiefs invariably promising to keep ears closer to the ground than hapless forerunners had done. Their first loyalty, however, was to the directors of the Soviet system, who insisted that in eastern Europe as in the USSR a monopoly of political and economic power be reserved for Communist Party officialdom. Any diminution of a ruling Party's "leading role" was indeed seen by Moscow as a threat to the integrity of security arrangements within the Soviet bloc.[6]

In early 1980 the Polish Communist Party head was Edward Gierek, and he then got high marks from a Soviet source for prudent methods of governance. Polish chiefs as a whole were acclaimed in a Soviet political manual for consulting with industrial workers before taking key decisions and for regularly visiting large firms to talk with the employees.[7] That laudation proved to be one of the ironies in which the history of communism is rich.

An economic crisis was brewing in Poland for several years. The command methods of running industry were a main source of a steady decline in production and growing shortages of goods. Mismanagement of big loans from Western banks had saddled the country with vast losses in the shape of wrong investments, useless licenses and unused machines that were imported for hard currencies. The rural areas were starved of investment capital and farmers not allowed to develop a proprietorial attitude towards the land. Warnings and proposals for economic reform that had been given by intellectuals were ignored in leadership circles.

So that funds be diverted to cope with debts and to import scarce materials, the Warsaw authorities on July 1, 1980 suddenly took drastic action to reduce heavy State subsidies of meat production. The increases in meat prices ranging from 30 to 90 percent were politically disastrous. Work stoppages began in protest and officials at first responded mildly with wage concessions. Gierek, however, resolutely told the nation on July 10 that new prices would not be reversed nor unauthorized wage increases condoned. A wave of strikes slowly rolled across various regions with generalized complaints about low wages, poor supplies and inadequate information about the reasons for shortages. The regime did not try to break the strikes, even though it had a strong internal security force at its disposal.[8]

One can accept at face value the statement later made by Soviet leaders to the effect that they had advised Gierek to be implacable in dealing with the strikers. "From the first days of the crisis," a Kremlin letter to Warsaw declared in 1981, "we believed that it was important for the Party to give a decisive rebuff to the attempts of the enemies of socialism to use the emergent difficulties for their far-reaching aims."[9] Evidently aware of the concern in Moscow but reluctant to launch a police crackdown, the Polish Politburo on July 18 appealed to striking railroad workers in Lublin, near the Soviet border: "the wave of strikes could arouse anxiety among our friends."[10] An incipient threat to Soviet lines of communication explains why a Polish Government commission headed by Deputy Premier Jagielski visited Lublin to investigate the situation (Warsaw. PAP. July 20, 1980).

Pravda's silence about the strikes may have been due in part to an outbreak of labor unrest within the USSR itself around the same time and the desire of Soviet leaders to embargo any news that might tend to encourage their own dissatisfied workers.

Unofficial sources in Moscow told foreign journalists that a two-day strike occurred in early May at the Gorky auto plant, about 250 miles from the Soviet capital. Vladimir Dolgikh, central Party Secretary (for heavy industry) was officially reported to have spoken in Dzerzhinsk, near Gorky, on May 31. One of the top Soviet ideologues, Pyotr Fedoseyev, addressed a June 12–13 sociology conference in Gorky and deplored harsh working conditions in the area. Nearly one-third of a sample group of workers admittedly had unfavorable hygienic conditions (noise and pollution) while skilled workers in particular were found to be demanding a better "moral-psychological" climate in work forces. The mood of Gorky workers, according to Fedoseyev, had improved since 1964, or Khrushchev's downfall, but he cautioned that comparisons had to be made with present-day needs.[11] Coincidental with this handwringing in Gorky, *Pravda* on June 12 ran a lead article on work forces and urged the creation of a "good attitude" by bringing order to food, health, transport and housing facilities.

A short time later (June 22), Vladimir Borisov, organizer of the unofficial Soviet labor union SMOT, was expelled from the USSR. Borisov, age 36, was one of several dissident workers who tried to organize free trade unions during the late seventies and were sent to jail or psychiatric hospitals. Interviewed in Vienna, Borisov said that there were many unpublicized strikes in his homeland, and he confirmed the stories of Soviet authorities usually giving in quickly to strikers and later arresting or firing the organizers (*Le Monde*, June 26, 1980).

Worker morale was discussed by a secretary of the Latvian Communist Party in the issue of the Soviet Party journal *Kommunist* cleared for printing on July 22, 1980. I. Strelkov in his article "Listening to the Voice of the Masses" lamented the many justified complaints of labor law violation. Offending managers were rebuked and the defense of worker rights was held up as a duty of officials.

The Soviet media blackout on Polish strikes may also have stemmed from a decision to await a personal report from Gierek during his annual summertime visit to Brezhnev in the Crimea. Gierek apparently sensed that his mettle would be questioned at the parley due to be held on July 31. As though to soothe uneasy Soviet leaders, the Polish Government at the end of July ordered the arrest of five members of the "Independent Poland Confederation," a self-proclaimed political party. But the joint communique of the Brezhnev-Gierek talks published on August 1 skirted the issue of Polish labor unrest.

Evidence of disquiet in Soviet ruling quarters did surface in the feature article of a Party ideological review cleared for printing on August 4. The author was "O.B. Borisov," a pseudonym for Oleg Borisovich Rakhmanin, first deputy chief of the Department for Liaison with Communist and Worker Parties in the Soviet Party Secretariat. ("Borisov" let slip his extreme conservatism by gratuitously defending Stalin in a book about Soviet-Chinese relations that he once co-authored.[12]) The August 1980 article fretted that "in a number of instances" the building of socialism was "accompanied by the emergence of occurrences alien to socialism." Apparently mindful of the Polish strife, Rakhmanin took a firm stand: "The lessons of history, connected with the events in Hungary in 1956, Czechoslovakia in 1968, and still more the fresh example of Afghanistan show what great importance attaches to the ability of the toilers' vanguard [the Party] to mobilize the people for defense of the revolution, relying here on the support of its friends and allies in the international arena, on class brothers."[13] This stern moralizing hinted that Polish leaders should not drift with the tide, as ill-fated Communists had done in Budapest and Prague, but come to grips with strikers and rest assured of Soviet military aid if necessary.

The escalation of protest in Poland during the week of August 10 nudged the Soviet elite into action. Almost all the drivers of the Warsaw Traffic Department went on strike. More than 50,000 workers, including 17,000 from the Lenin shipyard, walked out in Gdansk. Other strikes were reported in the towns of Lodz and Wroclaw. Strike committees were focusing on the right to set up free trade unions and publicity for grievances in official media. The Kremlin began to take precautions against the contingency of a breakdown of order in Poland. Soviet media had the following Poland-related items on August 15:

1. TASS announced Warsaw Pact maneuvers in the Baltic region and East Germany. Within ten days, 40,000 troops from Bulgaria, East Germany, Poland, Czechoslovakia, the Soviet Union and Hungary were involved in the war games, with Czechoslovak soldiers welcomed near

Dresden, only 60 miles west of Poland (East Berlin. ADN. Aug. 24, 1980).

2. *Pravda* ran a theory article with the buzzwords used to discredit the members of ruling Parties who were disaffected from Soviet centralism. Prof. Eduard Bagramov assailed "revisionist conceptions" hostile to "socialist practice"; "national 'models' of socialism" that were justified in terms of universal pluralism; and "fabrications" to the effect that "internationalism" or devotion to the USSR "and freedom are antipodes." This attack on reform Communists was reminiscent of those on Czechoslovak liberalizers in 1968, when Soviet journalistic broadsides were fired at the preachers of "various 'models' of socialism" and "new models of socialism."[14]

3. The Party newspaper *Sovetskaya Rossiya* carried an editorial giving an excuse for the imminent resumption of jamming of Western broadcasts. Hostile propagandists were accused of using the most modern technology for exerting influence on Soviet citizens. Youths were identified as a prime target because of their occasional "haste and maximalism" in evaluating events, as well as bent to "skepticism."

A fear of Polish contagion was suggested too by an editorial on trade unions in the August 16 *Pravda*. It ordained that an important criterion for rating the work of Soviet unions was "an attentive attitude towards the needs and inquiries of people, their complaints and statements." This token of concern about worker morale went beyond the language in a 1979 Party decree on unions which *Pravda* never saw fit to publish.

The Soviet leaders kept secret a concurrent effort to upgrade their military capability for coping with the worst in Poland should that materialize. (Only two Soviet tank divisions were stationed there under the Warsaw Pact and merely half the 67 divisions in the European USSR were in degrees of combat readiness between half and full strength.[15]) Reliable Soviet sources reported that army reservists in the Carpathian Military District bordering Poland were then hastily activated in a state of extreme urgency. The reservists were in the class one category (up to 35) with many given no opportunity to seek waivers. Police stopped trucks and autos and sent them to depots where military specialists gave assignments to drivers and vehicles. Similar abrupt tactics were reportedly used in 1979 to commandeer trucks before the Soviet invasion of Afghanistan.[16]

When Gierek left the Crimea for Poland on August 15 he probably thought that he had a Soviet mandate to reject at all cost the strikers' demand for self-governing trade unions. The TASS synopsis of Gierek's August 18 nationwide television speech as aired in *Pravda* on August 20 broke Soviet media silence on the Polish troubles and stressed Gierek's resolve to keep the Communist power monopoly in Poland:

Dwelling on the situation at certain firms of the Gdansk coastal area, E. Gierek noted the attempts to use work stoppages in the pursuit of hostile political goals, cases of certain irresponsible anarchistic and antisocialist elements inciting negative moods. We consider it to be our duty, he said, to state with all firmness that each act directed against the political and social order cannot and will not be tolerated in Poland. Nobody can count on concessions or even waverings in this question of principle.

(In concert with Gierek's hardness, the Polish police on August 20–21 arrested 14 prominent members of the unofficial labor advisory group "KOR" and Leszek Mosczulski, head of the Independent Poland Confederation.)

The Soviet elite kept up an illusion of Gierek's tight hold on authority, even though the foreign press was reporting that Polish workers were losing confidence in him and political associates advising him to step down. Calmly, *Pravda* registered the production successes in a number of Polish cities and the misgiving of honest workers about the economic distress (Aug. 22). Gierek's recent speech and an equally tough-worded letter of the Polish Party Secretariat to ordinary Communists were said to be the basis of efforts to rally the Party for an economic upturn (Aug. 24). The Soviet public was not told that Polish authorities reversed themselves on August 23 and recognized the Unified Strike Committee in Gdansk as a negotiating partner.

Gierek's slippage, however, could not be hidden long and was intimated by the report of a session of the Polish Central Committee in the August 25 *Pravda*. Gierek had spoken at the meeting, setting the main Party tasks and delivering the concluding remarks. But in the limelight was Politburo member and Party Secretary (for security and church affairs) Stanislaw Kania, who briefed the Committee on "the current social-political situation." Soviet insiders no doubt knew that Kania was not a protege of Gierek and had gone to Gdansk early in the crisis to persuade local officials that dialogue was better than confrontation. Still more distressing for the Soviet backers of Gierek was the news that Stefan Olszowski had profited from personnel changes announced at the Polish Plenum. Olszowski was named a Politburo member and Party Secretary, thus becoming one of the strongest figures in Warsaw. Only six months earlier, he was dropped from the Politburo and sent into diplomatic exile. A former foreign minister, Olszowski was reputedly a political hardliner who tended to favor economic reforms, or the granting of more scope to management initiative and the profit motive.

One of the Polish "kingmakers" who was likely to have offended Moscow at the time was Defense Minister Gen. Wojciech Jaruzelski. A Politburo member, he was rumored to have opposed Gierek's bid to hold a simple two-hour session of the Central Committee for information purposes only. Jaruzelski was said to have joined others who insisted that the Committee meeting be used for a debate that would fix responsibility for policy mistakes. The general, accordingly, could be blamed in part for undermining the Soviet loyalist Gierek by helping to remove several Politburo and Secretariat members (*New York Times,* Aug. 26, 1980). Looking backward, one can see that this was one of a series of signs of Jaruzelski's personal independence within a framework of dedication to the communist system.

Brezhnev returned to Moscow from the Crimea on August 25 and this may have insured that a self-criticism which Gierek had to perform was omitted from *Pravda*'s August 26 digest of the Polish leader's latest televised speech. Gierek had said: "We have called to key posts those comrades who perceived the growing irregularities earlier and tried to counteract them. *We did not heed their voice in time*" (PAP. Aug. 25, 1980. Emphasis supplied). *Pravda* merely quoted Gierek to the effect that "We have appointed to these key posts comrades who perceived in a timely way the growing difficulties and tried to overcome them." Gierek was still the Kremlin's man in Warsaw. But his position had become untenable after strikes spread to the mining and industrial region of Silesia, long the major base of his support. Soviet media on August 28 offset their criticism of Polish strikers as "antisocialist forces" with news that "special government commissions" or negotiating teams were operating on the strike-torn Baltic coast. This hinted at a peaceful outcome of the Polish labor strife, and that same day Brezhnev and deputy Party leader Andrey Kirilenko were relaxed enough to leave Moscow for short trips to the provinces.

At the same time, Moscow was not ready for a backdown in Poland that was anything more than temporary. TASS ignored the momentous fact that on August 30 the Gdansk strike committee and Government negotiators agreed on workers' right to form self-governing labor unions. The Kremlin thereby refused to legitimize the "Gdansk accords," an historic compromise in Party-people relations within the Warsaw Pact community. Polish rulers, for their part, had accepted the worker demand for independent unions with the right to strike and curbs on the official censorship, among other things. Worker delegates in turn had acknowledged the Communist Party's leading role in Polish society and Poland's adherence to the Soviet alliance system.

Icily, *Pravda* on August 31 notified that the Polish Central Committee had met under Gierek's chairmanship, was again briefed by Kania, and told something or other about the labor-management talks on the Baltic. A companion piece in *Pravda* summarized an article by U.S. Communist Party leader Gus Hall which blamed the strikes in Poland on "weaknesses" of leadership, implying that political mechanisms and policy guidelines there were essentially sound.

The inner ring of Soviet leaders met with Brezhnev upon his return to Moscow on August 31. A graphic in the next day's *Pravda* showed Brezhnev at an airport with KGB chairman Yuri Andropov, Foreign Minister Andrey Gromyko, Party Secretary (for ideology) Mikhail Suslov, Defense Mininster Dmitri Ustinov and Kirilenko. This sextet was apparently in unison that Polish chiefs would have to be coaxed into formulating a plan for evading implementation of the Gdansk accords. For an authoritative Soviet commentary on Polish events indicating that sentiment was carried in the September 1 *Pravda* above the signature "A. Petrov," or the pseudonym of *Pravda* chief editor Viktor Afanasyev. The article suggested that Polish authorities had unwisely agreed to "examine" the demands of antisocialist elements which were linked with subversive centers in the West. A conspiracy was supposedly afoot to cut workers off from the Communist Party and harm the cause of socialism in Poland.

As *Pravda* could not bring itself to declare that Warsaw had accepted the strikers' demands, so the Soviet State organ *Izvestiya* could not outrightly condemn the release of arrested dissidents in Poland as a consequence of the Gdansk accords. It attacked KOR leaders on September 2 as anti-Soviet extremists who were abusing national symbols and seeking to create "an atmosphere of 'free play of political forces.'" (The Czechoslovak liberals in 1968 were taxed with the same heresy.[17]) Similarly, a Moscow television commentator on September 2 stigmatized Lech Walesa, the Gdansk strike leader, as "one of the members of an opposition group."

Soviet misgiving and desire for a wedge to be driven between the Walesas and common workers may have underlain the treatment of Polish affairs in *Pravda* from September 3 to 6. The straight news was that "agreements [were] reached between Government commissions and inter-plant committees" on the Baltic coast, although the specifics were kept secret. Commentary was that negative phenomena were persisting: belief that Poland was ripe for a "process of liberalization" and a new "model of power." Social discord was also viewed as likely to hurt the Polish regime's military capability. But perhaps the agitators of dissension could be isolated, *Pravda* suggested, as the Polish working class at large still embraced the ideals of socialism.

Soviet ideologues were meanwhile following the example of the senior *apparatchik* Rakhmanin, who had raised the spectre of unravelling in Poland on the Hungarian and Czechoslovak patterns. The Prague Spring was recalled in a *Kommunist* review of a 1979 translation of a book by the Slovak Communist Vasil Bejda. An erosion of Party power was traced from the toleration of free-wheeling intellectual roundtables to the capture of mass media by enemies of the regime. The intervention of Soviet and allied forces allegedly prevented civil war and counter-revolution in Czechoslovakia (No. 13, cleared for printing Sept. 3, 1980). Professor Konstantin Suvorov of the CPSU Academy of Social Science raked over the Hungarian and Czechoslovak experiences in a lecture pamphlet. He did so to illustrate the "great peril" of "uncoupling" ruling Parties from the direction of State and public bodies such as trade unions. Suvorov warned that if a ruling Party got down to an equal footing with workers there could be "extraordinarily dangerous political complications."[18]

Soviet nonrecognition of the Gdansk accords was evinced anew in the September 6 coverage in *Pravda* of a national assembly session in Warsaw. The item ignored the new premier's commitment of his government to the terms of the strike settlement and promise of legislation to relax censorship controls. Nor did *Pravda* disclose that other speakers had ridiculed the strictly decorative nature of the Soviet-style parliament. What *Pravda* liked and duly reported was the premier's contention that time was needed to shape new economic policies, and the call of others to strengthen the Party's leading role in society (Cf. PAP. Sept. 5, 1980).

The same issue of *Pravda* contained what looks like a political allegory to the effect that it was necessary to reject an iron-back attitude toward the Polish strife and depend on intrigue to restore the *status quo ante*. A "historical" article in the September 6 *Pravda* marked the 100th birthday of Aleksandr Shotman, a relatively minor Bolshevik who perished in the Stalinist terror. Shotman was said to have once angered Lenin by physically striking a comrade who had deserted to the Mensheviks. Lenin later advised Shotman that "a fist in a dispute over principle is the most senseless 'argument.'" Lenin criticised Shotman for the "too hasty actions" of his Helsingfors Party committee during an attempted mutiny of Baltic sailors prior to the 1917 Revolution. In due course, Shotman "had learned caution and prudence, acquired the ability to ponder his actions beforehand, and to keep cool in the most critical situations." (It will be seen that at the close of the Polish drama in 1981 another seeming allegory in *Pravda* signalized a verdict by Warsaw to crush the domestic movement for social reform.)

A few hours after this sermon saw the light of day, Kania, great exponent of "caution and prudence," was named Party first secretary at an urgent meeting of the Polish Central Committee. Brezhnev apparently made the best of a difficult situation and sent a warm message of congratulations to Kania, which was featured in *Pravda* a day later, on September 7. Below the cable was a biography and photo of Kania, whose unanimous election and inaugural speech were noted in the inside pages. Brezhnev's description of Kania in his telegram of greetings may have been aimed at telling the new Polish leader what was expected of him. He was to be a "staunch fighter" for "strengthening the leading role" of the Party and champion the cause of "proletarian internationalism," that is, uphold the policy interests of the Soviet Union before anything else.

Kania certainly gave the Soviet leaders their due in his inaugural, read by a Warsaw television announcer on September 7 and published in *Pravda* September 8. The Soviet Party and Brezhnev personally were said to have taken an understanding view of the Polish situation and had faith that Poles would find a correct solution to their problems. Kania, 53, reassured the Kremlin elders that he would not embarrass them by bringing in too much new blood: the old cadres were praised to the sky after mention of different age groups in the Party. The Soviet alliance tie was exalted for having brought liberation to Poland in the Second World War and Kania portrayed it as a guarantee of secure postwar borders.

Above all, Kania seemed to promise that Poland's new, free trade unions would not be allowed to compete with the Party for ultimate power. He affirmed that the Party had gained valuable political capital by negotiating the strike settlements and vowed to implement the accords. But the new unions would have to respect "socialist positions" and act "in the single link of socialist democracy." These statements could have been read in Moscow as paying lip service to the idea of democratization and making a solemn pledge to recoup Party losses. But the Soviet hierarchy may have wondered if Kania would govern with a sufficiently tough hand. *Pravda* deleted from its almost full text of Kania's speech the following sentences: "The words were dropped in one speech or another here that I am to be the leader of the Party. No, comrades, the function does not make a leader of a man. And I am not so sure that our Party needs what the notion of leader means." In explanation, Kania said—and *Pravda* quoted him—that it was essential that the collective wisdom of the people function in all echelons of the Party. The implication of words that *Pravda* deleted from Kania's speech was that a Party chief in the Soviet bloc should mediate between social interest groups or bureaucratic lobbies, rather than strive to impose his own policy views. The omission hinted at a belief that Kania was mistaken to have posed as a mediator, or someone who could never roll back the free labor movement that had emerged on Polish soil.

Other omissions from the *Pravda* version of Kania's inaugural suggested that in Moscow he was viewed as too generous in making overtures to reformist and religious-nationalist elements. *Pravda* bluepencilled the underlined: "Today in our country, we can, and even must, discuss *and dispute* many issues; *we must change no small number of things."* A positive reference to "full self-governing" trade unions was excised. Kania's enjoinder to a search for ways to put the country on a sounder basis was printed, but without the prefatory word that, "We need to develop a great intellectual movement" to do so. The Soviet paper also approved of Kania's promise "to continue consistently our religious policy," but it excised a description of that policy as "enriched by the new experiences which have served our fatherland well." Was Kania too friendly toward the Polish-born Pope, who had visited his homeland in 1979 and fired up patriotic sentiment?

Even without the conciliatory notes that were omitted there was enough in the *Pravda* version of Kania's speech to have dismayed Soviet conservatives. Kania had devoted only a few words to the "antisocialist adversary" who "wants to use the emergent conflicts for aims that are contrary to what the workers desire and call for." The internal enemy was not lumped together with Western foes nor castigated for social disorder that had to be put down. Kania's relative neglect of the supposed pro-Western fifth column in Poland was very much at odds with the thrust of recent comment on Polish affairs in Soviet media. Thus, Soviet relief that Poland was growing calmer was probably counterbalanced by skepticism that Kania could lead a battle to rescind the new freedoms of Poles.

NOTES

1. *Planovoye khozyaystvo*, No. 2, 1978. Emphasis supplied.

2. B.P. Kurashvili, "Politicheskaya borba i eë zakonomernosti," in *Politicheskiye otnosheniya: prognozirovaniye i planirovaniye* (Moscow, 1979), pp. 66–67.

3. *The Military Balance 1980–1981* (International Institute for Strategic Studies, London, 1980), p. 16.

4. *Ibid.*, pp. 9 and 16, and *Yezhegodnik Bolshoy Sovetskoy Entsiklopedii (vyp. 25)* (Moscow, 1981), pp. 11 ff. and 330 ff.

5. Roman Szporluk, in *Crises of Political Development in Europe and the United States. Edited by Raymond Grew* (Princeton University Press, Princeton, NJ, 1978), p. 399.

6. Party supremacy and Bloc safety were linked in the following passage of the letter which the leaders of five Warsaw Pact signatories sent to Prague on July 15, 1968: "The might and stability of our alliances depend on the internal strength of the socialist system in each of our fraternal countries, on the Marxist-Leninist policy of our Parties, which perform the leading role in the political and social life of their peoples and states. The undermining of a Communist Party's directive role leads to elimination of socialist democracy and the socialist system. That creates a threat to the foundations of our alliance and the security

of our countries' community" (*Spravochnik partiynogo rabotnika.* [Moscow, 1968], p. 21).

7. *Lektsii po partiynomu stroitelstvu. Vyp. 3. Part. rukovodstvo khoz. str-vom, gos. i obshchestv. organizatsiyami i Deyatelnost part. komiteta i ego apparata.* (Moscow, 1980), p. 385.

8. Poland had 77,000 internal security and internal defense troops, including 21,000 construction troops, according to *The Military Balance,* p. 17.

9. "To the Central Committee of the Polish United Workers' Party," signed "Central Committee of the Communist Party of the Soviet Union," *Pravda,* June 12, 1981.

10. *Glos Ludu* as cited by "o.k." in *Neue Zuercher Zeitung,* July 22, 1980.

11. *Rabochiy klass i sovremennyy mir,* No. 5, 1980.

12. O.B. Borisov and B.T. Koloskov, *Sovetsko-kitayskiye otnosheniya. 1945–1970. Kratkiy ocherk.* (Moscow, 1971), pp. 5, 41–42, 48–49, 78 and 128.

13. *Voprosy Istorii KPSS,* No. 8, 1980.

14. See the articles by Soviet Politburo member Pyotr Shelest in *Pravda,* July 5, 1968; *Neues Deutschland* as cited by *Pravda,* July 15, 1968; and *Pravda* observer Yuriy Zhukov in *Pravda,* July 26, 1968.

15. *The Military Balance,* pp. 10–11.

16. Kevin Klose in the *Washington Post,* Dec. 2, 1980 dates the call-up to "3 1/2 months ago," or mid-August.

17. See Yuriy Zhukov in *Pravda,* July 26, 1968.

18. *Vsemirno-istoricheskoye znacheniye opyta KPSS* (Moscow, cleared for printing Sep. 4, 1980), pp. 58 and 75.

TWO

Outcries in Low Key

(SEPT. 10–NOV. 19, 1980)

Soon after Kania's rise to power, Western observers differed over Soviet thinking about Poland. President Carter's national-security adviser at the time would later remark about Polish affairs as he saw them in 1980: "Toward the end of September and certainly by early October, the situation began to look more ominous, with portents of possible Soviet intervention."[1] Diplomats in Moscow, however, failed to see the ill omens. In late October they reportedly believed that most Soviet officials felt that "the political struggle in Poland, though fraught with danger, is still at an early stage" and "the Polish leadership still has large reserves of power and influence to bring to bear" (*New York Times*, October 30, 1980).

The former Presidential aide does not offer any evidence for his sensing of an approaching squall over Poland at the turn of September–October 1980. His opinion might have been based on "intelligence reports" of unusual military activity in the USSR and East Germany which appeared in the press (*Boston Globe*, Sept. 18, 1980). The U.S. Secretary of State on September 19 described the activities as exercises. Other U.S. sources said the activities began to taper off on or about October 3, and by November 17 had ended (*Baltimore Sun*, Nov. 18, 1980).

A study of Soviet press materials suggests that in October 1980 those with a window on Red Square, figuratively speaking, had a clearer view of the Soviet political scene than others at the White House. It seems a fair conjecture that Soviet audiences were not being prepared for any major action against the independent Solidarity trade union—either by the Kremlin or the Warsaw regime—during the first 75 days or so of Kania's reign (September 5–November 19, 1980). The headings which

Pravda used for its dispatches from Poland were themselves important signposts of political attitude in Moscow.

As far back as the Hungarian revolt in 1956 the captions of *Pravda's* reports about it were a kind of register of the degree of Soviet concern. On October 29, 30 and 31, *Pravda* carried reports under the heading "Situation in Hungary." During those days Soviet troops began to move into Hungary and on November 4 a massive attack was launched to crush the rising. In 1980, *Pravda* got into the habit of signalling bad news by using the headings "Events in Poland" and "Situation in Poland."

At the height of tension on the Baltic coast and then during the politicking over Gierek's Party job, the unattributed or TASS items on Poland were run in *Pravda* with the captions "Events in Poland" (Aug. 28, 1980) and "Situation in Poland" (Aug. 29, Sept. 2, 3, 4 and 5, 1980).

The cited danger signal vanished from *Pravda* with the fall of Gierek, and would not resurface till November 19, or after Kania had made one concession after another to Solidarity and the Catholic Church. (It will be seen that *Pravda* was to flash the same sign of acute distress in late November, or just prior to great concern in Washington over the chance of Soviet invasion, and would do the same in the 10-day run-up to the imposition of martial law a year later.)

The real question for Soviet policymakers at the time may have been whether Kania had the grit to hamstring Solidarity and to tap the reserves of coercion at his disposal. This is to say that Soviet leaders, most of whom had been in office since the 1950's, had to wonder if it was a case of déjà vu with respect to eastern Europe. Would Kania follow in the footsteps of the Hungarian leader Imre Nagy in 1956 or the Czechoslovak leader Alexander Dubcek in 1968 and reconcile himself to internal liberalization "from below"?

Polish Politburo member and Deputy Premier Jagielski, who had negotiated the Gdansk accords on behalf of the Government, visited Moscow on September 10–11, 1980. A symbolic act stressing the Soviet fixation with the primacy of politics (centralized Party control) was the ushering of Jagielski to the office of Party grand ideologue Suslov. The host's mien was perhaps not too different from that in an interview he once granted to the daughter of his old political teacher: "Suslov moved nervously in his chair behind his desk. His pale hands, with thick sclerotic veins, weren't quiet for a single moment. He was thin, tall, with the face of a fanatic. The thick lenses of his glasses did not soften the manic look with which he pierced me."[2] Along with Brezhnev and Gromyko, Suslov was to see more of the Polish leaders than any other Soviet Politburo member during the next 15 months.

The Jagielski-Suslov meeting was attended by Rakhmanin of the Party Secretariat, who had recently commended Soviet armed interventions in the Warsaw Pact area and beyond. TASS claimed that Suslov and Jagielski had "exchanged opinions on questions of mutual interest" in a "warm and friendly atmosphere." After Brezhnev received Jagielski, TASS likewise said that the chat about bilateral relations had proceeded in a "warm and friendly atmosphere."

Since the official phrasing ignored "unity of views" it was suggestive of some discord, probably over matters other than a Soviet aid commitment to Poland amounting to $132 million in consumer goods and food. Jagielski was bound to be grateful for the largess, which the Kremlin may have conceived as a tool for the exertion of political leverage.

But Jagielski may have had thoughts of his own about Soviet policy counsel. Subsequent events allow one to speculate that Brezhnev and Suslov advised Jagielski along the following lines: Yes, dialogue with the misguided workers is essential for the time being. But you must be suspicious of the new trade unions and prevent their consolidation. Those bodies are a real or latent Trojan Horse of the imperialists. Both theory and practice instruct that unions not under Party control are an alien growth on the body of socialist society. We hope that major surgery can be avoided. Do, however, keep apart the workers and "dissident" intellectuals. Shake-up the Party and State apparatus. That will help you to regain the trust of the working people and to unify your own disorderly ranks. A further improvement of the economic mechanism is called for, but rein in the market forces. Use the clerics to obtain social peace, but limit their influence. Guard, too, the purity of the mass media, which the enemy will try to infiltrate. In general, don't rush ahead with new-fangled schemes.

The Soviet press insinuated that message to Polish Communists in the days ahead, largely by means of editorial selection, and it failed to convey any sense of the living processes in which all Poles were engaged.

Soviet journalists avoided like a plague the popular enthusiasm over the new freedoms of speech and assembly in Poland. Nor did they give any inkling of the dominance of youthful workers in Solidarity or the great appeal of the union's constant use of national symbols (flags and anthems) at its rallies. Soviet media likewise kept silent about the massive defections from the old trade unions to Solidarity; citizens' demands for religious teaching in the schools; occupation of local government offices to protest the arbitrary detention of social activists; lifting of bans on controversial articles, books and films; and agitation within the Party for an end to the corrupting practice of lifelong leaders.

The details of turmoil clearly fell in the category of "sensationalism" and had to be hushed up lest disaffected groups inside the Soviet Union become imitative or Party men fly into a rage over the tide of spontaneity rising a few hundred miles away. The political sophisticates in the lower echelons who distrusted Western broadcasts could gather from *Pravda's* references to "dramatic social tension" (Sept. 13) and "acrimonious talks" at Party committees (Sept. 17) in Poland that things were anything but normal. The facts, however, were certainly available to ranking Soviet personnel, either through the well-developed grapevine or confidential TASS summaries of world press comment.

Official public opinion about Poland and results of the Brezhnev-Suslov-Jagielski talks may have led the Soviet Politburo to conclude that no opportunity should be missed to stiffen Kania. The lead in this effort was probably taken by Suslov, who in the past was closely involved in press campaigns against various heresies and had general policy responsibility for "ideology." Suslov's direction of the handling of Polish affairs by *Pravda* would also help to explain the neo-Stalinist chords that were struck.

Delegates of hundreds of free unions met in Gdansk on September 17, 1980 and decided to register the entire new labor movement as one union called *Solidarnosc* (Solidarity), after the slogan of the Gdansk strikers. The impetus was an effort by local authorities to hinder founding committees of new unions, refusing them premises and harrying their organizers, which in turn led to many strikes (Warsaw. *Solidarnosc.* Special Supplement. Sept. 11, 1981).

"A. Petrov" responded to the formation of Solidarity with a warning in the September 20 *Pravda* that Gdansk had become a special target of West German revenge-seekers, who allegedly saw the city as virtually the new capital of Poland. The innuendo, it seems, was that Solidarity leaders and their dissident coadjutors might someday form an alternative government—the nightmare that assuredly was behind some of the worst Stalinist purges. There was a whiff of Stalinism too in the formula that "as the situation becomes more stable, there is an increase of the activeness of circles hostile to socialist Poland and their instigatory and subversive work." (Stalin had justified his mass terror policy in 1937 under the pretext that as the Soviet Union marched forward toward socialism class warfare had to sharpen inside the country.) *Pravda* seemed to be telling the Polish rulers to clamp down on the democratic intelligentsia that was helping Solidarity to chart its course.

Solidarity leaders and their consultants were in effect blackened as Western agents by a *Pravda* article of September 23 attacking Western broadcasters. V. Bolshakov charged that Radio Free Europe was a CIA front sending both direct and coded orders to antisocialist elements in

Poland. The station was purported to have been a co-ordinator of counterrevolutionary acts in Hungary in 1956 and to have advised antisocialist forces in Czechoslovakia from 1967–69.

An unusually large-size book review in the September 25 *Pravda* was relatable to such events in Poland as the drafting of a new law on trade unions (Sept. 23) and registering of Solidarity with a Warsaw judge (Sept. 24). Prof. G. Alekseyev lectured from a new collection of Lenin statements about trade unions. The master as far back as sixty or so years ago was said to have justly derided for all time "those who fought for so-called 'free' trade unions" under socialism. The idea of "independent" unions was said to have been rightfully scorned by Lenin as "either a bourgeois provocation of the crudest sort or an extremely injudicious thought, a slavish repetition of yesterday's slogans." The main task of unions in a socialist land was to ensure the development of production, and they could do so only under the Communist Party's "direct leadership." (Interestingly enough, Walesa was shown on evening television news in Warsaw on September 25, giving his first official press conference.)

Pravda exulted over the arrest of right-wing Polish dissident Moczulski in its September 26 issue. The existence of a "watershed" or great divide in Poland was averred a day later in another article signed "A. Petrov." On one side were arrayed "the patriots of socialist Poland and its friends," and on the other were the "hidden and open enemies." Here again was classic purge talk, the secret foes apt to be Party members who winked at what *Pravda* decried as unreasonable wage demands and treacherous plans for a national model of socialism.

The fulminations in Moscow had no appreciable effect on Polish realities. Solidarity's first nationwide warning strike, or selective work stoppages, was called on October 3. It was in reaction to bureaucratic harassment of the union and lack of access to the mass media, along with delays in abiding by the accords on pay increases. A flurry of local strikes continued through most of October and November. The main issue was wage increases, Solidarity leaders holding that a Government decree was not coordinated with them, and this was tantamount to violation of the Gdansk agreements (Warsaw. *Solidarnosc*. Special Supplement. Sept. 11, 1981).

Kania's refusal to be sterner towards his compatriots stands out from his October 4 report to the Polish Central Committee. The transactions of that meeting were summarized on no less than two-thirds of an entire page of *Pravda* (Oct. 7, 1980). The sweep of coverage suggests that quite a bit of Kania's diagnosis of systemic ills was gratifying to certain Soviet leaders.

Kania urged a new line of policy to raise economic efficiency and popular morale. Aside from the "atmosphere of edginess" that he noted at industrial firms, Kania listed a number of failings that marked the Soviet polity too. The problems included low labor productivity and poor discipline; shortages of food and basic consumer goods; inept planning and mismanagement of industry; neglect of the infrastructure of agriculture; stagnation of parliament and local government bodies; lack of public information about the sorespots of everyday life; and tangled lines of authority between Party and State offices. Brezhnev as a clear-sighted conservative in the spectrum of Soviet politics had lately been addressing the same issues in his capacity of Party chief and head of State.

But the Soviet chief would most likely have objected to Kania's political nostrums for easing the strain between regime and society. That much is clear from a comparison of *Pravda*'s version of Kania's report with the text given by Warsaw Radio on October 4. The Soviet editors repeatedly deleted Kania's expressions of willingness to share Party power with workers, professionals and young people. All references to such "partnership" and "co-management" were barred from the columns of *Pravda*. The same was true of Kania's raising for discussion a number of proposals to reform the innerparty regime. This included a definition of the duties of top Party bodies and leaders, as well as their relations with the nominally supreme policymaking organ of the Party, its Central Committee. Kania was even ready for a broad exchange of views on a question of major sensitivity to Kremlin elders: whether to limit the term of office for Party officials—and the readers of *Pravda* were spared the sight of that innovative motion.

Kania's speech had to be especially offensive to the most indurated conservatives in ruling councils from Moscow to East Berlin. It had too much about the need for "renewal" and was short on summons to "vigilance." Kania had promised to smooth the way for Poland's new trade unions and went no further than to say that "enemies of socialism" were merely pinning their hopes on the fledgling groups. The anticommunist centers abroad were just wishing to exploit the Polish crisis for their own ends.

Warsaw Pact leaders commented on the Polish troubles soon after Kania's speech and *Pravda* reported only the milder statements. Gustav Husak, general secretary of the Czechoslovak Party, spoke at a Central Committee session in Prague on October 7. He was accurately quoted in Moscow: "We stand firmly at the side of the Polish Communists and the fraternal Polish people and are convinced that they have enough strength to overcome the difficulties of the current period and beat back the drive of internal and external enemies of socialism."[3] True, this could not have been altogether comforting to the Poles: in the midst of the preparations for a march on Prague in 1968 the Kremlin and its allies were voicing sureness that Communists there would be able to neutralize supposed rivals for power.[4]

But the remark of Husak and its citation by *Pravda* had to be more gratifying for the Poles than a chilly blast from Husak's colleague Vasil Bilak. "We do not hide the fact," the Czechoslovak Party Secretary for ideology said, "that what is happening in Poland touches us very deeply, politically, ideologically, as well as economically." Bilak argued that counterrevolutionary forces were at work inside Poland and did not have to murder Communists in order to show their true colors. They did so by promoting social disunity and seeking to paralyze the authorities. Clearly alluding to the Polish August, Bilak saw behind the strikes a careful plan and ties between the strike committees and foreign centers. "We want to believe," Bilak said with an overtone of skepticism, "that both Polish Communists and non-Communists . . . will find a way out of the crisis."[5]

Vivid images of a dissolution of political controls in Poland were recorded by West German television and could be viewed by millions across the Berlin Wall. A jittery reaction in the German Democratic Republic's elite is clear from the speech that East German Party leader Erich Honecker made on occasion of his regime's 31st anniversary, October 6, 1980. Honecker warned that his country could not "remain indifferent" to events in Poland.[6] (Brezhnev in a speech of July 3, 1968, or about six weeks before the invasion of Czechoslovakia, said that the USSR "can and will never be indifferent to the fate of socialist construction in other countries.") A week later, Honecker told his Party officials that "antisocialist, counterrevolutionary forces" in Poland were threatening the system. "But one thing remains clear," he added. "Poland is and will remain a socialist country. . . . And together with our friends we will make sure of that."[7] Honecker's shrillness was ignored by *Pravda*, whose readers might have construed it as a bid for direct intervention in Poland by its alliance partners.

While the hawkish Bilak and Honecker were denied a Soviet platform for their rhetoric about Poland, another owl like Husak was granted that privilege. Romanian Party head Nicolae Ceausescu, who had to suffer labor unrest in his own domain a few years ago, criticized the Polish strikes in an October 15 speech to his Party Central Committee. Ceausescu, however, was sure that the Polish Party would repulse the antisocialist tendencies and be able to solve its problems (*Pravda*, Oct. 19, 1980).

In sum, a discussion was going on among the east European leaders about the character of the events in Poland. The Czechoslovak and

Romanian Party heads were taking a patient position; the East German chief and the top ideologue in Prague obviously wished to intensify the pressure on Kania. *Pravda's* airing of the less bellicose statements from allied capitals hinted at an enduring consensus in behalf of moderation at the Soviet Politburo. Consensus, of course, does not mean unanimity and there were soon a few tentative signs of divergence within the Soviet elite.

The synopsis of Brezhnev's speech to the plenary session of the CPSU Central Committee on October 21, 1980 had no mention of Poland. It is hard to believe that something so astounding as the liberalization in Poland could have drawn comment from the leaders of Communist Parties around the world and have gone unnoticed in the semiannual forum of Soviet Communism. It is wellnigh impossible to explain this silence and supposition is required: Brezhnev did say something but it was veiled to avoid offending one interested group or another; the Politburo was reappraising the Polish question; the cautious majority led by Brezhnev shrank from the prospect of a discussion by regional barons known for their intolerance of social nonconformity. One virtual certainty is that Brezhnev's clan was worried that Polish-type unrest might occur inside the Soviet Union if popular living standards were not improved more rapidly.

The Soviet leader urged a long-term Food Program at the Central Committee meeting and "sharp turn" of the economy at large in the direction of satisfying consumers. Still earlier, a theoretical article in *Pravda* (Oct. 2) argued against delaying the advent of full communism, or a high level of prosperity equally shared by all. Brezhnev's pro-consumer view would be set forth in another *Pravda* theory article (Oct. 31) which insisted that the material basis for satisfying human wants in the Soviet Union had been created and there was no room for complacence about the permanent shortages of the most basic household goods. A third theoretical piece (Nov. 21) stated that "undesirable social tension" could result from ill-conceived domestic policies.

Unverified but plausible is the report of a letter from the Soviet city of Tolyatti in which a dissident labor organizer tells of a lecture on world affairs that was held on October 30, 1980, at the factory where he worked. The speaker made the following comment regarding Poland: "It must be said that conditions here in our country are no better than those in Poland on the eve of the strikes. Here too, many administrative and Party officials adopt a haughty attitude towards the needs and requirements of the workers." The auditorium was said to have rung with complaints and wry humor about the political governing class (Radio Liberty Research. RL 470/81. Nov. 24, 1981).

What makes the report on Tolyatti workers credible is a decree of the Secretariat of the Soviet Trade Union Council adopted on October 14, 1980. The edict catalogued violations of law adversely impacting on working and living conditions of employees at the firms of various industrial ministries. It said that such breaches were evoking "the justified complaints of working people and conflicts with the administration of firms and organizations." The trade union committees were told to ride herd on negligent managers.[8]

At all events, the Brezhnev group in Soviet leadership had a special interest in opening the columns of *Pravda* to Kania's critical remarks on October 7. This identity of concern about popular discontent on the part of Kania and Brezhnev might have colored Brazhnev's outlook on the Polish situation. It may have disposed the Soviet leader to give Kania the benefit of doubt that others in Moscow would not. If there were opposite impulses among the Soviet leaders in regard to Poland, Party Secretary Kirilenko is likely to have sided with the hardliners in eastern Europe.

Kirilenko's devotion to a narrow political orthodoxy was indicated by a collection of his speeches and articles published in 1976. He was revealed to have cast aspersions on homegrown critics of Stalinism and to have lashed out at shirking workers in far harsher terms than Brezhnev usually did.[9] The editor of Kirilenko's book was I.P. Pomelov, one of the most dogmatic Soviet propagandists. On the eve of the Soviet-led invasion of Czechoslovakia, Pomelov in *Pravda* (Aug. 14, 1968) thundered against exaggerating national traits and rejecting the dominance of the Party. He was chosen to revile dissidents as "anti-patriots" and attack a foreign "campaign for the exit of Soviet citizens of Jewish nationality to Israel" (*Pravda*, Jan. 8, 1971).

A second edition of Kirilenko's book was reviewed in the September 13, 1980 *Pravda* and the article inveighed against "any and all attempts recklessly to defame real socialism." This could have alluded to Kirilenko's upset over the widespread censure of Soviet-style institutions in Poland. The Warsaw correspondent of *Pravda* would shortly take notice of the "reckless criticism" that Communists had to encounter (Sept. 21, 1980).

Kirilenko arrived in Prague one day after the Soviet Party Plenum and held talks with Czechoslovak leaders, perhaps to obtain pledges of aid for the damaged Polish economy. The militant Bilak escorted Kirilenko on a tour of the city, and the guest made speeches in Bratislava and Pilsen. Unusually, *Pravda* carried a photograph of Kirilenko with Husak (Oct. 23), and summaries of Kirilenko's speeches in the provinces were later published in *Pravda* (Oct. 24 and 25).

Kirilenko implied disquiet about Poland while he spoke in Pilsen, where the workers had once staged a violent protest over a currency reform, the first such outburst known to have occurred in eastern Europe during the post-Stalin era. Kirilenko said in his Pilsen speech that Communists had to solve difficult social tasks "in struggle against the intrigues of imperialism *and counterrevolutionary forces,* so to speak, under the fire of the class adversary" (emphasis supplied).

Kirilenko's return to Moscow roughly coincided with the out-break of a new squabble in Poland. Solidarity voted on October 27 to tell the Premier to come to Gdansk for negotiations on varied grievances or face new strikes. The primary demand of Solidarity was reversal of a Warsaw court decision to register the union legally if its statutes included a clause recognizing that the Party plays the leading role in the State and restricting the right to strike (*New York Times,* October 28, 1980).

Pravda overlooked Solidarity tactics and the conciliatory gestures of Kania that followed. Deputy Premier Jagielski went to Gdansk on October 28 and told Walesa that he could meet with the Premier in Warsaw on October 31. The Government, in turn, was informed that unless an agreement was reached on contested issues, a strike alert would begin on November 12 (*Washington Post,* Oct. 29, 1980). Gdansk was indeed coming to look like the second capital of Poland! But the Kania-chaired Politburo at its October 29 meeting warmly viewed Solidarity as "an irreversible element" on the national scene and instructed regional Party officials to avoid the obstruction of Solidarity activities (PAP. Oct. 29, 1980).

The absolute primacy of the Party bureaucracy was an almost sac-rosanct maxim for Soviet leaders. It is, therefore, hardly surprising that TASS announced on the evening of October 29 that Kania and Polish Premier Pinkowski would come to Moscow the next day on a "friendly working visit."

A guise of amity was put on display for the TASS photographer who was admitted to the room in the Kremlin where the Soviet-Polish summit was held. At the table were a smiling Kania and Pinkowski, along with an interpreter, and facing them in generally good mood were Brezhnev, the new Premier Nikolay Tikhonov, Gromyko, Party Secretary (for bloc liaison) Konstantin Rusakov, and First Deputy Premier (for foreign trade) Ivan Arkhipov.

In keeping with the superficial bonhomie, TASS reported an "at-mosphere of cordiality and unity of views." Brezhnev was clearly reluctant to see Soviet tanks hurled against Poland. The Soviet President "expressed the conviction of Soviet Communists, working people of the Soviet Union, that the Communists and working people of fraternal Poland will be able to solve the acute problems of political and economic development standing before them." Kania might have agreed to a Soviet

proposal that Solidarity be pressed to revise its statute and bow to
Communist Party supremacy in the court fight over its legalization. If
violence were to occur, the blame could be put on Western agents. That
is one interpretation which can be given to the lines of the TASS
statement which read: "The participants of the meeting resolutely
condemned the attempts by certain imperialist circles to wage subversive
activities against socialist Poland and interfere in its affairs" (*Pravda*,
Oct. 31, 1980).

Despite his outward poise, Kania was being ground between two
millstones, Solidarity and the Kremlin. He mollified the Soviets by
insuring that no joint communique was produced after a 14-hour meeting
of Government and Solidarity negotiators on November 1, 1980. Kania
accommodated Solidarity by vowing in a speech to workers in Nowa
Huta that he was committed to a partnership between trade unions
and the authorities in all issues, local and national. The second development was reported in *Pravda* November 7, and in the very same
news item a "typographic error" was made which had the effect of
diminishing the status of Kania. At one point in the dispatch he was
referred to as Party *"first"* rather than *"First"* secretary. One or more
of the Soviet Party Secretaries who read the daily copy of *Pravda*
apparently ordered the decapitalization of Kania's title in order to suggest
that Kania as appeaser of troublemakers should be overruled more often
or even be removed. (*Pravda* on October 11, 1964 heralded the ouster
of Khruschchev by unusually spelling his title *"first"* rather than *"First"*
secretary of the CPSU.)

In the meantime, the name of an old warhorse of Polish politics once
associated with anti-dissident and anti-Semitic brutality had returned
to the Soviet media in a favorable light. Mieczyslaw Moczar had
condemned the antisocialist elements upon becoming chairman of the
Polish war veterans and resistance fighters association (*Pravda*, Nov. 5,
1980). This may have been a straw in the wind that Moscow was casting
about for an effective rival to Kania.

As the strike deadline of November 12 grew closer, Solidarity was
tacitly menaced with Soviet connivance. Warsaw Radio reported on
November 8 and *Pravda* two days later that maneuvers had taken place
by units of the Polish Army and the Soviet Northern Group of Forces.
A documentary about the maneuvers was shown on Warsaw television,
albeit Western journalists were sure that the film was taken from the
archives.

Unobtrusively, a major shift occurred in the Soviet Army command
that can be linked to the tension in Poland. Col. Gen. of Tank Forces
Mikhail Zaytsev, commander of the Belorussian Military District, was
promoted to Army General (*Pravda*, Nov. 5, 1980). Zaytsev was later

identified as commander-in-chief of the Group of Soviet Forces in Germany. He traded posts with Army Gen. Yevgeniy Ivanovskiy, recognized as the top operational commander in the Warsaw Pact and natural leader of a Soviet thrust into Poland if it was decided upon by the Kremlin.

The presence of fleets of limousines at the Soviet Embassy in Warsaw on the morning of November 10 was indicative of high-level meetings (*New York Times*, Nov. 12, 1980). Moscow was no doubt involved somehow in the key decision, announced later that day by the Polish Supreme Court, to register Solidarity on virtually its own terms. The strikes set for November 12 were called off and a fresh breathing space was gained by all concerned.

Soviet policy planners were likely to have assessed Kania's latest retreat as a severe blow. The leadership of Solidarity was known to have been split into moderate and militant wings. Moderates, according to the Western press, were fearful of a violent reaction from Kania or Brezhnev if strike action was taken on November 12. They were overriden by radicals such as Andrzej Gwiazda, a onetime exile in Siberia, who discounted the danger of Soviet intervention. It stood to reason that Gwiazda was no less scornful of the Kania team, and convinced that Solidarity could with impunity go to the brink in disputes with the authorities. Soviet military maneuvers near Poland would have to be intensified, the planners might have concluded, so that the Gwiazdas be brought to their senses. As might be expected at a time of taking stock and canvassing, a deceptive calm hung over *Pravda's* reporting about Poland for about one week.

The Polish regime's defeat over the Solidarity registration issue was masked, and a line taken that Communist dutifulness was not lost sight of in Warsaw. A Polish Deputy Foreign Minister, writing in *Trybuna Luda*, was cited as having upheld the Soviet alliance tie and the Gdansk accords. The Government was still wedded to non-use of force for the settlement of internal problems, and the Soviet leadership approved of this stance. But the diplomat was said to have remarked impatiently that the crisis had gone on too long and might impact adversely on other socialist states: "We have a responsibility not only for the fate of our own people, but for the further development of the situation on the European continent." The lack of a political program could lead to structural collapse: "We have limited time and resources" (*Pravda*, Nov. 11, 1980).

The Polish Politburo and Premier were giving first priority to restoring the tempo of work at factories, according to a follow-up cable from the TASS office in Warsaw. In his speech to Party activists in Lodz, Pinkowski was critical of those who went too far in their proposals for policy change and others demanding more pay when the economy was crippled. (The reference was to striking hospital workers, teachers and postal employees.) Although the preparation and execution of management reform required time, it would begin in 1981 (*Pravda*, Nov. 13, 1980).

Significantly, the *Pravda* version of the speech by the Polish Premier did not mention that he welcomed the granting of legal status to Solidarity and looked forward to cooperating with the union. Warsaw's determination to keep Solidarity within bounds was suggested by the version of a *Trybuna Ludu* editorial in the November 17 *Pravda*. "We cannot agree," the Polish daily was quoted, "that trade unions be independent of the Party or become the 'sole genuine representative of the workers.'" *Trybuna Ludu* was also said to have recognized that there were no strictly domestic controversies in Poland: "The settlement of grave conflicts in our social life, the newspaper stresses, conflicts which have gone to the limits of risk, is an important part of the political situation in Europe." Thus, Polish leadership was implied to have in its ranks men who were aware of a need to safeguard the interests of allied states.

During the same week, an important political drama was acted out in Czestochowa, an industrial town and religious center in south Poland. Workers protested what they called an anti-Solidarity harassment campaign by the province governor since the union got legal status on November 10. The local citizens demanded the governor's removal and wanted a number of government-owned and private villas, including one belonging to the governor, to be turned over for use as kindergartens and nurseries. The governor finally offered his resignation and if accepted would have been the first time a governor had quit under pressure from irate citizens. The Polish Government cabinet went into session on November 17, presumably to discuss the revolt in Czestochowa (*Baltimore Sun*, Nov. 18, 1980). Kania had meanwhile met with Walesa and stated his belief that Solidarity had the qualifications to become an important link in Poland's socialist democracy (*New York Times*, Nov. 15, 1980).

The Vatican was also strengthening its hand in Polish life. It apparently obtained permission on November 14 to increase the circulation of the Polish edition of its newspaper *Observatore Romano* in Poland from 5,000 to 90,000. Warsaw Radio on November 16 carried the remarks of Pope John Paul II to a general audience that included Poles in which he expressed his joy that a wise and mature agreement had been reached in Poland.

The significance of warming relations between the Vatican and Warsaw as well as the Polish Pope's *de facto* endorsement of Solidarity cannot be underrated as a factor in the shaping of Soviet perceptions of the Polish scene.

In 1977, Cardinal Karol Wojtyla of Krakow, a year away from election as Pope John Paul II, openly supported the KOR dissident group after a local student in KOR was found beaten to death. Wojtyla offered the use of five Krakow churches to the "flying universities" that were spreading non-Communist ideas.[10] Since the Polish August, the Pope acted to increase Polish-language radio coverage of church affairs both through Radio Vatican and by including a correspondent from Radio Free Europe among the reporters accompanying him on his trips abroad (*Los Angeles Times*, Nov. 22, 1980). Solidarity leader Walesa, himself deeply religious, in early November listed people around Cardinal Wyszynski and the Catholic establishment as the primary intellectual advisers to the new union. Walesa also surmised that the Pope's visit to Poland in 1979 must have had an influence in provoking the wave of strikes a year later (London *The Guardian*, Nov. 6, 1980).

The growing challenge to central control of Communist Party membership and structure in Poland also had to be raising eyebrows in Moscow. By November, an estimated two-thirds of the Party rank and file had joined Solidarity. Activists in towns such as Torun were creating Party "coordination committees" which acted independently of the official regional committees. The radical *ad hoc* bodies were exerting pressure on conservative members of the regional apparatus and the main Party offices in Warsaw.[11] In Soviet parlance this was akin to "Trotskyism," or the fight for innerparty liberty that Lenin's closest associate of 1917 later waged against the Bolshevik majority headed by Stalin. One can be fairly certain that Brezhnev and his colleagues, for all their regrets about Stalin's purges of his own faction, were all Stalinists in the matter of defending the principle of hierarchy inside a ruling Communist Party.

Pravda said nothing about the Czestochowa protest, Kania-Walesa meeting, rejoicing of the Polish Pope, or decay of the Party edifice in Poland. But all that must have been tracked and deemed most vexing in the Soviet capital. For on November 19, *Pravda* exhibited its signal of rising tension in the western marches: "Situation in Poland."

NOTES

1. Zbigniew Brzezinski, *Power and Principle. Memoirs of the National Security Adviser 1977–1981* (Farrar, Straus, Giroux, New York, 1983), pp. 464–465.

2. Svetlana Alliluyeva, *Only One Year*. Translated from the Russian by Paul Chavchavadze (Harper and Row, New York, 1969), p. 47.

3. Bratislava. *Pravda*, Oct. 8, 1980 and Moscow *Pravda*, Oct. 9, 1980.

4. Cf. I. Aleksandrov in *Pravda*, July 11, 1968 and Letter of the Warsaw summit in *Pravda*, July 18, 1968.

5. Prague. *Rude Pravo*, Oct. 14, 1980.

6. *Neues Deutschland*, Oct. 7, 1980.

7. *Ibid.*, Oct. 14, 1980.

8. "On measures for increasing supervision of observance of labor laws and improvement of housing and living conditions of working people," in *Sbornik postanovleniy VTsSPS, 1980. Oktyabr-dekabr* (Moscow: 1981), pp. 112–115.

9. A.P. Kirilenko, *Izbrannye rechi i stati* (Moscow, 1976), pp. 95 and 496.

10. John Hellman, "The Prophets of Solidarity," *America*, Nov. 6, 1982, pp. 266–269.

11. See Bernard Margueritte's Warsaw dispatches in Paris *Le Figaro*, Nov. 7 and 20, 1980.

THREE

Trial of Nerves

(NOV. 19–DEC. 12, 1980)

Rarely has there been so much uncertainty about Kremlin intentions as in early December 1980. Reports were circulating that Soviet armed intervention in Poland was imminent. Even the resident foreigners in Moscow, hitherto calm about the state of Soviet-Polish relations, were apprehensive. Although the fears of a Soviet incursion proved to be unwarranted, a number of press anomalies suggest a Soviet debate over whether to bring the Polish crisis to a head.

The unity of policy decisions and personnel actions is axiomatic for Soviet Communists. Anyone chosen for a key post is assumed to be the kind of person who will be eager to perform the latest priority task given to his office from on high. *Pravda* on November 19, 1980 accordingly brought good news to those of its readers most worried about the confusion in Poland. Under the alarmist heading "Situation in Poland," *Pravda* told of Polish Party committee meetings that were stressing the necessity of taking "urgent measures for the full restoration by the Party of its leading role and authority in the nation." The language would serve to justify anything from ridding the Party of corrupt and incompetent people to arresting leading critics of the regime. The man and hour seemed to meet at a session of the Warsaw Party Committee held in the presence of Kania. Stanislaw Kociolek was installed as first secretary of the body, a selection soon protested by the Solidarity local in Gdynia on the Baltic coast. In a letter to the authorities, union officials charged that as Party leader of Gdansk in 1970 Kociolek was co-responsible for police violence against restive workers (*New York Times*, Nov. 23, 1980). Kociolek, of course, had always denied the charge, but he was clearly someone in the good books of Moscow: Kociolek would condemn all labor strikes as political in his speech to the critical meeting of the Polish Central Committee on March 29–30, 1981; he was later posted to the USSR as ambassador and invited to write for the Soviet Party press. *Pravda* supplemented the news of Polish cadres' plea for "urgent measures" and Kociolek's appointment with another TASS item reporting that *Trybuna Ludu* was angry over a swelling of worker demands. This was supposedly undermining the Gdansk accords and increasing tension in Poland. What *Pravda* did not choose to reprint were passages criticizing the Polish Government, which indicated that most Soviet leaders were still behind Kania.

The backing, however, was probably more grudging than ever after the Polish leaders on November 18 agreed to discharge the anti-Solidarity governor in Czestochowa. On the heels of a strike alert at 200 factories, a central minister was sent to Czestochowa to sign an agreement settling the two-week long dispute (Warsaw. Interpress. Nov. 19, 1980).

As in the discord over granting legal status to Solidarity, Kania was guilty of what is known in Soviet jargon as "capitulationism," or giving ground to the enemy on a point of principle. Politburo member and Party Secretary Konstantin Chernenko deplored just that among other Poland-related heresies in *Kommunist* (No. 17, cleared for printing on November 21, 1980). The director of Kremlin staff work extolled the Soviet Party as a model of discipline and "implacable struggle against all kinds of capitulationists." Like the ideologue Alekseyev in September, Chernenko invoked the authority of Lenin against "ideas of trade unions' 'freedom' from the struggle for the working class' ultimate goals and their 'independence' of all the working people's interests." In other words, Solidarity could never be integrated into the governing structure of Poland but had to be subjugated by one means or another.

Kania's indulgent policies and rejection of Fuehrerism in his inaugural made it possible too that he was the butt of other, unusual criticism. Ivan Pronin, a personnel expert of the Soviet Party Secretariat, wrote in the organizational journal of that body: "V.I. Lenin highly valued officials who had their own firm conviction and principled opinion. At the same time, Lenin always condemned indecisive, vacillating and unprincipled people who played the role of reconcilors of completely opposite views" (*Partiynaya Zhizn*, No. 23, cleared for printing Nov. 25, 1980).

A Kremlin wish to augment the shaky Polish leadership was suggested by *Pravda* giving more acclaim to that symbol of law and order Moczar. He was said to have shared with war veterans his displeasure with the slow pace at which the political climate in Poland was being normalized (Nov. 21). Moczar was also reported to have warned that no one had the right to insult Communists, and that unbridled emotions had never benefited Poles in their national history—a dark allusion to the crushing of popular uprisings by foreign powers (Nov. 23).

Even as Moczar was getting high marks for urging his countrymen to self-restraint, new developments in Poland were irritating the Soviet leaders. The functioning of the Polish railway system was becoming an apple of discord between Moscow and Warsaw. Striking railway workers in Warsaw and Gdansk briefly halted local commuter services rather than the international routes, as happened at Lublin in July. But *Trybuna Ludu* had to reassure Moscow on November 25 that labor problems would "never make it impossible for Poland to make good on its export and transit commitments." TASS shrugged off the optimism and in a November 24 dispatch from Warsaw asserted that a general strike on the Polish railways over Solidarity wage and jurisdictional demands "could affect the national interests, as well as disrupt transit railroad communications through Poland" (*Pravda*, Nov. 25, 1980).

The security police is the ultimate guardian of bureaucratic power and privilege in a state organized along Soviet lines. Without the wide-ranging activities of the security service and its accountability only to top leaders, it is hard to believe that pressures from below for self-government and civil liberties could be contained. Open criticism of the security police in Hungary (1956) and Czechoslovakia (1968) had fed the popular clamor for genuine democracy. Kremlin leaders, therefore, must have been excited by the extraordinary events in Poland from November 20–27 which threatened to breach the regime's most critical line of political survival.

The security police raided the Warsaw headquarters of Solidarity on November 20 and confiscated a copy of a confidential document on dissident groups. A volunteer printer at the headquarters was detained on November 21 in connection with the discovery of the document. Also arrested was someone who allegedly leaked the document while working in the state prosecutor's office. A strike was called at the Ursus tractor plant on November 24 to protest the arrests. The next day, November 25, Warsaw Solidarity leaders announced plans for a general strike in the capital on November 27. Their demands included the release of six imprisoned activists, in addition to the volunteer printer, and investigation of the security apparatus. Deputy Premier Jagielski met with Solidarity officials to prevent the dispute from getting out of hand.

The matter was so delicate that *Pravda* could not reveal anything like its full scope. Only on November 26, a day after the Warsaw Solidarity leaders demanded a probe of the security police, did *Pravda* disclose the incident which had ignited the furore. The Deputy General Prosecutor in Warsaw was said to have held a press conference and given unspecified details about the discovery of a "secret document" on Solidarity premises. The document contained "information that is a state secret" and investigation turned up the source of the leakage and persons who had duplicated and then publicized the document. The indicated persons were under arrest in accord with existing law, according to the TASS account.

The Soviet elite may have been very indignant over Kania's dawdling after the union had taken steps tending to demoralize the security apparatus. In the same November 26 issue of *Pravda* which told of the leaked-document episode, the Polish Government was adversely criticized. Speakers at a meeting of Communist trade-union officials with the Premier, TASS said, complained that "the Government sees in the old trade unions a 'scapegoat,' something which hinders the reaching of agreements with the new trade unions, 'Solidarity.' The mass media do not give the necessary attention to the work of the branch [old] trade unions, and more is written or said about 'Solidarity.'" The Communist union men were also reported to have deplored "opportunism," which in the context of events was a shaft at Kania's policy of going the extra mile to placate Solidarity.

Kania himself tried to mend relations with the old union leaders and their sympathizers in Moscow. *Pravda* on November 27 carried a short version of his speech at a parley with the labor bureaucrats in Warsaw. The message was not likely to have soothed the anxious minds of Kania's listeners. Dismemberment of the trade union movement in Poland was lamely regretted as a fact that was "negative, but objective." Kania did vent concern over the threat of a strike on the railroads, where stoppages could harm "our alliance ties," but he did not bring under fire the so-called antisocialist elements.

In contrast to the soft inflection in Kania's voice was a roar from the Polish Party's ideology journal that appeared in the same *Pravda* for November 27. Antisocialist forces were hit on grounds of intensifying their attacks on the Party and social institutions. A seizure of power was alleged to be the goal of these elements, who were inspiring the workers to make illegitimate economic and political demands. A cryptic passage in this TASS cable from Warsaw stated that Poles had "paid a heavy price in the years of Hitlerite occupation" for some unexplained "political game." This evidently harked back to the pro-Western sentiment of the prewar Polish government or the Warsaw revolt against the Germans in 1944, which had an anti-Soviet undercurrent. The intention was clearly to discredit critics of the present-day regime in Poland as persons liable to cause a national debacle.

The arm-twisting on stage and doubtless behind the scenes too was not entirely useless from the Soviet standpoint. Kania helped to defuse the explosive issue of police control by agreeing to the provisional release of the two workers charged with betraying state secrets. Walesa and dissident leader Kuron no longer dismissed the possibility that force might be used to break a major strike. The Solidarity chairman, addressing strikers in the Warsaw region, raised the spectre of a destructive "confrontation with tanks and rockets" of the Polish Government while Kuron warned of the danger of Soviet military intervention. The workers voted to end their strike (*Baltimore Sun*, Nov. 29, 1980).

If the Soviet Politburo met in these days of turmoil, the chances are that a decision was reached to mount a great campaign of psychological pressure on Polish society as a whole. A series of propaganda volleys would serve to complement military moves that were prepared weeks earlier in order to influence several key groups among Poles. (The Associated Press reported from Washington on November 25 that the Soviet Union had been improving the readiness of its forces near Poland, but there was no evidence that preparations for an attack were under way.)

Solidarity radicals were to be cowed away from their demands for higher wages and public scrutiny of the affairs of bureaucracy. Kania was to be hectored into opening his Party cabinet to men who wanted to restore social order as a precondition for enacting policy changes. Old-line Communists were to be encouraged in their resistance to the loosening of discipline while the innerparty reformers would be led to second thoughts. This hypothesis of Kremlin decision-taking would seem to be the best one in light of the twists and turns of Soviet propaganda that followed.

The opening shot in a campaign of pressure was *Pravda* summarizing on November 28 a statement of Polish war veterans that was recently sent to all ruling and civic bodies in the country. This manifesto derogatorily labelled the radical reformers (antisocialist elements) as Western hirelings and accused them of trying to destabilize the situation. Veterans were said to be "deeply concerned" by the persistence of social tension as a catalyst of economic difficulties and anti-regime attitudes. "We condemn any and all intrigues of the antisocialist forces," the veterans declared, adding "We have the moral right to demand a halt to anarchy. . . ."

The statement of Polish veterans was reminiscent of a pro-Soviet and anti-liberal resolution adopted in June 1968 at a nationwide mobilization of the Czechoslovak People's Militia, or Communist Party army. But the resolution was delivered to the Soviet Embassy in Prague and after *Pravda* had printed it there was a torrent of agreeing rhetoric from Soviet meetings and citizens (*Pravda*, June 21 and July 7, 1968). The new wrinkle was *Pravda*'s failure to reproduce the Polish document in verbatim form and subsequent absence of Soviet worker meetings in response to the airing of a mere summary. This novelty can be regarded as a sign of Kremlin reluctance to seek a showdown in Poland. At the same time, *Pravda* drove home the gravity of the Polish question by resurfacing the man who proved to be the ideological herald of the Afghanistan invasion.

Prof. Miran Mchedlov was deputy director of the Soviet Party's Institute of Marxism-Leninism. He wrote what turned out to be a lethal theory article for *Pravda*, November 16, 1979, on "Religion in the Present-day World." In it, Mchedlov attacked "enemies of people's power and revolutionary gains in Afghanistan (such as the renowned 'Muslim brothers,' agents of international imperialism and other reactionary forces)." A few weeks later, Soviet troops deposed Afghan President Amin, who was soon called one of the "agents of international imperialism." *Pravda*'s editors may have been told in November 1979 that they should use the important vehicle of an article on theory to impress upon Soviet officialdom the great danger to Moscow's security interests in Afghanistan.

Mchedlov appeared once again in *Pravda* (Nov. 28, 1980) with a theory article, pegged to the 160th birthday of Friedrich Engels but obviously written with an eye to the Polish crisis. Mchedlov warned:

> The experience of the practical building of socialism in various countries of the planet has confirmed that . . . an abstract, nonclass attitude towards problems of democracy, humanism, etc. leads only to a weakening of the new system, and in a number of cases even creates favorable opportunities for the action of antisocialist forces. The tactics of the latter have undergone an evolution. Heedful that in present-day conditions the success of "classical forms" of counterrevolution—armed uprising and violent destruction of the socialist system—is scarcely probable, they aim at paralyzing and decomposing it from within in order to attain a "peaceful" restoration of capitalism. The whole spirit of Engels' theoretical heritage and his practical activity teach a timely response to the change of tactics by the forces hostile to the working class and entire toiling people, to uncover their real intentions. This was and remains an important political and ideological task of the Communist and worker parties.

Although downplaying the peril of armed insurrection against socialism, Mchedlov hinted that the lives of Soviet friends in Poland could be put into jeopardy: Engels had often witnessed "the debauchery of the bloody terror of counterrevolution."

A section of the Polish powerholders was indeed paralyzed, and *Pravda* reported so on November 29. Some officials of the Party apparatus were said to be spending all their energy on self-flagellation and others were trying to wait-out the crisis in the quiet of their offices. (Reliable sources told of Polish functionaries who were then literally barricading themselves in Party buildings out of fear that they would be accosted

by disgruntled citizens.) Once more, *Pravda* alleged that patriots throughout Poland were asking the highest echelon to take "effective measures"
to curb public excesses.

Suddenly, on November 30, *Pravda* refrained from the use of its
indicator of a slump of Communist fortunes in Poland. The gloomy
caption "Events in Poland" or "Situation in Poland" had been manifest
from November 25 through November 29. The withdrawal of this danger
sign on November 30 coincided with *Pravda* informing that the Polish
Politburo had met on November 28, discussed the topic of a Central
Committee session and called for it to open on December 1. Soviet
leaders would seem to have heard from Kania that he would be mindful
of their concerns at the plenum. One might date to this time a Soviet
promise of additional economic aid to Poland and credits in convertible
currencies with a total value of $1.3 billion (Warsaw Radio, Dec. 1,
1980). This was not the kind of gesture that Kremlin leaders would
make towards a foreign Communist chief about to be excommunicated.

The Kremlin's receipt of new assurances from Kania would help to
explain why *Pravda* softened the text of a Czechoslovak newspaper
commentary on Poland that it summarized on November 30. "The
Positions of Socialism are Unshakeable" was *Pravda*'s title for an article
in the November 27 *Rude Pravo* marking the tenth anniversary of an
inquest into the Prague Spring. Both texts deplored "antisocialist aggressive trade unionism" in Poland, but expressed confidence that "the
socialist, patriotic forces of Poland" would do "everything vitally essential" to defend socialism. *Pravda*, however, poured oil on the troubled
waters by ignoring the Czechoslovak daily's harsh reference to "attempts
which, under the slogan of 'renewal' and overcoming 'deformations,'
are striving for nothing else but to exhaust and paralyze socialist power
and establish willfully or intentionally elements of petit bourgeois
counterrevolution."

The relative moderation of Soviet press comment on Polish affairs
was in tune with the presumed Kremlin decision to stage a show of
force around Poland, rather than launch an invasion, either directly or
by organizing a Warsaw Pact exercise in Poland as a ruse to neutralize
Polish forces.

The Moscow press on November 30 gave an intimation that Soviet
army commanders were about to perform an important political mission
that was related to the Polish crisis. *Pravda* ran an article for the 90th
birthday of Marshal Vasiliy Blyukher, legendary hero of the Russian
civil war and Stalin purge victim. It was quite different from the 75th
birthday piece, carried in the same newspaper on November 19, 1964.
(Blyukher was now said to have been born on December 1, 1890 and
not in November 1889.) Blyukher was described as a "mature *politician*

(*politik*), diplomat and military figure," who was an "outstanding miltary-*political* figure of the Leninist guard" (emphasis supplied). Another novelty was mention of the Red Army's conduct of "battles with the White Poles" in 1920, something which normally is not mentioned in Western biographies of Blyukher. The military newspaper *Red Star* also noted that Blyukher "took an active part in the solving of important general-Party and general-State problems."

The flexing of Soviet muscle on Polish borders was impressive enough to have ruffled the White House. President Carter writes in his memoirs: "Early in December [1980], not quite a year after Soviet troops had invaded Afghanistan, we became convinced that their military forces were preparing to move into Poland. . . . We were monitoring Soviet military preparations very closely. Fifteen or twenty divisions were ready to move; for the first time, Czech and Soviet forces were conducting night exercises together. The Soviets were surveying invasion routes, had set up an elaborate communications system throughout Poland, were conducting intensive photo reconnaissance flights out of Czecho-slovakia and East Germany, and were holding their military forces in a high state of readiness. . . . I sent Brezhnev a direct message warning of the serious consequences of a Soviet move into Poland."[1] The President's national-security adviser amplifies: "We learned that Soviet forces had been deployed in an offensive mode, sections of the East German-Polish and of the Soviet-Polish frontiers had been sealed off, and we had mounting indications of accelerated preparations in airfields, depots, and even hospitals."[2]

Western intelligence sources were reported to have picked up other measures taken by the Soviets, Czechoslovaks and East Germans in early December: moving command posts to forward positions along the Polish borders and fleshing out units with reservists from civilian life (Washington *Star*, Dec. 18, 1980).

The large scale of Soviet military preparations were clearly distressing to Ceausescu, independence-minded dictator of Communist Romania. Foreign Minister Andrei flew to Moscow from Bucharest on December 2 for an unscheduled meeting with Brezhnev. A "friendly" conversation between the two was reported on page one in the December 3 *Pravda*. Evidently Romanian fears of a Soviet thrust into Poland were allayed, or a formula denoting strain might have been used to characterize the Brezhnev-Andrei talks.

Simultaneously, Moscow dropped a strong hint that it had still not earmarked Kania for early removal. *Pravda* on December 3 allotted an entire half page to an account of Kania's December 1 report at the Central Committee session in Warsaw.

Kania had said some things that Soviet leaders disapproved of and these were kept out of *Pravda*. This was true of references to: conservative resistance to the line of policy renewal as undesirable; the imperative nature of concessions made to Solidarity by the Government; the legitimacy of the workers' right to strike and of independent, self-governing public bodies; the vital importance of innerparty democracy for the entire society; and the need for mechanisms (judicial, e.g.) to prevent a build-up of social discontent. The Kremlin was still hopeful that essentials of the old order would be recreated in Poland. But a Soviet decision to mark time was suggested by the overall editorial treatment of Kania's speech, as well as the vast coverage that *Pravda* gave to it.

Surely, if the Kremlin was planning some drastic action *Pravda* would not have undertaken a series of upbeat citations from Kania's address. The Polish leader was quoted to the effect that "Soviet comrades" possessed "the conviction that we will find a way out of the crisis." Solidarity was credited with being a "workers movement" and "movement of working people." The greater majority of its activists, members and sympathizers were praised as law-abiding citizens. Only a limited number of its chapters were said to be keeping alive a strike atmosphere and rashly threatening strikes. Only "some of the links" of Solidarity "were penetrated and are negatively inspired by groups and persons connected with centers of imperialist subversion whose aims are hostile to socialism and people's power."

The image of Kania projected to Soviet Communists on December 3 was that of aroused keeper of the flame of orthodoxy. Whatever his inner misgivings, Kania did bow to the strictures that Soviet leader Chernenko had indirectly levelled at him. "We shall act resolutely," Kania said, "against all symptoms of ideological capitulation, violations of ideological unity and actions against the Party's ability to act." The Party would not be allowed to become a "discussion club" and structures set up by ordinary Party members outside the existing hierarchy of committees would not be tolerated. Avoiding direct mention of the Czestochowa revolt, Kania assailed the practice of forcing changes in regional government or local management by threatening strikes and occupying official buildings. There could not, Kania said, be "two ruling powers" in the Polish state, and he tacitly expressed a readiness to use the security forces to resolve social conflicts if that became necessary. Kania did so by affirming that in Poland "A sharp class struggle is continuing"—a throwback to the pro-coercion dogma of Stalinist times.

The favorable publicity lately given to Moczar in *Pravda* suggested Soviet contentment with the Polish leadership reshuffle announced on December 2 at the close of the Warsaw plenum. Moczar and another order-before-reform man, Deputy Premier Tadeusz Grabski, were named voting members of the Politburo; the relatively popular Gdansk Party boss Tadeusz Fiszbach was made a nonvoting member. Ousted from the ruling clique were four holdovers from the Gierek period who reputedly belonged to a standpatter grouping. As always, the changes were simply listed in *Pravda* (Dec. 4) and not commented on so as to maintain the fiction of monolithic unity.

NATO diplomatic sources, according to Reuter on December 3, believed that Moscow did not intend to intervene at the current stage of the Polish crisis. Their view was supported by the fact that *Pravda* on December 5 issued a truncated version of an appeal of the Polish Central Committee to the nation. The summary mentioned "acute political crisis" and individuals with "counterrevolutionary intentions" whose plans would be foiled. But *Pravda* ignored the original document's extreme passages to the effect that "the fate of our nation and country hangs in the balance" and "Continuing unrest is leading our motherland to the brink of economic and moral destruction" (Interpress, Dec. 3, 1980). If Soviet public opinion was being readied for a major action in Poland it would have been a Polish military takeover of the reins of government.

The Polish Defense Ministry's Military Council met on December 3 and two days later *Pravda* reported that the Council had issued a communique. "Deep concern" was voiced about "the situation in the country, which represents a grave threat to social-economic life and the functioning of state bodies." The communique was said to have emphasized that "Further maintenance of such a situation could evoke grave negative consequences for the country's defense capability." The Council had set "tasks facing the armed forces" under the circumstances. This statement was reportedly heartening to an East German policy expert, who told an American correspondent on December 4 that authority had broken down in Poland and that the National Guard would be called to reestablish order if a similar situation existed in the United States (*New York Times*, Dec. 5, 1980).

The East German's estimate of the Polish situation was shared by many high-level officials in the Soviet Union and eastern Europe, to judge from the presence of some key security leaders at the Warsaw Pact emergency summit held in Moscow on December 5. Defense and interior ministers were in the delegations representing the Soviet Union, G.D.R. and Poland. But the order of listing of Soviet delegates in the summit communique was by itself suggestive of a consensus for restraint at the pinnacle of the alliance. As though the use of economic and propaganda leverage would move Kania to take action for regaining control in Poland, the USSR delegation was officially listed as: Brezhnev, Premier Tikhonov, Party Secretary (for ideology) Suslov, KGB chairman Andropov, Foreign Minister Gromyko, Defense Minister Ustinov and

Party Secretary (for Bloc liaison) Rusakov. There may of course be other angles to this list of Soviet leaders, which puts Suslov out of alphabetical order so that he outranks Andropov. But it could have been framed to dovetail with the text of the summit communique, which unmistakably hinted that Kania should be given more time to put his house in order.

Polish Communists and people, the summit communique declared, "will be able to overcome the difficulties that have emerged, and ensure the country's further development on the socialist path." One could have read in a number of ways, menacing or supportive, the allied assertion that Poles "can firmly count on the fraternal solidarity and support" of Bloc members. The lone certainty one could glean from the communique was that power in Warsaw would not be allowed to slip out of the hands of persons responsive to the wishes of Moscow: ". . . Poland has been, is and will remain a socialist state, a firm link in the general family of the lands of socialism."

Rightly or not, the White House was focusing on Soviet military capabilities for intervening in Poland and the clandestine reports about their utilization. The national-security adviser of President Carter describes the vigil on Poland from December 5 as follows:

> On Friday, December 5, at 9:10 a.m., I received a secure call from [Director Central Intelligence] Turner informing me that according to reliable information a number of Soviet divisions were scheduled to enter Poland on Monday morning. . . . At the SCC [Special Coordination Committee] meeting, held at 4 p.m. on Saturday, Turner informed us that it was anticipated that Soviet divisions would enter Poland in the next forty-eight hours and that this would be accompanied by a crackdown by the Polish Communist regime on the Solidarity movement. The Agency judgement was that there would be national resistance and considerable bloodshed. . . . The NSC [National Security Council] convened at 9 a.m. on Sunday in the Cabinet Room. We again reviewed intelligence information indicating that the Soviets would move into Poland under the guise of a "peaceful exercise" and that this would be combined with a simultaneous massive crackdown against the Solidarity movement. . . . The situation remained tense for the next several days, with intelligence agencies indicating that the scope of the Soviet intervention might be even greater than anticipated. Additional divisions were identified as ready to move, and . . . preparations included advance storage of fuel supplies, the unfolding of tents next to field hospitals to provide more space for likely casualties, and the forward deployment of assault forces, including paratroopers.[3]

President Carter jotted down in his diary on December 8, 1980 with respect to Poland: "Brezhnev has not answered my hot-line message. This is the first time that has occurred."[4]

Brezhnev left Moscow on December 7th for a short visit to India. In his absence, a startling dispatch was filed by the TASS office in Warsaw and broadcast by Moscow radio on December 8. The dispatch was reportedly scheduled for prominent display in the major Soviet newspapers on the following day. But it did not appear either on the main television newscast in Moscow on the night of December 8 or in the Soviet press on December 9.

TASS alleged that in various parts of Poland "counterrevolutionary groups, operating under the cover of branches of the 'Solidarity' union, have turned to open confrontation" with Party and management. A "campaign" had supposedly begun in a number of Solidarity committees "to replace trade union workers by persons who openly adhere to antigovernment positions." "These and other facts," TASS said, "show that counterrevolution is leading the situation in the country toward further destabilization and aggravation of the political struggle." In particular, TASS declared that "so-called 'protectors' of workers' interests" at a plant in Kielce, south of Warsaw, had ousted the management and guards. Party activists who stood up to the rebels "were missing," that is, were abducted or murdered.

The TASS report was fabricated. Interpress, the Polish information agency, and the local Solidarity chapter in Kielce denied that accusation. One Solidarity branch called it "a complete lie . . . aimed at misleading Polish, Russian and world opinion" (*Washington Post*, Dec. 9, 1980).

The TASS canard was at variance with the essentially clean bill of health that Kania had given to Solidarity a week earlier and which *Pravda* seemingly approved. It also tended to demolish the veiled thesis in the September 6 *Pravda* that what was going on in Poland was a "dispute over principle" in which it would be "senseless" to use a "fist." The Soviet news agency was in effect claiming that Solidarity was driving for power and it was suggesting that a clampdown was necessary.

Was the TASS alarm of December 8 triggered only for the Polish leaders so as to intimidate them, or was it the work of a pro-interventionist faction in Moscow which was eager to stir up Soviet audiences, and did moderate forces at top level soon short-circuit the signal for action?

A number of anomalies, taken in their entirety, suggest that in Brezhnev's absence some members of the Soviet elite were using the propaganda machine to promote their own policy opinions. Defense Minister Ustinov stole Brezhnev's thunder and became the first Politburo member to comment directly on the Polish situation. Speaking at a Party conference of the Moscow Military District on December 10, Ustinov urged "vigilance" in the face of "the attempts of reactionaries to inflict harm on the positions of socialist countries, in particular socialist Poland" (*Pravda*, Dec. 11, 1980). The same copy of *Pravda* had an inflammatory slogan in a book review that concerned the smashing of the Prague liberals in 1968. The slogan exhorted to "struggle to strengthen the front of confrontation with anticommunism and anti-Sovietism on an international scale." On the same day too, anti-Solidarity feeling was running high among certain editors at Radio Moscow. The station on December 11 transmitted two versions of an article in the Polish military newspaper *Zolnierz Wolnosci*. The second version omitted the italicized words in the following passage used during each of the broadcasts: "The Party, all patriots, and the overwhelming majority of all Poles have declared and are saying 'yes' to the process of renewal, to necessary and obligatory economic reforms and to necessary changes in the trade union movement *including Solidarity*. They are saying 'no' to political subversion, anarchy, chaos and all attempts to turn Poland from the socialist path of development" (emphasis supplied). The effect of dropping Solidarity from the category of approved phenomena was to associate it with disintegrative tendencies, that is, something which an interventionist group in the Soviet hierarachy would have desired.

Brezhnev returned to Moscow from India on December 11 and the impression of uncertainty was heightened by *Pravda* on December 12 running the following announcement:

IN THE CPSU CENTRAL COMMITTEE
On results of the meeting of leading figures
of the Warsaw Treaty member states held in Moscow
on December 5, 1980.

To approve the results of the meeting of leading figures of the Warsaw Treaty member states, as well as the activity of the Soviet Union's delegation headed by comrade L.I. Brezhnev at this meeting.

Apparently, the Politburo held a regular Thursday session on December 11 and this was the text of the resolution that had been adopted. The procedure itself was normal on the heels of important bilateral or multilateral talks, but it was quite unusual for a Politburo document of this kind to lack a "political evaluation" of the talks. Underscoring the irregularity were reports in the Soviet press from December 8 through 12 on discussions of the Warsaw Pact summit at Politburo sessions in Warsaw, Prague, East Berlin, Budapest and Sofia. Each of those reports had restated the Bloc leaders' confidence that the Poles themselves would be able to surmount their crisis. (Romania's Ceausescu and his colleagues did so the following week, according to the December 18 *Pravda*.)

Disorder in the status indicators of Soviet leaders crowned the unusual developments of December 8 through 12. KGB chief Andropov continued to outrank Party Secretary Chernenko in the line-up of Brezhnev's colleagues who bid him farewell on occasion of his trip to India, according to the photograph in *Pravda* December 8, 1980 (Cf. *Pravda*, Sept. 1, 1980). Chernenko, however, took precedence over Andropov in a similar array of leaders welcoming back the Soviet President which *Pravda* depicted on December 12, 1980. Assuming a Polish policy tie-in, as one can, the relatively moderate stance Chernenko took in his public remarks about the crisis from start to finish tends to raise the possibility that in Brezhnev's absence he brought influence to bear to restrain the more aggressive ruling groups in Moscow.

The anomalies do not necessarily serve to confirm the rumor cited in the Preface that in December 1980 the Soviet leadership was divided over an invasion of Poland. But it is intriguing that cross-currents abounded while Soviet armies gathered at the western frontier. The historian of the future may uncover the truth about this Kremlin muddle, if the Brezhnev-led Politburo kept minutes of its proceedings. For the moment, a hunch is that Soviet leaders were arguing among themselves over how long to endure the tumult in Poland, and the vehemence of their controversy played havoc with the routine workings of the propaganda system in Moscow. In sum, the Soviet elite could have taken several alternative courses of action during the three-week period under review.

It might have done little more than criticize those responsible for labor unrest on the Polish railways and others demanding social control of the security police in Poland. The probable consequence would have been to embolden the Solidarity radicals to go further and weaken the Warsaw regime in its struggle to keep control of most economic and administrative centers. If this virtual do-nothing approach was taken, Soviet influence in eastern Europen would have fallen, and social discontent might have led to the testing of especially unpopular regimes in the area.

The Kremlin had the second option of organizing a show of force along the Polish borders with a view toward frightening Solidarity, stiffening the Kania team and raising the stock of hardline Communists. The likely outcome of such a gambit was unforeseeable, but probably more rewarding than that inherent in choice 1.

The third possibility for Moscow was to use the display of force to induce Polish leaders to declare a state of emergency. Solidarity leaders would be arrested, the union put under ban, and civil liberties drastically curtailed. This, of course, was done a year later and "worked" insofar as bloodshed within Poland was rare and the international reaction did not gravely impair Soviet interests. This step, however, was riskier than posturing with tanks and hoping for the best. Civil war might have broken out and required the engagement of Soviet troops.

A fourth choice was military intervention. The imponderables of such a move were considerable. Was the Soviet Army already set to move? In the case of Czechoslovakia, the Soviet practice was to exercise its entire invasion force before using it. In early December 1980 the Soviets had reportedly exercised each of six armies on five different fronts surrounding Poland. But they had only begun to hold coordinated maneuvers of entire fronts as an entity, and were just nearing the completion of various readiness tests. Also, the assigning of some Soviet personnel to Polish army units was only beginning.[5] Still another question was if a new, pro-Soviet government could be formed quickly in Poland and would have any sizable support in the population. If not, as seemed likely, the Soviet Army commanders would have to set up an occupation regime. That meant courting the twin dangers of violent clashes with Poles and the demoralization of Soviet servicemen. Kremlin strategists also had to weigh the possibility of NATO trade sanctions and the likelihood of some defections from their "peace movement" in the West if Poland was invaded. Washington might have played the China card with a vengeance.

The usual dovetailing of a propagandist's intent with the policymakers' aim in a dictatorial setting suggests that Soviet leaders vacillated between alternatives 2 and 3—military/psychological pressure to "sober up" the Poles or to cause the imposition of martial law in Poland. Once the November 26 Pravda had blessed Polish internal criticism of the Warsaw Government, everyone had to know that policy choice 1—immobilism—had been rejected.

The political preparations for armed intervention or martial law were at first not in evidence. That can be gathered from a number of peculiarities in Soviet media output in early December. There was: an absence of reports that factory meetings in the USSR were echoing the anger of Polish Communist loyalists over Solidarity misdeeds; forsaking of the high-crisis heading for TASS dispatches from Warsaw; moderating of an outcry from Prague about the sinister plans for "counterrevolution" in Poland; the granting of much publicity to Kania's tougher-than-usual speech of December 1; and the toning down of the strident appeal for discipline from Polish authorities to the people soon after Kania spoke. The peculiarities make suspect the warnings of Soviet intervention described by Brzezinski as coming from "covert intelligence sources" that aroused disquiet at the White House from December 5.

It is true that the groundwork for a martial-law decision was laid by Pravda reporting the communique of the Military Council of the Polish Defense Ministry (December 5) and TASS alleging that Solidarity had embarked upon a ruthless effort to take over factories (December 8). But this is insufficient reason to conclude that all along the purpose of the Soviet military build-up around Poland was to force the Warsaw Government to proclaim martial law. Only at the Soviet Politburo meeting on December 11, it seems, did certain Kremlin leaders press for drastic action of the kind not envisaged in the directives supplied to propagandists in the past two weeks or so. That hypothesis rests on the string of anomalies noticeable from non-publication of the December 8 TASS dispatch on Solidarity thrusting to power through the Politburo's blank resolution of December 11 on the Warsaw Pact summit.

Thus it appears that most of the Soviet rulers were wedded to the safest course of policy, which was to conduct psychological warfare against almost the entire Polish nation. To theorize about the relative strength of the different forces which together produced this decision would be an exercise more wearisome in the attempt than useful in the achievement. A surmise is that miscalculation underlying the invasion of Afghanistan a year earlier and acceptance of the folk wisdom One War at a Time was a most weighty factor that put a damper on Soviet aggressiveness.

NOTES

1. Jimmy Carter, *Keeping Faith. Memoirs of a President* (Bantam Books, New York, 1982), p. 584.

2. Brzezinski, *Power and Principle*, p. 465.

3. *Ibid.*, pp. 466–467.

4. Carter, *op. cit.*, p. 585.

5. See the summaries of a report by Les Aspin, chairman of the US House of Representatives' intelligence oversight subcommittee, in the *Washington Post* and Washington *Star*, Jan. 2, 1981.

FOUR

The Pillars in Jeopardy

(DEC. 12, 1980–MAR. 4, 1981)

Soon after the seemingly inconclusive meeting of the Soviet Politburo on December 11, 1980 there were further signs of discord among Kremlin leaders over the Polish question. Some, it appears, urged the immediate arrest of dissident intellectuals advising Solidarity, or a crackdown on the labor movement itself. Others evidently wished to delay action and let conservative bureaucrats in Poland go on hindering the activities of Solidarity till the union was devitalized. Internal Polish trends did not have an entirely predictable effect on Soviet collective thought. Brezhnev and *Pravda* escalated criticism of disruptive influences at the end of 1980, although relative calm had settled over Poland. A torrent of protest actions, many not authorized by nationwide Solidarity, burst forth in January 1981 and the response of Soviet propagandists was varied, probably due to squabbling in Moscow. The advent of Polish Defense Minister General Jaruzelski to the post of premier as social tension was easing in February raised the prospect of the formation of an alliance of nationalists and reformers. This development seems to have compelled Soviet leaders to close ranks and agree upon more pressure on Kania to deal a blow at the suspected brain trust of Solidarity.

"Dangerous Provocations" was the title of an Aleksey Petrov article in the December 18, 1980 *Pravda*. The article was ostensibly a riposte to statements in behalf of Polish sovereignty made at the NATO Council session which ended in Brussels on December 12. Actually, it served the interest of all Kremlin leaders, who needed an alibi for armed intervention in Poland in the event of the collapse of the Warsaw regime.

Petrov accused NATO of a readiness to go over from the ideological subversion of Poland to military intervention. NATO armed forces had supposedly rehearsed, in exercises, "alternative methods of military intervention in the event of so-called 'crisis situations' arising in the countries of eastern Europe." The NATO leaders, Petrov charged, wanted the Polish situation to "pass out of the control" of the Communist authorities and to see Poland "plunged into chaos and anarchy."

What *Pravda* seemed to be arguing between the lines was an updated version of the old imperialist doctrine of contingent necessity. European and American empire-builders of the 19th century had used this idea to lend authority to colonial ventures in Africa and Asia. It was rightful, the expansionists held, for a great power to move into nearby unstable areas coveted by rivals. Now the USSR, *Pravda* was suggesting, would be acting correctly if its armies invaded Poland in the event of the fall of its client government there; otherwise, the hostile West would fill the power vacuum in the center of Soviet Europe.

Running parallel to the strategic alibi-making were no doubt some important differences in Soviet ruling circles over the making of a tactical action plan. The disagreements can be discerned from press comment on Poland which featured incompatible doctrinal statements about the nature of domestic strife inside a socialist country. Disarray of that kind has traditionally reflected policy struggles in the Soviet hierarchy.

The commentators were faithful to orthodoxy and recognized as legitimate a conflict of interests in socialist societies. But one spoke of "antagonistic and non-antagonistic contradictions" while the other would go no further than to acknowledge the existence of "non-antagonistic contradictions." In Marxist terms, "antagonistic" conflicts are irreconcilable struggles and must be settled by violent action. "Non-antagonistic" conflicts, however, can be mitigated through mutual compromise or the conduct of a prudent policy.

In the context of Polish events, which each commentator was discussing, this variation was a signpost to divergent opinions of Solidarity-Government relations and what the Soviet Union should do next about Poland. The believer in "antagonistic" conflicts was likely to imagine that a battle of annihilation was raging between the worker movement and the Communist Party. He would tend to advocate the harshest measures for the elimination of Solidarity. Anyone seeing only "non-antagonistic" conflicts in Poland would have favored a strictly political contest with Solidarity.

The pro-confrontation view was aired in a yearend review of world affairs in the Party journal *Kommunist*. Vadim Nekrasov stated that, "By its very essence the building of socialism is a process of resolving essentially new socioeconomic and ideological tasks and overcoming *antagonistic* and non-antagonistic contradictions" (No. 18, cleared for printing Dec. 18, 1980. Emphasis supplied). Nekrasov impressed on the minds of his readers the existence of "crisis processes of a political nature" and "acute political crisis" in Poland. He attacked the "antisocialist forces" that were "attempting to shake the foundations of the new society" and pointed up the "manifestations of open antisocialist activity by counterrevolutionary groupings."

In contrast, a similar survey by Sergey Vishnevskiy in the December 28 *Pravda* was remarkably bland. "Socialism is a young and growing social organism," Vishnevskiy wrote, "in which not everything has kept its ground and in some respects it still bears the stamp of past historical epochs. Tasks which are new in principle and complex must be solved through the resolution of internal non-antagonistic contradictions, under the fire of imperialism and its agents." Vishnevskiy, unlike Nekrasov, spoke of mere "difficulties" rather than "crisis" phenomena in Poland, and he avoided use of the emotive words "antisocialist" and "counterrevolutionary."

Disunity among the Soviet leaders would also help to explain why only one of them had directly referred to Poland outside the framework of bilateral talks in Moscow. It will be recalled that a summary of Brezhnev's speech to the October 1980 session of the CPSU Central Committee ignored Poland; Kirilenko alluded to it in his blast at "counterrevolutionary forces" in a speech made in Czechoslovakia during the same month; and Chernenko restricted himself to a seemingly indirect criticism of Kania ("capitulationism") in the November 1980 *Kommunist*. Only Ustinov, the civilian Defense Minister, clearly identified Poland as a flashpoint in his speech to military Communists on December 10, 1980.

Chernenko had a second chance to discourse about Poland in a speech to the Cuban Communist Party congress in Havana on December 19. But this candidate for the ripening successsion to Brezhnev may have wished to evade a clash with one wing or other of Soviet bureaucracy and he skirted the Polish issue. Chernenko made only a vague reference to the "export of counterrevolution" by the Western powers as something that was "impermissible" (*Pravda*, Dec. 20, 1980). Fidel Castro must have heard grim news about Poland from Moscow or Soviet guests. In his keynote speech, Castro spoke of an "explosively dangerous situation around Poland" and appears to have sniped at Kania: "When it is necessary to rectify mistakes, this must not be done by means of concessions to the external and internal class enemy." Like the hardliners in Moscow, Castro said that "victory" had to be won in Poland against the "antisocialist and counterrevolutionary elements." Castro, however, seemed eager to keep in the good graces of all the Soviet leaders. On one hand, he expressed only "hope" that the Polish Party could "with its own forces change the situation," and on the other he firmly voiced the "conviction" that worthy Poles on their own would overcome "incipient failures" (*Pravda*, Dec. 19, 1980).

At that time in the Soviet Union, local Party officials working nearest to Poland were beginning to show the concern of their East German and Czechoslovak brothers about the threat of political fallout. The Latvian Party journal warned against the reform communist (Revisionist) idea of leading a socialist country on the basis of "equal partnership" between the Communist Party, free trade unions and youth leagues, which together would make "mutually acceptable decisions." This "false, speculative and dangerous thesis" was said to benefit only "class enemies of the working people" (*Kommunist Sovetskoy Latvii*, No. 1, 1981, cleared for printing Dec. 22, 1980). Even the Kremlin moderates would have endorsed this anti-pluralist viewpoint, which belied the joint statements indicating that leaders of the USSR and Poland were in substantial ideological agreement.

One more of those empty announcements was in the works as Polish Foreign Minister Czyrek prepared for a meeting in Moscow with Brezhnev and Gromyko on December 26, 1980.

On the eve of this meeting, *Pravda* was sending mixed signals about the conditions in Poland. Kania reportedly told the first session of a commission to prepare for an extraordinary Party congress: "The public mood in our country . . . is improving, although only slowly. . . . There have been no strikes for a long time" (Dec. 23). But on the same day, *Pravda* quoted *Trybuna Ludu* on the need to "put an end to anarchy in the country's socioeconomic life." The second report exaggerated the scope of civil unrest, and was most likely inspired by critics of Kania. It was also in tune with the skepticism of certain Soviet officials that Kania would ever get up enough nerve to face down Solidarity.

Within hours of Czyrek's arrival in the Soviet capital, *Pravda* effectively rejected the validity of the Solidarity experiment. The jurist M. Baglay signed the theory article "Trade Unions in the Conditions of the Socialist Society." He linked the slogan of free unions with such internal enemies of Lenin as the Mensheviks and Socialist Revolutionaries, most of whom were exiled or later liquidated by Stalin. Baglay said that recent events in Poland had testified that industrial strikes played into the hands of anti-socialist elements. Unequivocally he declared that trade unions in the socialist countries must always work under the Communist Party's ideological and political leadership. Whatever the differences in their forms of organization, the trade unions in all socialist countries, Baglay concluded, had to make common cause (*Pravda*, Dec. 26, 1980).

Comparison of the TASS statements on the Brezhnev-Czyrek talks and the Brezhnev-Kania encounter in October is suggestive of rising Soviet dissatisfaction with the Polish rulers. The latest statement contained a new reference to the harmful schemes of "reactionaries," as well as "imperialists," which could have meant clerical forces led from Rome.

Another new note highlighted the importance of Warsaw Pact ties and Socialist Internationalism, reflecting perhaps a Kremlin demand that Soviet military officers be given a wider berth in the command structure of the Polish armed forces.[1] As in October, Brezhnev was said to be confident that Polish Communists would surmount internal difficulties. (Gromyko was to follow suit in an article on Soviet foreign policy in *Kommunist* No. 1, cleared for printing Jan. 9, 1981.) There was no mention of "unity of views" in the TASS report on the Brezhnev-Czyrek talks, which could have signified that tempers were frayed (*Pravda*, Dec. 27, 1980).

At year's end, the Soviet press offered more divergent judgements about Poland. On December 30, *Pravda* reported on an alarming open letter to all Polish Communists from veteran Party members assembled in the Silesian industrial center of Katowice. The letter bristled with terminology from the Stalinist glossary: "*camp* of struggle for peace, democracy and socialism" (emphasis supplied), "political two-facedness," and "opportunists." The "forces hostile to socialism" were allegedly trying to "heat up the atmosphere in the country still further" and to increase "the threat of counterrevolution." That same day, however, a contributor to the weekly magazine of the Government newspaper *Izvestiya* more soberly and accurately restated Kania's words about an improvement of the atmosphere. "Life is gradually returning to normal," reassured *Nedelya* (No. 1, 1981, cleared for printing Dec. 30, 1980).

The Polish calm was short-lived. Strikes and sit-ins broke out in many towns during January 1981. Organized and unattached groups raised demands for workfree Saturdays; legalization of the farmer's trade union (Rural Solidarity) and the Independent Association of Students; publication of information on Solidarity via radio and television; removal of corrupt and anti-Solidarity officials; shares of the old labor unions' assets; and the transfer of Party offices and police stations to the health service. Solidarity's annual report later accused the Government of having provoked the uproars by violating the agreements it made with strike committees during the past summer (Warsaw. *Solidarnosc*. Special Supplement, Sept. 11, 1981).

The protests were closely followed in Moscow. *Pravda* accented the use of Solidarity's strike weapon and the production losses resulting from the union's Saturday-work boycotts (Jan. 10–28). Use of civil disobedience as a lever to dislodge unpopular bureaucrats was another focal point of interest (Jan. 10, Feb. 1 and 7, e.g.). The vilification of security police was so rankling that mention of it in a speech by Politburo member Grabski was relayed to the Soviet public although much of the original text was ignored (Warsaw Radio, Feb. 9, 1981 and *Pravda*, Feb. 11, 1981).

A good indicator of Kremlin anxiety, as usual, was display of the crisis heading "Situation in Poland." That rubric was used in the January 10 and 11 *Pravda* for the first time since the end of November 1980. Similar press alerts were called on January 21 and 30. But the week or so leading up to the decision for Polish Defense Minister Gen. Jaruzelski to serve as Polish premier was a time of exceptional disquiet in Moscow: *Pravda* ran its scare headline on February 1, 2, 3, 6, 7 and 8. This equalled the highwater marks of Soviet agitation about Poland, in the days from Gierek's decline to Kania's rise (Aug. 28 and 29, Sept. 2, 3, 4 and 5, 1980), and at the time of ferment over the security police-control issue (Nov. 25, 26, 27, 28 and 29, 1980).

The hue and cry was not fully warranted. Government and nationwide Solidarity negotiators agreed to a 42-hour work-week and on Solidarity's access to the media on January 31. Solidarity leaders accepted the agreement on February 1 and suspended a one-hour warning strike scheduled for February 3. The temperature in local hotspots—Bielsko-Biala, Jelenia Gora, Rzeszow and Ustrzyki Dolne—appears to have been dropping (Warsaw. *Solidarnosc.* Special Supplement, Sept. 11, 1981).

Was the acerbity of *Pravda* headline writers a sign of the Soviet leaders' disgust over the latest fallback of Kania? That is conceivable in view of the fact that on January 30 TASS reported a Polish Government statement warning that authorities would act to stem spreading labor unrest, but deleted the final paragraph in which the government confirmed its readiness for talks and desire to improve relations with the trade union movement. Aversion to Kania's flabbiness seems to be a more reasonable explanation of the belated vehemence in *Pravda* than one which posits the creakiness of the Soviet propaganda machine.

Whatever the reason for Kremlin hystrionics, a pointer to Moscow's commitment to the restoration of Soviet-type controls in Poland was the nature of official visitations to Warsaw from the USSR and related media comment.

Marshal Viktor Kulikov, commander-in-chief of the Warsaw Pact Joint Armed Forces, was received by Kania and Premier Pinkowski on January 13. Gen. Jaruzelski also took part in the conversations, according to the next day's *Pravda*. Warsaw Radio added that the conclave was attended too by the Soviet chief of staff of the Warsaw Pact forces and the Soviet representative of those forces for the Polish Army, along with the chief of the Polish general staff and the chief inspector of Polish Army training. One can surmise that Kulikov wished to promote closer cooperation between the two armies in advance of any possible decision for martial law or Soviet intervention.

The second Soviet visit in January was preceded by a rumbling of the Suslovists. Censorship relaxation in Poland was too great a heresy for *Pravda* to have dwelt upon candidly. The foreign press monitors in Soviet agencies, however, must have been reporting their findings to senior Party executives. The Politburo accordingly could learn that a new surge of printed matter in Poland was "exploiting errors and deviations," promoting "defeatist moods" and undermining "trust in the idea and practice of socialism" (Warsaw, *Zolnierz Wolnosci*, Jan. 5, 1981).

The ire whipped up in high Soviet places by reports from the screeners of Polish publications is suggested by Vasiliy Stepanov's essay "V.I. Lenin as Journalist and Editor" in *Kommunist* (No. 1, cleared for printing Jan. 9, 1981). Stepanov, one of the editors of Suslov's books, listed the duties of a Communist journalist: "struggle against revisionists, nationalists and other anti-Marxists masquerading their views as Marxism . . . anarchistic laxness"; "Criticism . . . must be distinct from nihilism, self-contempt and maliciousness . . ."; "sharp and unmasking irony . . . reveals the essence of any and all conciliatoriness, which is political parasitism." Stepanov alluded to the Prague Spring and to current-day Poland from the perspective of Soviet history:

Such Lenin materials as . . . "Letter to G. Myasnikov" which deal with the bourgeois understanding of freedom of the word are very important at present too for our press, the bearer of Leninist traditions. Replying to Myasnikov, later on expelled from the Party, who had demanded total freedom of the press in Soviet Russia for all political parties and groups, including monarchists, with the aim, as he said, of uncovering defects in the Party and State, Lenin wrote that there has never been and cannot be in a class society such broad freedom of the press as the socialist state insures. Press freedom in conditions whereby the bourgeoisie has been defeated but not destroyed, he noted, is "freedom for the *political organization* of the bourgeoisie" against the working people (see *Complete Collected Works*, Vol. 44, p. 79). The rightfulness of this Leninist tenet is certified by many *lessons of the past and present* . . . (emphasis supplied). You wish to heal the Party, Lenin wrote to Myasnikov, and have begun to reach for medicine which leads to certain death. One must struggle with the defects in the Party and State with proletarian, Party means. Otherwise it is possible to be deceived and drawn into the swamp of the bourgeois mode of thought and bourgeois way of life.

Leonid Zamyatin, head of the International Information Department of the Soviet Party Secretariat, led a delegation to Poland from January 13 to 20. The group discussed with Party and media officials "questions of ideological work and Party guidance of the mass media" (*Pravda*, Jan. 21, 1981). Zamyatin reportedly expressed displeasure over Polish media coverage of internal developments since August.[2]

The choleric Nekrasovs and Stepanovs were joined by others during the early weeks of 1981. Vladimir Lomeyko, a Novosti news agency writer, stigmatized the Polish intellectual dissidents in the newspaper of the USSR Writers Union and seemed to attack Communist officials who failed to have them bridled. "The astonishing thing," said Lomeyko, "is that there are still naive people who have not completely grasped just where the silver-tongued sirens of extraclass freedom are inviting Poles to go, or what the strategy of permanent chaos threatens not just for Poland but also for peace and stability in Europe" (*Literaturnaya Gazeta*, Jan. 21, 1981). Lomeyko's refusal to pinpoint the location of the "naive people" left open the question of whether he was aiming at the Kania team or some in the Soviet leadership.

The extreme conservatives of the Writers Union in the Russian Republic gave a sounding board to hardline publicist Yevgeniy Bugayev, onetime editor of the journals *Kommunist* and *Party Life*. He melded the reformist tendencies in Poland with the ill-starred challenges to Soviet dogma in Hungary and Czechoslovakia. The "well-known events in certain socialist countries in 1956, 1968 and 1980," Bugayev warned, gave proof that anti-Communists had devised a blueprint for decomposing socialism from within. The scheme called for turning a ruling Communist party into just one of many partners in the political arena, obtaining assistance from the West, and rallying the internal forces of counterrevolution (*Oktyabr*, No. 2, cleared for printing Feb. 11, 1981).

A similar effort to inflame Soviet opinion was made by a public lecturer in Leningrad sometime in early January. The speaker berated Solidarity as an "anti-Soviet labor union" that had received hundreds of thousands in pounds sterling from Great Britain. Solidarity chairman Walesa was flayed for making antisocialist statements, and it was vowed that counterrevolution would be no more successful in Poland than it had been in Hungary and Czechoslovakia (Personal source).

As a rule, *Pravda* was not allowed to make the borscht so peppery. It is true that *Pravda* on February 7 carried a TASS item from Warsaw that was likely to be almost as disturbing for Soviet bureaucrats as the false cable of December 8, 1980 alleging a Solidarity campaign to take control of factories. In Jelenia Gora, close to Czechoslovakia and East Germany, Solidarity strikers were said to be making the political demand that regional Party leaders be ousted for their misconduct. Solidarity members in Rzeszow had supposedly wrecked the premises of an unfriendly journal and broken into the offices of a factory manager and Party secretary; a strike committee was urging farmers not to market their products since a governmental commission had refused to register Rural Solidarity. In Legnice, the Soviet garrison town, a Solidarity founding committee had threatened a transportation strike if several

Party bosses were not removed. Solidarity leaflets in Warsaw and other towns were said to be instructing people on how to harass Party members. "These and other facts," declared *Pravda*, "attest that counterrevolutionary forces are in essence going over to a *frontal attack on the Party*" (emphasis supplied).

In general, however, there were some qualitative differences between the overall coverage of Polish affairs by *Pravda* and the remarks of the fire-eaters. The polemical thrusts at soft Communists ("naive people") were missing from the Party daily. Walesa was shielded from direct criticism. And the Polish case was not so starkly bracketed with the Hungarian and Czechoslovak episodes.

Aside from the eloquent silences, *Pravda* took a decidedly non-interventionist stand on January 29. It cited the French President to the effect that Poland should be allowed to solve its own problems, with due consideration of its geographic and strategic position. The editors did not exercise their right to designate this opinion as merely that of the foreign leader who had expressed it.

The Kremlin's military deployments near Poland were consistent with a view that the Poles had begun to show political restraint. Sometime in February, the 25 or so Soviet Army divisions along Polish frontiers were put on a much lower state of alert than they had been (*New York Times*, Jan. 9 and Mar. 6, 1981).

Aware or not of the indecision and acrimony in the USSR, Kania stuck to his line of social accommodation. The police were ordered to clear demonstrators from public buildings they had occupied only in towns near the Soviet border. The Church was welcomed as an intermediary in bargaining sessions with protestors. Although the Government was still reluctant to grant legal status to Rural Solidarity, it threw ideology to the winds and recognized the permanence of individual land ownership in the countryside (Warsaw. *Solidarnosc*. Special Supplement, Sept. 11, 1981).

Kania apparently wanted the day-to-day affairs of government to be run by someone of his centrist thought and respected. The idea of banking good will in Moscow by elevating a Soviet-trained military man could also have played a role in the Party nomination of Gen. Jaruzelski as premier on February 9. (Premier Pinkowski, reportedly a colorless and shallow figure, had lately discredited himself by brashly rejecting the resignations of corrupt local officials whose removal was demanded by strikers and who lost their posts after more talks.) Jaruzelski retained his defense portfolio when the parliament formally confirmed his appointment on February 11.

Jaruzelski was indubitably a more complicated personality than the world was led to believe from repetition in the Western press of a vow he allegedly made that Polish soldiers would never again be allowed to shoot at Polish workers as had been done in 1970. A West German historian has claimed that Jaruzelski once adhered to Gen. Moczar's political clique known as the Partisans. The members of this group were said to be characterized by "an almost military severity, even brutality, in their mode of governing and by a decided hostility to discussion and culture which was aimed particularly against liberals and centralists."[3] But a sympathetic portrait of Jaruzelski was sketched by the liberal chairman of the Polish Journalists Association, Stefan Bratkowski, who knew the highest leaders in Warsaw during 1980–81. He described Jaruzelski as "an intellectual and a soldier through and through, whose lot it was to become a politician." Bratkowski was convinced that Jaruzelski wanted to begin economic reforms as soon as possible when he became premier, but ran into opposition from entrenched bureaucrats (Amsterdam. *De Volkskrant*, Oct. 3, 1981). Solidarity sources were to recall that with the appointment of Jaruzelski to the premiership the Government's authority "clearly increased" and talks could begin on a wide range of labor and social issues (Warsaw. *Solidarnosc*. Special Supplement. Sept. 11, 1981). Solidarity leaders were unstinting in their praise of Jaruzelski. Bogdan Lis, a union militant, told an interviewer that Jaruzelski was one of the top leaders "willing to compromise" (Stockholm. *Dagens Nyheter*, Feb. 25, 1981). Richard Kalinowski, deputy chairman of Solidarity, spoke of Jaruzelski's "reputation for honesty and moderation" (London. *Financial Times*, Feb. 27, 1981). Walesa said of Jaruzelski: "I respect him. I think he is a good man, a good Pole" (Paris. *Le Monde*, Mar. 21, 1981). On the other hand again, a darker picture of Jaruzelski is in the recollection of Klemens Szaniawski, world expert on mathematical logic and chairman of the Association of Artistic and Intellectual Creators. He negotiated with the Polish leaders on a new censorship law in April 1981 and described Kania as "urbane and sincere but not always well informed," Jaruzelski as "a shadowy, silent and impenetrable figure but haughty and touchy" (Brussels. *Le Soir*. July 24, 1981). The overall impression one gets from circumstance and commentary is that Jaruzelski remained what he seemed to be at the moment of Gierek's teetering: a Polish nationalist and judicious disciplinarian rather than power-crazy fanatic subservient to Moscow.

Whatever the innermost thoughts of Jaruzelski, new evidence of fear in the midst of Soviet officials working close to Poland shortly arose. The Ukrainian Party Congress, managed by Soviet Politburo member Vladimir Shcherbitskiy, went into session around the time of the change of Government in Warsaw and gave a preview of the chilly talk about Poland that would mark the CPSU Congress due in a few weeks time.

A fierce attack on Solidarity and its friends was made by Vitaliy Sologub, head of the Ukraine trade union council:

> Our trade unions, putting at the center of all their activity the interests of the working man, regard as their primary duty the concern for an upturn of production. This is the most important feature of the activity of trade unions in a socialist society. And it is understandable that nothing other than exasperation and indignation can be evoked by the intrigues of enemies of the working class who, speculating on the demagogic slogans of the independence of trade unions, sacrilegiously preach to the trade unions of socialist countries how they should work further, whom to defend and how to do it. As is known, various antisocialist elements, dressed in the toga of champions of human rights, speculating on the sacred feelings of proletarian solidarity, abusing the trust of workers, and incited by the more reactionary imperialistic and clerical forces, would like to pit the trade unions against the Marxist-Leninist parties and socialist state, and thereby attempt to weaken the socialist system from within. This will never happen. (*Applause*).
>
> The true intentions of these, so to speak, well-wishers, will be ultimately understood even there where today some people have succumbed to their political demagogy. History teaches that the source of strength of trade unions lies in unshakeable fidelity to class principles, to the banner of proletarian internationalism, and in the leadership of the Marxist-Leninist party (*Pravda Ukrainy*, Feb. 12, 1981).

The consensus of watchful waiting at the Politburo in Moscow evidently forbid direct mention of Poland by Sologub, and absence of similar vitriol at other republic-level Party congresses may have been due to a wish to mask any gap between the center's lenient approach to the Polish disorders and growing perplexity among the local cadres.

Hardly a shred of empathy was shown toward the Polish innovators at the all-Union Party Congress which opened in Moscow on February 23, 1981. Soviet Party congresses are largely ritualistic celebrations of economic plan fulfillment. Called only once in five years, the meetings are attended by as many as 5,000 delegates from the power and prestige elites of the USSR, along with hundreds of foreign Communist officials. The speeches are manifestly designed to instill pride in achievements and arouse enthusiasm for the tackling of new tasks. But the real thoughts of orators are sometimes visible in spite of the outward show of confident optimism and unanimity.

Brezhnev, who delivered the Report of the Central Committee, misrepresented and internationalized the Polish crisis from its origin to the present day. Initially, he averred, elements hostile to socialism were stimulated by conditions rooted in imperialist subversive activity and mistakes in domestic policy. At the moment, opponents of socialism supported by outside forces were stirring up anarchy and seeking to channel events into a counterrevolutionary course. "The pillars of the socialist state are in jeopardy," Brezhnev intoned.

The Soviet President did laud the Polish leaders for efforts to redress the critical situation. They were trying to heighten the Party's effectiveness and increase contacts with the working people, as well as draft a program to restore to health the Polish economy. Brezhnev, however, said not a word about the "line of agreement" or "socialist renewal." Recalling the Warsaw Pact summit of December 5, 1980, Brezhnev ignored the expression of faith in Polish rulers which was in its communique. Brezhnev said only that the Bloc summit had given substantial political support to Poland and demonstrated that it could rely on allies. Essentially hardline rhetoric followed. "We will not abandon fraternal, socialist Poland in its hour of need," Brezhnev declared, "we will stand by it." The Soviet leader went on in the same vein of supra-national politics: "Let no one doubt our common determination to secure our interests, and to defend the socialist gains of the peoples" (*Pravda*, Feb. 24, 1981).

The heads of foreign Communist delegations began to go to the rostrum on February 24 and Kania had to listen to speeches by Castro and Vietnam Party leader Le Duan. Neither saw anything auspicious happening inside Poland.

Castro arraigned imperialism for seeking to tear Poland away from the socialist community. Western states were openly provoking the country's political destabilization and inflicting inestimable social, moral and material harm on it (*Pravda*, Feb. 25, 1981). Le Duan too viewed Poland exclusively through the lens of East-West rivalry, denouncing imperialists and world reactionaries for hatching plans to meddle in Polish affairs. "But these are vain endeavors," he said, without going into the specifics of rescue (*Ibid*).

Kania in his speech tactfully rejected the version of Poland's travail which purported the involvement of malicious foreigners and their Polish accomplices at every step of the way. He depicted the Polish August as a strictly internal protest that stemmed from political ineptitude at the highest level. Only later, Kania felt compelled to say, was the massive societal criticism exploited by forces that were hostile to socialism, openly counterrevolutionary and supported by subversive imperialist centers. These enemies of socialism were trying to take command of the new trade unions and to set them against the Communist Party. They sought to maintain tension, produce anarchy and disorganize public life.

Kania's thesis of healthy criticism from below compounded by sinister plotting enabled him to argue for a dual policy. The main concern of Polish leaders, he said, was to ensure a political solution of social conflict. After that, the authorities were determined to do everything necessary to stop the dangerous actions of those instigating disruption. As Kania put it: "We have enough patience for the Party line to be supported by all honest Poles, all patriots. But we also have enough resolve in struggle with enemies, in defense of socialism."

Kania reverted to and magnified the non-interventionist formulas that Brezhnev had used in his talks with Polish visitors to Moscow in October and December 1980. He thanked the Soviet Party for belief that Poles would be able "independently to solve Polish problems in the spirit of socialism." Kania next insisted that "we have sufficient resolve and power to see that counterrevolution does not succeed in Poland" (*Ibid*).

Resting his case, Kania prematurely left the Kremlin Palace of Congresses. He visited a Warsaw factory on February 26 and sought to allay fears of an internal clampdown or Soviet incursion. Kania told a meeting that he had found "appreciation" in Moscow for using "exclusively political means" to resolve Poland's problems, as well as "anxiety" over what might happen next (Interpress. Feb. 27, 1981).

The anxiety in Moscow that Kania spoke of remained conspicuous at the Soviet Party congress. Lithuania's Party first secretary said he was following the Polish situation with "uneasiness" and looked forward to a "rebuff to the attempts of imperialistic interference" (*Pravda*, Feb. 26, 1981). The head of the USSR Writers Union twisted the confidence-in-Poland slogan so that Kania's first duty was to deliver a "rebuff to the counterrevolutionary threat," and then to hurdle the shortfalls of production (*Pravda*, Feb. 27, 1981).

The allied speakers from Eastern Europe seemed to be divided over how much more time to give the Poles. Honecker of East Germany, Husak of Czechoslovakia and Zhivkov of Bulgaria did not mention Poland, which hinted at an unwillingness to mar the gala festivities with an outpouring of bitterness (*Pravda*, Feb. 25 and 26, 1981). Ceausescu of Romania was also silent, and it is impossible to tell if he was only self-serving in declaring that he championed "the right of each Party to determine independently its own political line" (*Pravda*, Feb. 26, 1981). Only Kadar of Hungary would again go on record in behalf of the view that Poles themselves would get out of difficulty (*Pravda*, Feb. 25, 1981).

In the back of many skeptical minds could have been the question of whether a deadline ought to be set for a Polish solution of the troubles inside Poland. A Soviet leader whose career and writings are suggestive of hardline thinking was Boris Ponomarev, central Party Secretary in charge of relations with non-ruling Communist parties. The 75-year-old ideologue may have prompted the Nigerian speaker at the Soviet congress to make an original contribution to the relevant discussion: "As is well known, antisocialist elements are financed and directed by forces outside of Poland. It is very important that the Polish United Workers Party with the help of socialist community countries find *at a given time* the true path of resolving its internal problems" (*Pravda*, March 4, 1981. Emphasis supplied).

A single plea for statesmanship was made by the Italian Communist leader John Carlo Paietta. He specifically endorsed Kania's appraisal of the Polish situation and implored Kremlin leaders to adopt a hands-off policy. Paietta of course drew no applause with the following entreaty: "The demands of the workers combined with the criticism and self-criticism of the Polish Communists themselves must lead to a renewal, and in our view the Party and government of Poland have already embarked on it. We assume that a politicial solution of the question, reinforced by the approval and support of the people can and must, with full respect for independence and autonomy of the Polish people, ensure the socialist development of Poland, renewal and national independence, for which this people has sacrificed so much" (*Pravda*, Mar. 2, 1981).

In analysis, the uniqueness of Paietta's speech at the Soviet congress—giving moral support to the Polish liberalizers—allowed for an inference about Kremlin expectations. The observer could see an almost unanimous verdict of Kremlin stage managers to deny ideological respectability to the political reformation in Poland. The reforms themselves were blackened in a manner which made them appear to be a threat to the interrelated doctrinal and strategic interests of the USSR. An implicit corollary was that political power which had slipped away from the Communist machine in Warsaw to authentic social bodies had to be returned to its original guardian. How the rebinding of Polish society was to be accomplished had to remain obscure, given the Soviet Union's self-image of peacefulness and the self-esteem of many foreign Communists. But the documents of the Moscow congress indicated that Soviet leaders intended to keep importuning the Warsaw Government to regain lost ground.

Nevertheless, it was unexpected that Kania had to return to Moscow a day after the Soviet Party congress had ended for a March 4 meeting of Polish and Kremlin leaders. This was the third such conference since the birth of nationwide Solidarity less than six months earlier.

The gravamen that Soviet security was imperiled by developments in Poland was suggested by the new order of precedence for listing the Soviet leaders at the March 4 meeting. In December 1980, Brezhnev's colleagues present at the Warsaw Pact summit were ranked so as to stress the importance of those responsible for economic and ideological affairs. Now, pre-eminence was given to the heads of the security police and foreign relations apparatuses.

Dec. 5, 1980	*Mar. 4, 1981*
Brezhnev	Brezhnev
Tikhonov	Andropov
Suslov	Gromyko
Andropov	Suslov
Gromyko	Tikhonov
Ustinov	Ustinov
Rusakov	Rusakov

(The otherwise identical seating arrangement of the Soviet leaders—left to right: Ustinov, Andropov, Tikhonov, Brezhnev, Suslov, Gromyko and Rusakov—at the two meetings leaves small doubt that the protocol revision was made to accentuate the importance of security matters.)

In contrast, Kania downplayed the role of the gendarmerie, not bringing along to Moscow the minister for internal (police) affairs, who was at the Warsaw Pact summit in December 1980, or his deputy. The inclusion of conservative Politburo member Zabinski, Party boss of Katowice, in the Polish delegation can be read as a symbolic gesture of concern for ideological rectitude. Or perhaps the Soviet leaders wanted Zabinski to be present for the sake of heartening their own kind of people in the Polish power structure.

In any event, the Poles had to make concessions that were far-reaching if only rhetorical. The most important was recognition of the old Soviet canon of the limited sovereignty of Soviet-orbit governments, which *Pravda* had reaffirmed after the 1968 invasion of Czechoslovakia and got to be known as the Brezhnev doctrine. As stated in the TASS report of the March 4 meeting, the participants agreed that, "The socialist community is indissolvable and its defense is a matter not only for each state but for the entire socialist coalition as well." Thus, Kania and Jaruzelski acknowledged the right of the Soviet Union to intervene by force if necessary to safeguard what the Soviet leaders understood to be socialism in Poland.

The Soviet recompense for this blank check from visitors was a vote of confidence in them that smacked of an ultimatum. The Polish Communists were said to have the resources to "turn the course of events and eliminate the dangers hanging over the Polish people's socialist gains." The meaning of this harsh phrase seemed to be that Kania should bow to the demands of his police chiefs rather than those of restive groups in the population. If he did so, the latest Soviet prophesy that Poland "was and will be a dependable link of the socialist community" would be fulfilled.

The impression conveyed by formulas used at the March 4 summit in Moscow is that a Soviet journalist was truthful when he later told a Western colleague in Warsaw: ". . . we have had problems with the present leadership [of Kania and Jaruzelski] whose carelessness and inefficiency—we told it so in Moscow—really went beyond all bounds" (*Le Figaro*, Mar. 31, 1981).

The March 4 summit is not likely to have been harmonious. TASS reported a "common approach," but not "unity of views," of the participants. The Soviet side or absent leaders of the Polish security police might even then have been engineering the most serious provocation against Solidarity throughout the union's short history.

NOTES

1. "Senior Soviet officers are being inserted quietly into key posts throughout the Polish armed forces, according to Western intelligence sources. Some of the officers, particularly generals, wear their regular uniforms, the sources say, but others are in Polish military uniforms so as to be less obvious to outsiders. Their assignment is believed to be to look over the shoulders of Polish officers both to offer suggestions and to be in position to try to prevent the Poles from getting together to resist a Russian invasion, should it come. 'We saw the same pattern in the summer of 1968 in Czechoslovakia before the invasion, and again in the fall of last year in Afghanistan,' one American official said" ("Senior Soviet Officers Taking Polish Army Jobs." By William Beecher. Washington *Star*, Dec. 18, 1980).

2. *Chronology. Soviet and Soviet-proxy Involvement in Poland. July 1980-December 1981* (Special Report No. 94. U.S. Department of State, Bureau of Public Affairs, Washington, D.C.), p. 2.

3. Hans Roos, *A History of Modern Poland From the Foundation of the State in the First World War to the Present Day* (Alfred A. Knopf, NY, 1966), pp. 257–258.

FIVE

A Bid for Martial Law?

(MAR. 5–APR. 10, 1981)

The alignment of Soviet propaganda after the Moscow summit suggests that Kremlin leaders welcomed an act of violence in Poland which almost sparked a confrontation between Solidarity and the regime. A police assault on Solidarity activists in the town of Bydgoszcz was preceded and followed by Soviet media charges that Solidarity represented a danger to the internal security of the Polish state. Soviet military moves accompanying the propaganda were seemingly intended to pressure Kania and Jaruzelski into imposing martial law as a counter to Solidarity's threat to call a general strike in protest over the Bydgoszcz affair. The military information then available to US analysts did not allow for a unified conclusion about the chances of Soviet armed intervention once Polish leaders refused to alter their course of liberalization. And it is still too soon to decide how close the Kremlin was to direct intervention at this critical juncture.

Solidarity chairman Walesa and Premier Jaruzelski met for the first time on March 10. Their talks centered on local disputes and a series of police attacks on Solidarity supporters across Poland. Agreement was reached to establish a Solidarity-Interior Ministry commission to investigate the charges of police harassment.

If the two strong personalities Jaruzelski and Walesa had a firm grip on the governing bureaucracy and labor movement, respectively, it might have been posssible to cement the nascent alliance of commonsense and patriotism. But a crisis of authority was wracking the Solidarity federation and the elite. Disputes among union radicals and moderates were paralleled by others dividing conservatives and reformers within the Communist Party. The endless social conflicts were fought out against a background of havoc in the economic sphere.

Shortages of industrial raw materials and spare parts were universal in the wake of severe cutbacks in imports due to financial stringencies. Foodstuffs were becoming increasingly scarce for ordinary citizens, especially in small cities, as farmers were getting ever smaller returns for their efforts. The constant meetings and strikes were making a bad situation worse insofar as worker productivity was concerned. In brief, an atmosphere of nervousness and irritation was building in large sections of the populace.

The tensions in regime-people relations and inside the political governing class of Poland gave to Soviet leaders a good opportunity to apply their well-developed skills of manipulation. It would be surprising if an Andropov or Suslov did not begin to think along the following lines: directors of the Polish Interior Ministry might be encouraged to continue the physical attacks on Solidarity activists. The events of November 1980 had proven that one such incident might drive the union to overreact and call for a general strike. If the Warsaw government was forced to choose between letting Solidarity in effect run the country or itself adopt a hardline policy, the most likely response would be to declare a state of emergency. Alternatively, doctrinaire leaders might challenge Kania for the top Party job, secure it and restore old-style discipline. Either way, military pressure from the Soviet Union was bound to be indispensable for the support of Moscow's friends and intimidation of its foes.

The reluctance of Warsaw leaders to betray their promises of reform to the nation was intimated in a report on a Polish Politburo meeting which *Pravda* carried on March 7. The session discussed Moscow's Party congress and Soviet-Polish summit. The CPSU was alleged to be confident that Polish authorities "have the opportunities and forces in order to eliminate the dangers hanging over the gains of the Polish people." Actually, the TASS statement on the March 4 summit had said that Soviet leaders expressed confidence that Polish Communists had "the opportunities and forces *to turn the course of events*, eliminate the dangers hanging over the socialist gains of the Polish people" (emphasis supplied). The reaction was suggestive of more faltering in Warsaw and a reminder was served to Polish leaders in the *Pravda* editorial for March 8 that at the Moscow summit they were "filled with resolve to turn away the grave threat hanging over the socialist gains of their country."

Soviet media comment on Poland during the weeks prior to the Bydgoszcz affair was virtually tailored to a Kremlin plan for settling accounts with Solidarity and the political reformers organized around Kania. The editors of *Pravda* were clearly under orders to ignore creative happenings on the Polish scene, for example, the Walesa-Jaruzelski meeting and peaceful settlement of local disputes. Solidarity was to be portrayed as a lawless organization disposing of a private army and consorting with rabid anticommunist groups. *Kommunist* had the task of discrediting on grounds of ideological scruple the milder version of socialism that was taking root in Poland.

The March 8 *Pravda* alleged that "armed groups" had been created by the right wing of Solidarity's leadership. This was an overblown account of an event in the provincial city of Wroclaw, where the Solidarity chapter formed a "worker's guard" to protect the leading dissident Michnik from police who were trying to serve a prosecutor's summons on him. The truth was evidently twisted to make it appear that Poland in 1981 was going down the road of violence-ridden Hungary in 1956.

Pravda on March 13 charged that a "nest of antisocialist forces" was sheltering under the wing of Solidarity, which had gotten CIA funds for the production of leaflets and subversive literature through the conduit AFL-CIO. Certain leaders of Solidarity, *Pravda* declared on March 14, were involved in a campaign to free from custody the right-wing dissident Mosczulski. He was supposedly linked with foreign-based conspirators who were readying "terrorist groups" for operations in Poland that would be directed against the State administration, police and security service.

The intolerable nature of Polish renewal at large was an undercurrent of materials compiled for *Kommunist*. Aleksey Shibayev, chairman of the central council of Soviet trade unions, in the course of a discussion of the role of unions, tended to put Solidarity beyond the pale: "Socialism's ideological opponents have frequently tried and are continuing to try to direct their thrust against the most important principle of trade union building under the conditions of socialist society—the trade unions' recognition of the leading role of the Communist Party. These actions are similar to the attempt by the Mensheviks, Socialist Revolutionaries and other opportunists—an attempt exposed by Lenin—to 'liberate' the trade unions from the Party's influence and make them 'independent' of the political parties and state" (*Kommunist*, No. 4, cleared for printing Mar. 9, 1981).

CPSU Secretary Ponomarev censured the notion of a ruling Party machine sharing power with other bureaucratic or social groups. Obviously reproving Kania's defense of "partnership" with labor, peasantry, youth and the Church, Ponomarev affirmed:

It is well known that somewhere there exist conceptions framed for the purpose of eliminating the ruling party in a socialist country from the position of exercising a determining influence on the formulation and execution of social policy, and making this policy a subject of the so-called free play of "pluralistic" forces. Acceptance of such conceptions would doom the new society's development to zigzags and vacillations that are dangerous for its very essence. This would lead the society away from the socialist path and realization of socialism's ideals (*Kommunist*, No. 5, cleared for printing Mar. 23, 1981).

Spelling out the meaning of Ponomarev's "zigzags and vacillations" was the article of Kiev political economist Vilen Mazur. He attacked "the idea of independent, autonomous trade unions which are called upon to oppose the socialist state and Communist Party, using strikes as a means of struggle for upturn of the members' living standards." Mazur argued that such unions run counter to the basic Communist principles of planned investment ratios, full employment, and payment according to performance. Free unions and political pluralism under socialism were equated with the Social-Democratic or Menshevik outlook which the Western powers allegedly wished to filter into the Soviet bloc (*Ibid.*).

Reminiscences about Lenin were also pegged to the Solidarity revolution. The only infallible Soviet leader prior to Brezhnev was said to have demanded that trade-union head Tomskiy be expelled from the Bolshevik Central Committee and Party for having failed to challenge "an anti-Party resolution in the spirit of the trade unions' independence from the Party" at a meeting of the Bolshevik caucus at the 1921 congress of trade unions. Lenin fought the innerparty "Worker Opposition" group, which had "demagogically thought about the independence and freedom of the trade unions," and proved such talk reflected "petty-bourgeois anarchism." The passage about Tomskiy approved of Lenin having "literally raged," shown "wrath," and turned "dark as a storm cloud" with eyes that "literally flashed lightning" (*Ibid.*) This was a very different image of Lenin from that presented in the *Pravda* of September 6, 1980, which had the Old Man warning that "a fist in a dispute over principle is the most senseless 'argument.'"

War games were being played in conjunction with this propaganda offensive. A command-staff exercise of Warsaw Pact forces was scheduled for the second half of March (*Pravda*, March 11, 1981). The exercise, codenamed "Soyuz-81," was to be run in sections of Poland, East Germany, the USSR and Czechoslovakia. Senior staffs were to improve their ability to work smoothly in joint operations. Although such tuneups were routine, the continuing local unrest in Poland and Soviet anxieties made the latest one seem to be shades of that in June–July 1968, or just prior to the invasion of Czechoslovakia. One wonders if Soviet personnel in the Soyuz-81 area and beyond were lectured along the lines of a fighting article that was soon to appear in a journal of the USSR Defense Ministry:

The political parties of the working class, especially the CPSU, are at the center of the ideological attacks by bourgeois and revisionistic propaganda. Among the basic directions of attack is struggle against their leading role in society's development. History offers many examples and reveals too the means with the aid of which enemies of peace and progress try to reach their goal. One of the examples is the events in Czechoslovakia in 1968. Healthy forces in the Communist party and in the state with the support of the fraternal Communist and worker parties of the socialist countries with the Soviet Union and CPSU at the head were able to defend the revolutionary gains of the Czechoslovak people and to strengthen the leading position of the Communist party. Now antisocialist elements in Poland, entrenched in the so-called "Solidarity" trade union, supported by violent enemies of the Polish people abroad, are trying to make a massive attack on Communists and the party of the working class (*Voyennyy Vestnik*, No. 4, cleared for printing Mar. 26, 1981).

The Polish news agency reported on March 19 that Soyuz-81 was in progress and that Polish and other Pact forces would fulfill their duty to defend socialism.

On the same day, March 19, an event that was to shake all Poland occurred in the northern city of Bydgoszcz, 120 miles from Warsaw. "Bandits and sadists" were Walesa's epithets for some 200 police who severely beat Solidarity activists while evicting them from a government building. Walesa, however, expressed confidence in General Jaruzelski and cautioned against Solidarity rushing into a general strike to display outrage (A.P., Mar. 20, 1981).

What is astounding was the swift reaction to the Bydgoszcz incident at the offices of *Pravda*. Just a day later, March 20, a front-page editorial on Soviet bloc relations cited Brezhnev's remarks about Poland at the recent Moscow Party congress. The only change in paraphrased text had Brezhnev say that Polish Communists and workers could "fearlessly" —rather than "firmly"—depend on their allies in an hour of need. The word "fearlessly" was taken from a different passage in Brezhnev's Report, and hinted that Polish authorities were expected to muster the courage to hem in Solidarity in light of the Bydgoszcz affair. The Polish Interior Ministry and Politburo took steps in the direction that Moscow was pointing. Solidarity headquarters in Warsaw reported on March 21 that police had beaten up four bus drivers as they were pasting up union posters at the bus depot about the incident in Bydgoszcz (Paris. AFP Mar. 21).

The Kania-led Politburo met on March 22 to discuss planned strikes over the Bydgoszcz uproar. A statement denounced extremists for sowing distrust toward the security service and police, which was said to have acted properly in Bydgoszcz. Solidarity activities were criticized as increasingly political and the union hit for creating anarchy by illegally substituting for state bodies. But the statement had the imprint of the dual policy that Kania set forth at the Soviet Party Congress. Social conflicts would be settled through dialogue and energetic actions taken to insure the calm necessary for continuing the process of renewal. The statement could even have alluded to the danger of Soviet-instigated mischief when it appealed for everyone to "counter possible provocations." Kania seems to have given the Kremlin its due under the press of events that he could not fully control.

Kania's desire to prevent matters from coming to a boil was perhaps matched by the hesitation of some at the top of the Soviet Party. All of the major Soviet dailies on March 22 ran a TASS item from Warsaw with the ominous headline "Situation in Poland," the first of its kind in almost six weeks, or since February 8. The original item had a notably shrill sentence: "The Solidarity leader L. Walesa at a meeting in Bydgoszcz came up with an *instigatory* assertion that the situation that has developed there is 'more serious than it was in August'" (emphasis supplied). The implication was that Walesa had favored a general strike, even though he had warned against that move upon in arriving in Bydgoszcz. A TASS correction, however, omitted the word "instigatory," and in so doing spared Walesa the image of rabblerouser. *Pravda* and some other newspapers carried the corrected verion of the TASS report, deleting the word "instigatory." But the Government daily *Izvestiya* and Party organ *Socialist Industry* included the word. A technical mishap could explain the divergence, but *Socialist Industry* on April 5 and 9 would again be at odds with *Pravda*, omitting sentences from TASS items that were favorable to the cause of social peace in Poland. Was Kirilenko, the Politburo overlord of industrial management, ready to go full tilt for the destruction of Solidarity? In any event, *Pravda* underlined its moderate stand on March 22 by approvingly citing West German Foreign Minister Genscher to the effect that after visiting Warsaw he recognized as correct the Polish leadership's choice of political means to cope with its internal problems.

Whatever the qualms in Moscow, the Soviet leaders bore down on Kania to be tough after Solidarity on March 24 proclaimed a warning strike for March 27 and an open-ended general strike for March 31. The union's decision was taken in spite of Deputy Premier Rakowski having informed Solidarity on March 22 that the Warsaw Pact maneuvers were extended "because of the situation in Poland" and union actions could bring in Soviet tanks. The annual report of Solidarity would refer to the March 24 decision as "rather impetuous" and made following "some serious disagreements" (Warsaw. *Solidarnosc*. Special Supplement. Sept. 11, 1981).

A crescendo of Soviet media attacks on Solidarity began with the TASS announcement of March 26 that the Polish Central Committee would convene on March 29 to discuss the state of the nation. The first-magnitude crisis heading "Situation in Poland" or "Events in Poland" was inserted over each of the TASS dispatches from Warsaw that *Pravda* ran from March 27 through March 30. Significant precedents for such alarmist coverage were in the periods from September 2 through 5, 1980, or the eve of Gierek's ouster from the Party leadership, and November 25 through 29, 1980, or just before the invasion scare of early December.

The common feature of all these materials was a *de facto* allegation that Solidarity had declared war on public officials and was preparing for a takeover, with the connivance of media workers. TASS levied charges that a host of leaflets were openly menacing Communists; the police and security organs were the targets of a hostile campaign (Mar. 26); pickets in the four-hour strike had kept managers out of firms; Walesa was boasting of his union's power; nationwide television was relaying strike instructions; the Polish army daily viewed the antisocialist elements as a fifth column (Mar. 27); Solidarity's posting of guards around the building where union-Government talks were held showed that it was usurping the State's law-keeping functions (Mar. 28); Solidarity leaders and other extremists were compiling black lists of security and police employees, setting up road blocks, trying to seize post offices, television transmitters and food stocks (Mar. 29).

The March 29 item did everything but say that Polish authorities were on the verge of declaring martial law. Sessions of the Politburo and steering committee of the parliament were held "in connection with the sharp increase of tension in the country." A decision was taken to assemble the parliament on April 2 "for discussion of the grave situation." In addition, the first secretaries of regional and town committees of the Communist Party had met and discussed "questions relating to the provocative actions of 'Solidarity' leaders." The Central Committee plenum which Kania opened on March 29, it could also be gathered, was going to put its imprimatur on a martial law decision.

What the mass audience in the USSR could not learn from TASS reports was that a show of Soviet force was being mounted in and near Poland. A State Department briefer noted that there were indications that Warsaw Pact units had been placed on a high state of alert and large-scale ground force movements had begun to show up around Poland. Newly deployed communications units had tied in all the military commands in a large area of the western USSR, Poland, Czechoslovakia and East Germany (*New York Times* and *Washington Post*, Mar. 30, 1981). These preparations for possible military intervention were apparently made to assure Polish leaders that they could act "fearlessly" to ban Solidarity.

The Kremlin's chagrin and perhaps underlying caution was hinted by TASS's reaction to the great defeat which Polish hardliners suffered at the March 29–30 plenum in Warsaw.

The existence of a conservative opposition to Kania was an open secret inside Poland. Yet on March 10 the Yugoslav paper *Borba* in a cable from Warsaw reported sharp differences in the Polish Party. Conservative forces in the apparatus were said to be strong and to be expressing their anti-reformist opinion vigorously. An open letter from Bratkowski, chairman of the Polish Journalists Association, to all primary Party units was quoted in the Western press on March 25 (Paris. *Le Monde*) and released by the Polish news agency at the opening of the latest plenum. Writing as a rank and file Party member, Bratkowski criticized "the men who want to introduce fear in the Party apparatus— fear of their own Party and of the people, pointing to themselves as the only ones capable of protecting the apparatus from the loss of positions and influence. These are the men who try to set the forces of public order in conflict with their own community so as to preclude all other ways out except confrontation. These are the men who present themselves to our neighbors as being the only force capable of guaranteeing the durability of our alliances and of the state system." Bratkowski denounced "our hardliners" as "not representing any program except the concept of confrontation and disinformation." While refusing to mention any names, Bratkowski referred to and urged the ouster of "comrades among these men who occupy the highest positions in our Party" (Warsaw. PAP Maritime Press Service. Mar. 29, 1981).

Politburo members and Party Secretaries Grabski and Olszowski identified themselves as the hardliners at the 18-hour plenary meeting. They took strong exception to a moderate keynote report by their colleague Barcikowski. Grabski in effect saw Poland as Russia had been under Kerensky in 1917, arguing that "dual power has now become a fact," and he claimed that "even armed terror" was often used against public officials (*Trybuna Ludu*, Mar. 30, 1981). Olszowski pretended that State bodies were subject to "continuous dismantling" and that Solidarity leaders, departing from their legalized statutory principles, were now "standing on the grounds of creating a political party" (*Ibid.*). No one followed the lead of Grabski and Olszowski in quite the same way, and reliable Polish sources later said that the duo was not ousted at the plenum because a letter from the Soviet Central Committee urging Party unity was read out and backed up by a telephone call from Brezhnev to Kania during a recess (*New York Times*, Apr. 14, 1981).

Yet, not a word about Grabski or Olszowski was dropped in the March 30 TASS account of the plenum which *Pravda* carried the next day. The item was relatively short and divided almost equally between summaries of the keynote report and the resolution, without any selections from the 44 speeches made in the discussion period. (Kania's concluding speech was digested in the April 1 *Pravda*.) Conceivably, Soviet leaders did not accept as final reversals the March 30 agreement of Solidarity and Government delegations to forestall the general strike scheduled to start on March 31. The Kremlin may still have hoped to use its military movements to drive Kania into invoking martial law. In that case it would have been inopportune for Soviet media to have boosted the foremost critics of the Party head when reporting on the Central Committee meeting.

Soviet military movements led to an increase of U.S. concern over Kremlin intentions on April 3. Alexander M. Haig, Jr., recalls:

The intelligence community reported unusual Soviet troop movements toward the Polish frontiers from East Germany, Czechoslovakia, and the USSR itself. These included infantry and armored columns and airborne formations. The twelve Soviet divisions normally stationed in and around Poland appeared to be in a high state of readiness. Soviet aircraft evaded Polish radar by flying beneath it and entered Polish airspace. Soviet troops had been moved into Warsaw to protect the compounds in which Soviet personnel were housed. . . .

These were ominous signs, but did they constitute a pattern? In the State Department operations center, we asked ourselves the obvious questions: Were the Russians moving in? Were they raising the level of intimidation? Was this a prelude to a declaration of martial law by the Polish government? I considered postponing my trip to the Middle East, scheduled to begin that evening. At the end of a long day, however, it appeared that Soviet troop movements had abated. Whatever Moscow's purpose had been, it did not on this particular Friday include an invasion of Poland. We stood down the watch. . . . (Haig, *op. cit.*, p. 244).

But others kept the vigil and were not of one mind whether the Kremlin was near to a decision for direct intervention in Poland. Some were cited in the U.S. press to the effect that the origin of an airlift to Soviet bases in Poland and the nature of the equipment unloaded indicated the deployment of special forces of the kind that went into Afghanistan in advance of the 1979 invasion to secure key positions. Analysts looked to the Czechoslovak case and opined that the Soviet buildup would have to continue for another week or 10 days before a full-scale invasion was set into motion. That much time would be needed for the Soviets to have 30 or 40 divisions (350,000 to 500,000 troops) to overwhelm the 210,000-man Polish army. Colleagues, however, advised that Soviet forces might be committed to action sooner on a piecemeal basis. A few speculated that Premier Jaruzelski had put out the story of his "temporary indisposition" and need to reschedule the parliamentary session from April 6 until April 10 so that he could prepare for a Soviet onslaught (*Washington Post* and Washington *Star*, Apr. 4 and 5, 1981).

It is impossible to determine if the Soviet Politburo was at the brink of taking military action. Soviet press comment did have some unique notes which could have been sounded to justify a move into Poland.

The first direct criticism of the Polish Party in Soviet media surfaced on April 2 with *Pravda*'s exclusive information dispatch called "Antisocialist Assemblage." Dissident and Solidarity leaders were pilloried for having given an anti-Marxist and anti-Soviet tone to a seminar at Warsaw University at the end of March. The speakers had allegedly extolled fascism as a suitable lodestar for Poland. Party organizations were scored for having failed to deal even an ideological rebuff to the seminar participants. "Some people in Poland," it was argued, "are still expressing doubts as to the existence of antisocialist forces in the country." This echoed the complaint of Novosti writer Lomeyko in *Literaturnaya Gazeta* in January, and signified an escalation of rhetoric for *Pravda*.

The label of fascism was affixed on Bydgoszcz Solidarity leader Rulewski in a TASS cable from Warsaw that *Pravda* ran on April 3, and under the crisis banner "Events in Poland." Rulewski was tarred as someone once jailed for trying to cross the frontier illegally and a reckless driver who had lately killed a pedestrian. The Rulewski family had assumed German citizenship in World War II and the father had fought in the Hitlerite army against the USSR, according to *Pravda*.

A piercing cry was emitted from *Izvestiya* on April 5. Its Warsaw correspondent was saddened that the hopes of September 1980 for a speedy correction of mistakes had not come true. Poland was almost economically bankrupt and KOR/Solidarity extremists were using terror to seize positions in all spheres. Events of the last few days had proved that "the 'creeping' counterrevolution has risen to its feet and attained its full height. It has not so far met with perceptible resistance." But there was reason to believe that Soviet leaders were not in sufficient agreement to take the plunge of armed intervention.

The April 4 *Pravda* included some optimistic news from a TASS dispatch about local Party meetings in Poland. Politburo member Barcikowski was cited to the effect that the decisions of the latest Plenum "will have long-term consequences for the Party's consolidation and for restoring its efficiency in the new conditions." Zabinski, Politburo member and Katowice Party boss, had spoken in a similar vein: "A strong government, enjoying the support of the whole people, and strong trade unions, by means of joint activity, in Zabinski's opinion, can lead the country out of this profound crisis." But these encouraging lines of Polish leaders were deleted from the TASS item as published by the CPSU organs *Socialist Industry* and *Sovetskaya Rossiya*. It may be hazarded that editors who ran the remarks were acting for Soviet leaders who felt that Kania and Jaruzelski should be given more time to work out their problems. Others, who excised the remarks, may have done so in accord with the opinion of leaders who doubted the wisdom of continued forbearance.

As noted, Kirilenko may have enjoyed a special relationship with the hardline editors of *Socialist Industry* by dint of his policy responsibilities for economics. Since Kirilenko regularly attended key sessions of the Russian Republic's Supreme Soviet Presidium, the same could be said about his influence with the editorial board of *Sovetskaya Rossiya*.

Kirilenko would have been a logical choice to attend the Czechoslovak Party congress opening in Prague on April 7. He had addressed the last such meeting in 1976 and visited Prague in October 1980. But a major anomaly cropped up on April 5 with Brezhnev's departure for the Czechoslovak congress at the head of a Soviet Party delegation. Brezhnev had not journeyed to eastern Europe for a Party congress since 1975, when he spoke at the Polish rally.

In retrospect, the April 6 *Pravda* can be seen to have effectively dispelled any fear that Brezhnev was going to Prague to tell his allies of a Soviet plan to invade Poland. Its "Letter to Warsaw" was remarkably mild. A Moscow professor told his namesake on the Polish Central Committe that he agreed that the PUWP was "the sole force able to overcome the present crisis." Polish students in Moscow were said to "share entirely and completely the policy of the present-day leadership" in their homeland.

The signs of Kremlinology also failed to harmonize with an assumption that Brezhnev went to Prague to herald intervention. *Pravda*'s photo of the Politburo send-off for Brezhnev showed the relatively low standing of Kirilenko, who was associable with an aggressive stand on the Polish question. Entirely missing from the scene was the harsh ideologue Suslov, whose latest article, pegged to the Moscow Party congress, was evasive and stood clear of the confidence-in-Poland line, for all that might have been worth (*Partiynaya Zhizn*, No. 8, cleared for printing Apr. 7, 1981).

A schism in the Warsaw Pact over whether to use force to return Poland to the fold of orthodoxy can be adduced from the dissonance between the speeches of Husak and Brezhnev at the Prague congress. Husak ranked Poland in 1981 with Hungary (1956), East Germany (1953) and Czechoslovakia (1968)—in that order—as examples of Western efforts to rip a country out of the socialist community. The stern liquidator of the last vestiges of the Prague Spring is likely to have listed Hungary out of chronological order to stress the evil of violent anticommunist methods, as Czechoslovak propagandists were doing in their latest tirades against the Poles. Husak averred that inside Poland the antisocialist forces were striving to accomplish nothing less than a counterrevolutionary coup. The political crisis was said to be growing more acute as counterrevolutionary elements were creating anarchy in political life. Husak restated the doctrine of limited sovereignty within the Warsaw Pact system: "The defense of the socialist system is the cause of each of the socialist states, but at the very same time it is also the general cause of the states of the socialist community, which are filled with resolve to defend their interests and the socialist gains of their people" (*Pravda*, Apr. 7, 1981).

Brezhnev certainly gave no benefit of doubt to the West, but he did not crudely rake up memories of past Soviet interventions. Nor did he stress the perils of the situation in Poland. Brezhnev gave a qualified vote of confidence to the Kania team, saying that it would be able, "one must suppose," to foil the schemes of enemies. In the next breath, the Soviet leader rallied to the side of Polish Communists: "They will be able to defend the cause of socialism, the true interests of their people and the honor and security of their homeland" (*Pravda*, Apr. 8, 1981). The qualifier "suppose" might have been a gesture to hardliners everywhere while the stronger follow-up was reflective of the Brezhnev clan's more trusting viewpoint. If so, Brezhnev's personal intervention was thought essential to lay down the line of confidence-in-Poland, which Suslov was repudiating.

(The present writer finds plausible a rumor from East Berlin in the *New York Times* for April 8, 1981 that three members of the East German Politburo—in charge of relations with other Communist parties, defense and state security—had urged military intervention by the Warsaw Pact because Solidarity had such size and momentum that it could not be co-opted or reoriented by the weakened Polish apparat.)

Within hours of Brezhnev's speech, TASS announced that Warsaw Pact exercises had ended. The disclosure that Pact forces commander Marshal Kulikov of the USSR had led the games could have brought to mind that his predecessor had directed a similar one just before Czechoslovakia was invaded (*Pravda*, July 12, 1968 and Apr. 8, 1981). That may help to explain why some U.S. officials were still uncertain about the immediate objectives of Moscow (*New York Times*, Apr. 8, 1981).

But it seems that the balance of forces in Moscow was weighted too heavily against the doctrinaire circles. Their last gasp was to keep out of a sympathetic press organ, *Socialist Industry*, on April 9 the pro-Kania words in a TASS item from Warsaw that *Pravda* ran a day earlier: "The Party has launched a principled struggle for putting Poland on the road of stabilization and further development in the spirit of socialism's ideals." Aside from having obtained the building of a military framework for possible intervention at a later date, the hardliners got little more than a request from Jaruzelski to his parliament on April 10 for a suspension of the right to strike for two months (Interpress. Apr. 10, 1981).

Precedent can give no assurance as to Soviet intentions. But it is noteworthy that certain propaganda efforts which the Kremlin made on the eve of the Czechoslovak invasion were not in evidence during the Polish intervention threat of April 1981.

"Aleksey Petrov" was conspicuously missing from the columns of *Pravda*. In contrast, the equally authoritative "I. Aleksandrov" was highly visible before the tanks rolled into Prague. He vilified both "certain leading figures" and the Party Presidum of Czechoslovakia for their complacency in the face of a mortal political threat (*Pravda*, July 11 and Aug. 18, 1968). The silence of the foremost Soviet observer on Polish affairs may have been due to a desire to keep the Poles off balance or to a shaky consensus at the CPSU Politburo.

In the case of Czechoslovakia, much ado was made about the "concessions" of Prague leaders to the antisocialist forces and the high risk of them sticking to that course (*Pravda*, July 22 and 25, Aug. 14, 1968). Ringing the tocsin against a policy of concessions to enemies was a Stalinist device to gain internal support for the launching of repressive actions, as for example at the time of the Kremlin Doctors' Plot in 1953. The failure to utilize this ploy against Kania in March-April 1981 could have been a deliberate token of sufferance.

Military activities were given much publicity on the eve of the Czechoslovak invasion. Aside from the command-staff exercise in June and July 1968, there were dry runs of communications and supply units, along with a disclosure that reservists were taking part (*Pravda*, Aug. 11, 12 and 17, 1968). The Soyuz-81 coverage in Soviet media was less elaborate. This discrepancy too may have been fraught with meaning for Soviet newspaper readers accustomed to stereotyped modes of expression.

In fine, the propaganda accompaniment to Soviet saber-rattling around Poland during March and April 1981 suggests that martial stirrings were designed to induce the Warsaw powerholders to impose a state of emergency. But there can be no certainty about the inner discussions among Soviet rulers which almost certainly preceded Brezhnev's dramatic trip to Prague. The threat of direct intervention, after all, would reportedly be a topic of private conversation at an imminent meeting of the number-two Kremlin leader and his Polish hosts.

SIX

Divide et Impera

(APR. 12–JUNE 12, 1981)

The entire body of Soviet propaganda during this period of relative social calm in Poland leaves little doubt that Kremlin leaders were still intent upon rolling back the reform movement. A strong effort was made to energize divisive forces in the rising triarchy of Communist Party, Solidarity labor union and Catholic Church. Discord was to be sown between Party and union activists, radical and moderate reformers inside the Party cells, and conservatives and liberalizers among Warsaw leaders. The instruments of Moscow's splitting tactics included media campaigns, official visits, and perhaps KGB incitement of dissension. Beneath the consensus on strategy in Moscow, there appears to have been a revival of policy debate involving procrastinators and others seeking a quick end to the upheavals.

What Solidarity chroniclers would call a "quasi-peace" reigned in Poland from April through July. The Bydgoszcz affair was a political hornets nest which could not be settled and public discontent of a local nature continued to simmer around it. Many incidents were still sparked by police bullying in the provinces, and there was an outbreak of protests in the prison system. But intensive negotiations were held between the Government and Solidarity even on police matters, and the revolt of private farmers ended with the legalization of Rural Solidarity (Warsaw. *Solidarnosc*. Special Supplement. Sept. 11, 1981).

A sign of good prospect for national cohesion on a reformist platform was the character of regime eulogies of the late primate and friend of Solidarity, Cardinal Wyszynski, who died on May 28. The national Party organ *Trybuna Ludu* praised Wyszynski as "one of the architects of the new social contract" represented by the Gdansk accords (May 19). Party chief Kania extolled the late Cardinal as "great priest," "great patriot" and "man of dialogue" (Warsaw Radio. May 30).

The Kremlin knew that it had to disorganize the emerging informal coalition of major forces in Polish society and politics. Soviet media were not allowed to criticize the Catholic hierarchy nor did they go so far as East Berlin radio on April 21 and outrightly claim a tacit alliance of Solidarity leaders and Communists who demanded freedom within the ruling party. Moscow propagandists, however, made it appear that a great danger was raised by anti-Party Solidarity members and anti-Leninist Communists. Over a span of eight weeks or so, Soviet journalists assailed about equally the parallel reform movements headed by Kania and Walesa.

Suslov began another of his drives for orthodoxy with a speech to the congress of the East Germany Party on April 12. Unlike G.D.R. leader Honecker, Suslov avoided direct reference to Poland, but strikingly warned that "any deviation from our revolutionary teaching entails ruinous consequences" (*Pravda*, Apr. 13, 1981). This implied assessment of Polish events turned out to be gloomier than one given to the East German rally by the senior Bulgarian official Doynov, who aired the "conviction" that Poles would be able to "muster the forces to resist decisively the internal and global reactionaries" (*Ibid.*, Apr. 16, 1981).

The image of staunch Polish Communists caught in a crossfire between Solidarity extremists and Party liberals was drawn in *Pravda* on April 13. A dispatch from the Warsaw correspondent of the paper cited a worker Communist's complaint that "we experience great psychological pressure from Solidarity." Others supposedly denounced "some in the PUWP who would like to make use of discussions to force through views alien to a Marxist-Leninist party, while covering their apostasy with a fine flourish of pseudo-Party phrases about ideological pluralism and the 'partnership' of different political forces." The charge of betraying prior convictions was vintage Suslov, and scoffing at power-sharing could be read as censure of Kania, who had championed the idea.

The same *Pravda* staffer visited the industrial center of Katowice and on April 15 took the same line. On one hand, telephone calls were said to have been made to Party activists which threatened them as well as their families. Solidarity leaders were reputed to have asked for a boycott of the local Party paper, which had criticized the union's activities. On the other hand, there were "weak and vacillating people among the Communists," even if not many resided in this particular area. (Katowice was soon to become a focal point of dogmatic opposition to Kania.)

Soviet chauvinists—and there are many—could be expected to agonize over the exclusive *Pravda* item of April 15, "Provocative Gathering." The mass shooting of Polish prisoners of war at Katyn forest near Smolensk during World War II was reported to have been the topic of speeches by the organizers of a meeting in Warsaw cemetery. *Pravda* stated that speakers gave the Nazi version of the crime, or blamed the Soviet authorities even though a USSR commission of inquiry had established Nazi guilt and its findings were widely known. "Antisocialist, counterrevolutionary elements" were held responsible for this "anti-Soviet witches' Sabbath."

But there were cautionary remarks about the Polish situation. Zamyatin of the CPSU foreign propaganda bureau used the confidence-in-Poland line during a Moscow television commentary on April 18. The Kremlin's limited effort to subdue Polish reformers was indirectly justified by a tale of U.S.-China relations in the April 19 *Pravda*. Defense Secretary Weinberger had reportedly intimated that the United States was ready to begin arms shipments to China "if the development of events in Poland were to become disagreeable for Washington," that is, if the Soviet Union were to intervene directly. Alluding to the time of the initial Soviet invasion scare, *Pravda* quoted Senator Percy to the effect that he believed that in December 1980 the White House had sent to the Defense Department a list of armaments that might be sold or transferred to China.

Mikhail Zimyanin, Party Secretary for culture, was relaxed in his keynote report to a week-long seminar of Agitprop workers that opened in Moscow on April 20. Zimyanin devoted little more than 100 words to the most protracted crisis in the history of Soviet Europe. He assured that Polish patriots led by the Communist Party were waging an intensive political struggle for bolstering socialism in Poland and enjoyed the full support of the Soviet Union.[1] Politburo member Chernenko also hinted in his Lenin Day speech of April 22 that it would be wrongful to get too excited about the Polish troubles. He mocked at "the hullabaloo" about Poland and ignored the widely-condemned evildoers there. Chernenko rounded instead on Western politicians who were trying to destabilize the country (*Pravda*, Apr. 23, 1981).

The gloomier side of things was necessarily pointed up by the sudden visit of Suslov and Party Secretary for bloc relations Rusakov to Warsaw on April 23, or in the very midst of the all-Union conference of propaganda workers. Polish officials reportedly did not even know that Suslov was coming until his plane was already in the air (*New York Times*, Apr. 30, 1981). One reason for the rush may have been the announcement of April 22 that the Polish Central Committee would meet on April 29. Calls for the ouster of hardline Politburo members Olszowski and Grabski by such a plenum were heard on April 15 at a meeting of 750 radical Party democratizers from all over Poland in the city of Torun (Paris. AFP. Apr. 16, 1981). Suslov may also have gotten some backing to dramatize the Polish heresy by a surprise visit to Warsaw just when ideology was again in the spotlight.

The TASS communique on Suslov's mission avoided the use of any phrase that might have created an impression of interference in the internal affairs of a fraternal Party. It informed that Suslov, Rusakov and Soviet ambassador Aristov had talks with Kania and other Politburo members. A host of platitudes about the defense of socialism, Soviet-Polish cooperation and Western scheming was recorded. But the description of the atmosphere at the meeting as "cordial, Party-like" was suggestive of disunity and belied the caption "Friendly Visit" (*Pravda*, Apr. 24, 1981).

Soviet sources later disclosed that Suslov in Warsaw held forth on "overcoming the disturbance of the ranks of the PUWP, defending its cadres against enemy attacks and defending people's rule by every means" and "the rising tide of anti-Sovietism" in Poland.[2] Foreign journalists reported that Suslov's encounter with Polish leaders was a stormy one. There was disagreement on the vigor of the Polish Party in combatting democratic influences. Suslov wanted the election of delegates to the forthcoming Party congress to be open and uncontested. The visitors were warned that a Soviet invasion of Poland would meet with armed resistance.[3]

Upon the return of the Suslov party to Moscow on April 24, Rusakov went back to the ideology seminar at CPSU headquarters. His detailed version of events in Poland was a blending of alarm and hope. The crisis was said to be "grave and dangerous." Mass media were being penetrated by antisocialist elements, which were fomenting nationalism and anarcho-syndicalism. Hostile and inflammatory leaflets were inundating the country. Party and police were subjected to slander on a regular basis. The upshot was that a large segment of the populace was confused.

Solidarity, according to Rusakov, had become an organized political force that was essentially paralyzing the authorities. Many of the union's local branches were pawns of the counterrevolutionary KOR. The dissidents were using "well-known methods of silent, creeping counterrevolution," that is following the example of Prague Spring activists, in their quest for a political takeover. Solidarity's draft program (published April 14) was vilified as an attempt to switch discussion away from legitimate topics to be addressed at the next congress of the Polish Party. The Draft was especially condemned for demanding a lifting of the curbs on private ownership and supposedly for seeking the legalization of an opposition to the Party.

Rusakov saw exceptional danger lurking within the Party itself. What he termed "the opposition" in society was said to be manipulating "unstable opportunist elements" among Party members. It had begun subversive work at the grass roots in order to send agents as delegates to the Party congress and to impose a defective program on the congress.

Rusakov put the hazards into the context of world politics. It "needs to be understood," he argued, that the crisis in Poland was not confined within national boundaries. Imperialism was trying to change the balance of power in Europe to its advantage. This statement of Rusakov could have been a rebuke to Soviet Party members in the lower ranks who might have taken a hands-off-Poland attitude like that of the Italian Communist speaker at the recent Party congress in Moscow. (A similar intrepretation can be given to the polemic at a roundtable of Soviet ideologues on April 23, 1981: it would be "wrong" not to see a linkage of current-day phenomena with old battles in Soviet Russia against the Mensheviks, Worker Opposition, Right and national deviationists, according to *Voprosy Istorii KPSS*, No. 7, 1981.)

Rusakov did move near to the undaring position of Chernenko when he commended the Warsaw rulers for endeavoring to thwart the pluralists. He approved of the Polish leaders "putting forward the slogan of 'renewal of socialism'" and under it straining "to restore and strengthen relations with the masses, overcome the mistakes of the previous leadership and normalize the situation in the country." Soviet militants were told not to despair: "It would be a mistake to believe that the entire Polish working class follows the Solidarity trade union, even less its extremist figures. Yes, Solidarity does include millions of people. But the views and beliefs of the absolute majority of them are far from the antisocialist goals of Solidarity's counterrevolutionary advisers." In other words, it was still possible to erode the mass base of Solidarity and to avoid resort to the mailed fist. Rusakov further encouraged his audience to think that anti-Communists in Poland were beginning to encounter rebuffs in different strata of society and the Polish Party had people with whom it could fight jointly to consolidate the system.[4]

If there was any rift in the Soviet establishment about ultimate goals of the Kremlin's Polish policy it would almost certainly have barred the airing of a fiercely anti-reformist editorial in *Kommunist* No. 7 (cleared for printing on April 24). The article had the zealous title "May They Live Through the Ages," referring to the name and cause of Lenin. Obloquy was heaped on "critics of Marxism-Leninism" who were "trying to pepper the monolithic bastion of scientific socialism with the buckshot of 'socialisms' of the nationalist variety" and "the false followers of socialism who are trying to eat away at the monistic scientific concept of the socialist system with the acid of ideological and political 'pluralism.'" Departures from Soviet-style socialism were viewed as indicative of "infantile utopianism or malicious intentions." The editorial urged distrust of "the irresponsible slogan 'freedom of criticism'" as it

was put forward by "opportunists," who absurdly complained that
Marxism was "growing 'decrepit.'" Lenin was held up as a shining
example of how Communists had to be "merciless toward ideological
opponents." The immediate objective of Moscow, however, was to stave
off the demise of law-and-order politicians in Warsaw.

Clearly pegged to the imminent meeting of the Polish Central Committee was an attack on the radical-reformist foes of Olszowski and
Grabski in the April 26 *Pravda*. The crisis heading "Situation in Poland"
was affixed to a TASS item from Warsaw accusing "revisionist elements"
of "inspiring a campaign to discredit Party officials." The reformers
were also assailed for insisting on the creation of "horizontal structures,"
or discussion groups of Party members from all walks of life that would
be independent of Party staffs under centralized control. *Pravda* alluded
acridly to one of the Torun crowd, Zbigniew Iwanow, who was expelled
from the Party in December, as one of those who wanted to immobilize
the Party.

Underscoring the widening breach in Soviet-Polish relations, Kania
eschewed criticism of the Torun Party dissidents in his report to the
Central Committee plenum on April 29. It is not possible to say
confidently if the Soviet leaders finally agreed that Kania had tied himself
irrevocably to national communism and so become unacceptable as the
helmsman of an allied state. The vast cuts in the TASS summary of
Kania's report do indicate at the least that Moscow had great misgivings
about the Polish leader.

The Soviet editors heavily expurgated Kania's text in behalf of inner-
Party freedom and socialist democracy. His calls for breaking with tested
tradition and subordinating the Party machine with its lifelong leaders
to elected committees fortified with new blood were cloaked. The Polish
chief's virtual motto was likewise thrown into the shade: "Democracy
is not a gesture by the authorities to the community, but a great and
growing requirement of society." Soviet displeasure was shown towards
Kania's onslaught against bureaucratic overprivilege: Only the original
text contained an appeal to broaden access to higher education for the
children of workers and peasants. The same was true of Kania's stress
on the importance of using the profit motive in agriculture and running
industry on a less centralized basis.

In addition, the Kremlin patently despised Kania for his building of
bridges to Solidarity. Yet in the wake of Suslov's visit to Warsaw, *Pravda*
(April 26) had carried a TASS item with comment on the visit by
Trybuna Ludu (April 25–26) which ignored a line that "agreement has
gained the upper hand over conflict" in Poland. Now, *Pravda* hid from
its readers the references of Kania to Solidarity as "an organization of

millions of people of good will" and to examples of "good, useful cooperation" between the union and Government.

Kania's pledges of loyalty to Soviet ideas may no longer have been credible in Moscow. That may help to explain the omission of some verbal guarantees on vital issues from the Kania speech as published in *Pravda*. These included a defense of the Party apparatus's grip on major job appointments (*nomenklatura*): "The Party will preserve its influence on filling posts in the key links of our life." Missing too from the Soviet version was a promise that "the Party will never renounce either the right to inspiration or control over the means of information and propaganda." (A Soviet media workers' delegation led by State Radio and Television Committee chairman Lapin would visit Poland May 12–16, indicating Moscow's continued annoyance on that score.)

But the rendition of Kania's speech in the April 30 *Pravda* was extensive, occupying about one-fifth more space than was given to the Polish plenum held a month earlier. Evidently the Soviet faithful had to be comforted that Poland was not leaderless, or the Kania team notified that it was expected to measure up to definite standards of political conduct. In any case, the sanitized text of Kania's address highlighted as the real problems of Poland the existence of an economic depression and weakened executive power stemming largely from Solidarity having overstepped the limits of its by-laws. Was the Soviet newspaper reader to extrapolate that it was only a matter of time before famine and unemployment would turn the Poles away from their non-violent revolution?

The best news for Moscow at the Polish plenum was resignation of top leaders other than Olszowski and Grabski. By merely noting that Kania had made a concluding speech, *Pravda* on May 1 concealed that new Politburo members Gabrys and Wronski were workers, though not Solidarity members. The evasion also served to mask the identities of a new non-voting member of the Politburo (Masny) and a new Secretary of the Central Committee (Cypryniak). They were regional Party secretaries who were promoted, Kania said, as "the first step toward expanding local representation" in the supreme Party bodies (Warsaw Radio. Apr. 30, 1981).

The next opportunity for moves to refurbish the Polish elite would be the special Party congress which the April plenum scheduled to run from July 14 to 18. A reflex thought for everyone in East and West was the decision of the Prague Spring leaders to call a special Party congress for September 14, 1968, only to see it aborted by the Soviet invasion launched almost a month earlier. Significantly, *Pravda* on August 20, 1968, or hours away from the invasion, speculated that no more than 25 percent of the Party Central Committee in Czechoslovakia could expect to be re-elected at the forthcoming special congress. Not even that many might survive in the Polish Central Committee after an event that Kania had billed as "the congress of workers."

On the surface, there was little to indicate that Soviet defense planners were doing much more than enhancing the army's capability for the contingency of intervention. The foreign press quoted "Western attaches" in Warsaw as saying that Soviet troops in southeastern Poland were constructing an extensive network of communications facilities. "We are seeing a lot of buildup in communications," one analyst noted, pointed on a map to several towns and a suburb near Warsaw and added: "These would come in very handy if there were a need to use forces in the country" (*New York Times*, May 5, 1981).

But some ideologues and generals were seemingly agitating for the Kremlin to play its military card. The outline of a history of the Czechoslovak Party that was published in Moscow in 1979 was belatedly reviewed in *Kommunist* No. 7, cleared for printing on May 5. The same insidious groups that Soviet propaganda had claimed to be at work in Poland since August 1980 were recalled to have spearheaded a campaign of wrecking against Czechoslovakia in 1968: Western intelligence services, revisionist Communists and antisocialist forces. The internal subversives at the behest of Western masters had ignited popular discontent over regime mistakes and defects. One position after another in Party and State was allegedly seized by the enemy, who was attacking each basic principle of socialism. Party and society were cast into a "severe crisis" which could have resulted in open counterrevolution and civil war. Senior officials and ordinary citizens, supposedly, could not get the authorities in Prague to take measures against the danger and sent to the leaders of fraternal Parties a request for "international aid in the cause of defending socialism." The positive response to this appeal was claimed to have served the interests of all concerned. This "historical" review, it seems, was tantamount to asserting that it was high time for Kania's critics in Poland to ask for the help of Soviet forces.

The military representatives in the Soviet Central Committee may also have included partisans of direct intervention. Marshal Ivan Bagramyan had written an essay for the April 1981 issue of the literary journal *Znamya* that dwelt on the career of Stalin's Polish viceroy, Marshal Rokossovskiy. The Polish-born Soviet hero was said to have been named commander of the Polish army in 1949 after Poland's President "insistently requested" his assistance for the strengthening of national defense at a time of heightened threat from the West. Bagramyan may have been hinting that there was good precedent for the Kremlin to send a military governor to Warsaw.

A short time after he favorably recalled Poland in the age of satellite communism, Bagramyan suggested that Soviet forces could occupy that country without causing the devastation of its industry or themselves becoming demoralized. He did so in an article entitled "Our Remarkable Compatriots. Story about Marshal Konev." The essay appeared in *Znamya* No. 7, delivered to the compositor on May 16 and cleared for printing on June 11. According to Bagramyan, Stalin told Konev in December 1944 that "liberation of the industrial heart of Poland must be conducted in a special way. . . . All measures had to be taken to save it from destruction." Konev then "understood even more his responsiblity for preserving this property of the Polish nation." In his subsequent campaign in Silesia, Konev allegedly shunned textbook tactics in order to "save the factories, plants and mines." The Germans in Krakow had "mined everything," but they "did not succeed in blowing things up." Konev's problem with troop morale was not an easy one, but

> Ivan Stepanovich also paid maximal attention to Party-political work. The soldiers had to go into action beyond the frontiers of the Homeland, on the territory of Poland, where the ideology of bourgeois society was still strong, and the population was subjected to the massive influence of fascist propaganda for a period of five years. Here each soldier had to show by his entire conduct the advantages of socialism over the society of private ownership.

Thus, Bagramyan appears to have been suggesting that Brezhnev like Stalin before him could safely run the risk of invading Poland. He did not need to fear the ruin of factories, mines and ports or that his troops might fall victim to anticommunist ideology.

It is true that Bagramyan in 1981 was 83 years old and only a general inspector at the Defense Ministry. But someone at the top was keeping him in the public eye. Bagramyan signed an article on military paintings in the January 4, 1981 *Pravda* which repeatedly lauded the trait of "decisiveness." The unveiling of a bronze bust of Bagramyan in his hometown and the Marshal's vitality at the ceremony were reported in *Pravda* on May 31. Bagramyan's signature appeared too at the close of a World War II book review with anti-Western notes in the June 13 *Pravda*. (A Bagramyan-Suslov tie is possible: Bagramyan commanded the forces of the First Baltic Front in 1943–45 and the Baltic Military District in 1945–54; Suslov was chairman of the central Party Bureau for Lithuania in 1944–46.)

Brezhnev may have listened not long ago to the enticing schemes of his general staff for a quick victory in Afghanistan. Almost a year and a half later there was still no light in the Afghan tunnel. The Soviet

President was apparently still determined to fight one war at a time, if he could help it.

Barring resort to its military option, the Kremlin had to signal Polish leaders that in the run-up to the special Party congress it could not endure a purge of hardline friends. The report-back and election meetings at local level would have to name Politburo members and regional secretaries as delegates to the congress. Moscow evidently demanded too that congress delegations include a sizable number of activists beholden to the apparatus mainstays.

One message along those lines was sent in the May 4 *Pravda*. It took the form of a letter from a war veteran-pensioner living in a town of the Odessa region. He and his comrades were said to be following the events in Poland "with emotion and uneasiness." The antisocialist elements, richly endowed by the West, were supposedly trying to use the report-back and election campaign in the Polish Party and preparation for the special congress. Spreading chaos and anarchy, they were doing everything to destabilize the situation. But the Polish Communists would foil the plans of the enemy, and the people of Poland were alleged to be capable of defending their revolutionary gains. In all, a "time of anxiety" had arrived.

A second sign that Moscow could not abide organic reform was the disapproving silence of Soviet media about a basic document summarized in *Trybuna Ludu* on May 8: "Programmatic Assumptions for the Ninth Extraordinary PUWP Congress." This manifesto had begun with a scathing critique of the sham democracy practised in Parties and Governments of the Soviet alliance system. The draft program urged, above all, that the Party be freed of centralized domination and cooperate as a partner with self-governing organizations of working people. Partnership was to distinguish the relationship of Party officials to media editors, trade unionists and young people. A thorough change of investment policy was demanded: The consumer was promised a shift of economic priorities, away from emphasis on heavy industry and towards light industry and agriculture. A breakthrough was to be made in creating small-scale industry and services. Within the nationalized sector, the Draft envisioned more decision-making rights for managers and a narrowing of wage differentials. Cultural freedom was in effect proclaimed to be essential.

The new politics of accommodation in Poland seem to have been condemned in the theory article which *Pravda* ran on May 8. Vadim Pechenev, a consultant of the Propaganda Department in the CPSU Secretariat, discussed the Soviet concept of socialism and preached "struggle against the now quite modish attempts to counter real socialism with various types of subjective 'ideal models' of a society which has

never existed anywhere but which is passed off as 'genuinely socialist.'"
The implicit advice to Kania was that any variety in Polish institutions
and policies had to be within the limits of the Soviet pattern.

A protest against the loosening of cultural controls in Poland as
sanctioned by the draft PUWP program was lodged by Feliks Kuznetsov,
first secretary of the Moscow writers union. The second and final part
of his report on a trip to Warsaw was run in *Literaturnaya Gazeta* for
May 13. Kuznetsov sympathized with the old conservative writer Pu-
trament, who was allegedly hooted down from the rostrum at a recent
special congress of Polish writers. That kind of "intolerance, anarchy
and diktat" was found to be very typical of those campaigning loudest
of all for democracy. Kuznetsov further charged that rightwing forces
in Poland were trying to wage a struggle for public opinion via waverers
within the Party. Destructive actions were becoming more frequent in
the spheres of education, science, creative and student circles, and the
mass media. (A glowing review of Kuznetsov's latest books in the May
8 *Pravda* showed that this paragon of intellectual conformity was valued
in the main Party offices.)

Co-ordinated with Kuznetsov's massive article in *Literaturnaya Gazeta*,
apparently, was a shorter item in the May 13 *Pravda* which also equated
freedom of expression with license. A cable from the paper's Warsaw
correspondent entitled "Provocative Exhibition" condemned a public
display of native *samizdat* and Western books glorifying dissidents, as
well as caricatures that were mostly of an antisocialist and anti-Soviet
character. A book fair to be held in Warsaw on May 17 would reportedly
feature the open sale of such literature. (The East German news agency
ADN on May 11 reported the book show and notified that exhibits
included "trash" by Aleksandr Solzhenitsyn, "who holds ultrareactionary
views.")

In spite of the limited success of the Suslov mission, the Soviet elite
still viewed personal contacts as a prime means of exerting pressure
on recalcitrants. A delegation of Soviet Party officials headed by Nikolay
Petrovichev visited Poland from May 18 to 23. Petrovichev was first
deputy chief of the Organizational-Party Work Department in the CPSU
Secretariat and a prolific writer on the theme of Party structure. He
had come to discuss Party congress preparations and was later received
by Kania (PAP, May 18 and *Pravda*, May 24, 1981). If Petrovichev had
watched the evening news on Polish television for May 18 he would
have heard excerpts from a Kania speech to the effect that "there can
be no retreat from" and "there is no turning back from" the new course.

The next visit to Warsaw by a high Soviet official coincided with an
offensive by conservative forces in Poland. Warsaw Pact commander
Marshal Kulikov met with Kania and Jaruzelski on May 30. The meeting

was reportedly held in "a friendly atmosphere" and stressed the importance of military cooperation (Warsaw Radio. May 30, 1981). It is hard to believe that the enormous throngs that Kulikov saw at the public funeral of Cardinal Wyszinski did not shake the Soviet marshal and reduce whatever ardor for intervention that he might have nurtured.

On the eve of the Kulikov visit the Polish youth newspaper *Sztandar Mlodych* (May 28) carried a text dated May 15 called "Declaration of the Katowice Party Forum under the regional PUWP committee." Sharpening the criticisms in the Soviet press, the Declaration hit at Kania and urged a reversal of the Party line:

> The threat of a revisionist coup d'etat in the Party has been growing hand in hand with the passive and, in effect, acquiescing, posture of the PUWP leadership. Some members of the Central Committee and the Congress Commission have even been inspirers and protectors for revisionists and Party-splitting forces. That has been evident from their statements, from the anti-Party line assumed by the Party press. . . .
>
> The further passiveness of the PUWP leadership and the hostile activity conducted by antisocialist centers within the Party and society is threatening incalculable domestic and international consequences, is directly jeopardizing the unity and security of the socialist community, and is providing imperialism with conditions for freely disposing of the revolutionary and national liberation movements. We call on the Politburo and Central Committee to take resolute steps to avert the threat of counterrevolution in the country.

The most poignant of a series of ripostes to the Katowice Party Forum in Polish media struck at its members as hitherto "dormant antediluvian dinosaurs" who were "encouraging the Party authorities to repeat the Czechoslovak experience and to ask for help" from the USSR (Warsaw. PAP Maritime Service. May 31, 1981).

The ideologue of the Katowice Party Forum was Wsiewolod Wolczew, a naturalized Pole descended from a Bulgarian father and a Russian mother. He was a Party secretary in the eastern regions of the country in the late 1950's and gained notoriety by having Western books burned in a marketplace. Wolczew in the 1970's was an associate professor of political studies at the university in Katowice and took on as aides a number of compromised bureaucrats (*Neue Zuercher Zeitung*, June 11, 1981).

KGB chief Andropov's role model could hardly have been Platon Zubov, the youthful lover of Catherine the Great. But Andropov may have played a no less important part in the machinations that led to the Declaration of the Katowice Party Forum than Zubov did in the case of the Targowica Confederation. In 1792 a group of Polish nobles who had recently lost political privileges got into touch with St. Petersburg and proclaimed a "confederation" at Targowica, Poland. The act of "confederation" denounced the new constitution of 1791 which had diminished the magnates' power, demanded the restoration of ancient Polish "liberties," and appealed for aid to Catherine. Some 100,000 Russian troops crossed the Polish frontier two weeks later.[5] In 1981, Wolczew and others of the Katowice Party Forum may have acted at the instigation of the Soviet or an allied security service.[6]

KGB concern that the democracy delirium in Poland might have an adverse impact on Soviet youth was recently suggested by Col. Gen. Viktor Chebrikov, KGB deputy chairman. Writing for the April issue of the Young Communist League journal (*Molodoy Kommunist* No. 4), Chebrikov warned that "enemies of socialism" were seeking to suborn Soviet young people with "provocative slogans about the 'conservatism of the old cadres,' who are allegedly hindering the 'democratization,' 'liberalization' and 'humanization' of socialism" and "ideas about the need for so-called 'political pluralism' . . . the 'expediency' of creating within socialism's political system 'competing' organizations, societies and unions in opposition, of course, to the CPSU."

That kind of worrisome talk could have flowed at a secretive conference of KGB officers that was held in Moscow on May 25–26. Andropov spoke to the meeting and Brezhnev made a rare appearance (*Pravda*, May 27, 1981).

Whether or not by accident, a stiffening of the Soviet propaganda line on Poland is noticeable after the KGB conclave. As late as May 17, *Pravda* cited the Mongolian Communist ruler as softly reciting to his Party congress the confidence-in-Poland shibboleth, with CPSU Politburo member and Secretary (for agriculture) Gorbachev looking on. A few days later, however, the chairman of the West German Communist Party was reported to have struck a much harsher chord at his Party congress, which was attended by Ponomarev, CPSU Politburo candidate and Secretary (for liaison with nonruling Communist Parties). The German Party leader went far beyond his Mongolian counterpart and warned that the danger to socialism in Poland "will not in the least diminish if concessions are made to the antisocialist forces, something which has been occurring until this day." This remark anticipated the favorable publicity for the hardline Katowice Party Forum in Soviet media, and was even followed by an augury of a major Kremlin pronouncement of June 5: The interests of the entire socialist community supposedly demanded "a halt to the threatening danger of counterrevolution in Poland" (*Pravda*, May 30, 1981).

The TASS account of the Katowice Party Forum's stand which *Pravda* ran on June 2 had the crisis headline "Situation in Poland" and supported the band of malcontents. The item falsely claimed that a meeting of the Forum was chaired by new Politburo member Gabrys, identified as a miner by profession, doubtless so as to lend respectability to the affair. Kania's stewardship of the Party was damned by virtue of a unique assertion that since August 1980 "more significant damage was done to the Party than in the whole of the seventies." The pre-congress guidelines of the Politburo were blasted for lacking such essentials as a class approach to events, mention of private property as the root of political evil, and express stipulation of the directive nature of Party leadership of the working class. Contrary to the spirit of all major Party documents adopted under Kania, the Katowice Party Forum was warmly quoted as stating: "We must use the universal methods of the construction of socialism and not erect a Polish socialism."

The Kania team replied with disdain on June 2. At a press conference in Warsaw, Politburo member and Secretary Barcikowski said that a session of the ruling body had decided that Katowice Party Forum materials "do not serve the cause of unity," "contain accusations which cannot be accepted," and "polarize stances." Journalists were also told of a convulsion in the report-back and election campaign, completed in 187 out of 205 large Party organizations: About 90 percent of the members and candidate members of regional Party committees were people who had been elected to Party office for the first time or after a break of one or two terms of office (Warsaw Radio. June 2, 1981).

Pravda's response was to issue two articles under the crisis rubric "Situation in Poland" on June 5 and 6. The first was datelined Sofia and based on a signed article in the Bulgarian Party paper *Rabotnichesko Delo* (May 31). "A diarchy actually exists in the country," the TASS item thundered, "and attacks and insults against police and State security organs have become more frequent, crime is increasing and anti-Soviet moods are being fanned." The second article, supplied by TASS in Warsaw, defended the Katowice Party Forum. A new document by the Forum was said to have been published in the army newspaper *Zolnierz Wolnosci*. One passage had the ring of a swipe at someone at the very top: "those political chameleons who often change their views, getting at the head of each routine renewal and avoiding responsibility for their prior activity." Kania was "at the head" of the latest rectification drive and he might have been the target of this invective.

Any suspicion of Defense Minister and Premier Jaruzelski having sided with the pro-Moscow forces in Katowice or *Zolnierz Wolnosci* was dispelled by the attack on both him and Kania in a Soviet Party letter sent to the Polish Central Committee, and obviously adopted by the Politburo or Secretariat. "S. Kania, W. Jaruzelski and other Polish comrades" were said to have "expressed agreement with our point of view" on the need to strengthen authority across the board. "But nothing has changed," the letter added, "and the policy of concession and compromise has not been corrected." The letter gave a picture of Poland as a land in the throes of a vast anticommunist conspiracy, with the plotters able to gain control of most sensitive institutions, for example the mass information media.

Polish leaders were told that with little more than a month remaining before their special Party congress, the antisocialist forces were increasingly setting the tone of the Party election campaign. "Casual people who overtly espouse opportunist points of view" were often found "to lead local Party organizations and figure among delegates to conferences and to the Congress." At the same time, Party stalwarts were being shunted aside and few worker Communists named to attend the congress as delegates. A political massacre of Soviet collaborators might be in the offing: "It cannot be excluded that during the congress itself, an attempt could be made to strike a decisive blow against the Marxist-Leninist forces of the Party in order to liquidate it."

A broad hint was made that Kania should be ousted: "What is needed now is to mobilize all the healthy forces in society to resist the class adversary and combat counterrevolution. This requires, first of all, a revolutionary will within the Party itself, among its activists and its leadership. Yes, its leadership. Time will not wait. The Party can and must find within itself the forces to reverse the course of events and return them to the proper path even before the Ninth PUWP Congress" (*Pravda*, June 12, 1981).

The Soviet warning letter resembled too closely one that Warsaw Pact leaders sent to Prague in July 1968 for Kania to have disregarded it. In 1968 the crucial words for Prague were: "the offensive of reactionaries, supported by imperialism, against your Party and the foundations of the social system of the Czechoslovak Socialist Republic is threatening to push your country off the road of socialism and consequently threatens the interests of the entire socialist system";[7] in 1981 the key phrase for Warsaw was: "The offensive of hostile antisocialist forces in the Polish People's Republic threatens the interests of our entire community, its cohesion, its integrity and the security of borders— yes, our common security." The Polish Politburo met on June 7, 1981 to discuss the Kremlin letter and decided to convene an emergency session of the Central Committee for June 9. That was reported in the June 9 *Pravda*, which gave the agenda as "Current-day situation in the country and preparation for the 9th extraordinary Party congress."

Soviet pique over the results of the Central Committee meeting held in Warsaw June 9–10 could be gathered from the unusually brief press coverage. *Pravda* for June 12 merely informed that Kania had read the

Politburo report to the plenum and the session ended after a debate. Kania's closing speech was ignored, and there was a terse reference to "crisis in the Party" as well as country. The same issue of *Pravda* ran the Soviet warning letter to Warsaw, and a TASS summary of the plenum resolution was carried in the CPSU paper on the next day.

Comparision of the TASS summary with the original edict of the PUWP Plenum as aired by Warsaw television on June 11 shows the Kremlin's total rejection of the Polish experiment. The reprinted passages were those critical of moves to de-Sovietize the Communist party in Poland and to tolerate freedom of expression along Western lines. A massive tightening up was the professed objective of the PUWP which Soviet leaders underscored. Missing from the TASS digest of the June Plenum resolution were countervailing—and no doubt more sincere—gestures of friendliness to reformist elements in Solidarity and the Party.

The decision to avoid a summary of Kania's report and to publish the June 5 letter indicated that he had become unacceptable to Soviet leaders. Kania had said many things in line with the dire message from Moscow, and gave what turned out to be a sincere pledge to replace lax media executives. But he also restated the moderate conviction that patience was needed in building a national consensus for "socialist renewal."

The masking of stormy debate at the Polish Plenum from Soviet eyes could have reflected the Kremlin's fear that ordinary members of the CPSU might envy the freedom of discussion allowed to the governing class across the frontier. Very little was put above criticism as a series of speakers blasted everything from Solidarity to the Politburo and Party First Secretary.[8] Grabski flatly stated that Kania was not supplying adequate leadership and even charged the Party head with violations of collective rule. The Soviet hawks appear to have been chastized by a local boss who warned that "the enemy" was setting a trap by trying to "make us use force" and "One of the elements of such a trap would be an intervention either of the Polish Armed Forces or a Soviet intervention in Poland."

Kania withstood the attack of pro-Soviet officials thanks largely to a groundswell of patriotic feeling. All of it was not idealistic. Roman Ney, a central Party Secretary, betrayed a healthy instinct for self-preservation: "If we carried out a change in the Party leadership today, it is my conviction that this would be regarded by the entire Party and the public as a change forced on us by our allies. Such a change will be regarded as a turning back from socialist renewal. We must not do this." An anti-Solidarity voice, that of Szczecin Party leader Stanislaw Miskiewicz, had conceded that "Today most of our people are against the Party—against us," hinting that many worried about a new wave of social protest if Moscow's clients were given the power.

With vision of hindsight, one can see that military speakers at the June 1981 Plenum in Warsaw gave a ray of hope to Soviet leaders. Even Jaruzelski was pained by the "destabilization" of political life and "spiral of collapse" forming in the economy. His fellow officers were no less disturbed over the weakening of the country's defense potential because of loosened social discipline. The Soviet publication of the June 5 letter from Moscow to Warsaw was evidently calculated to encourage such reform skeptics and to legitimize any new putsch that might be staged against Kania.

NOTES

1. *Za vysokoye kachestvo i deystvennost ideologicheskoy raboty: Materialy Vsesoyuz. seminara-soveshchaniya ideologicheskikh rabotnikov. M., 20–25 apr. 1981 g.* (Moscow, 1981), p. 65.

2. Mikhail Lebedev talk on Moscow Radio in Polish to Poland, July 7, 1981, and "Statement of the CPSU Central Committee and USSR Government," Warsaw Radio, Sept. 18, 1981.

3. Belgrade. *Borba* and Paris. *Le Monde*, Apr. 25, 1981; *Washington Post*, June 25, 1981 and Aug. 21, 1983.

4. *Za vysokoye kachestvo*, pp. 239–243.

5. Michael T. Florinsky, *Russia: A History and an Interpretation* (Macmillan, New York, 1955), Vol I, pp. 536–538.

6. An East German tie is possible. Unlike TASS, ADN reported on November 5 that Wolczew as a leader of the Katowice Marxist-Leninist seminar at the Party college of the Katowice regional PUWP committee addressed a local meeting celebrating the 64th anniversary of the Bolshevik Revolution. ADN also ran the meeting's ultra-orthodox letter to G.D.R. chief Honecker.

7. *Spravochnik partiynogo rabotnika. Vypusk vosmoy* (Moscow, 1968), p. 20.

8. Speeches delivered at the Plenum were reported by Warsaw Radio, June 9–11, 1981; PAP, June 10–11, 1981; *Trybuna Ludu*, June 10, 1981 and *Zycie Warszawy*, June 11, 1981. The Kania-Grabski power struggle was described in the *New York Times* and *Washington Post*, June 11 and 12, 1981, and *The Christian Science Monitor*, June 16, 1981.

SEVEN

Congress Without a Vision

(JUNE 14–JULY 31, 1981)

Soviet pressure on Warsaw continued after the Kremlin letter of June 5, and was evidently still meant in part to split the varied social interests that acting together might have gotten Poland out of impasse. Commentators were not in unison about the competence of Polish leaders, suggesting a continuance of divided counsels in the Kremlin. But a drumfire of propaganda was kept up against Solidarity and Party reformers while Gen. Jaruzelski, his cabinet and the Polish Army were shown favoritism as potentially stabilizing elements. With the special Party Congress drawing nearer amidst fresh incidents of labor unrest, Soviet military moves resumed and Gromyko was sent to confer with the Polish leaders. Kania felt constrained to take a few steps backward on the sensitive issue of media control and election of delegates to the Congress. Although the Polish leader defended the essentials of reformism in his keynote to the Congress, the hostility of Moscow towards democratization can be regarded as a prime factor that led to the Congress avoiding bold proposals that might have helped the regime to gain a degree of public trust.

The opinion of some, if not many Poles about the Kremlin letter was registered in the national assembly speech of Deputy Karol Malcuzynski, a famous author, on June 12. He said tactfully that "the picture of the situation in Poland as described in the CPSU Central Committee letter is in many respects biased. It is based on bringing forth negative phenomena, processes which alarm our nation, but it overlooks the achievements of renewal, its therapeutic trend affecting both the nation and the state and the consolidation of the social foundation of socialism in our country" (Warsaw Radio. June 12, 1981). The weakened and fear-ridden regime can therefore be assumed to have distanced itself still further from its societal base by having recognized as valid the stern judgements set forth in the Kremlin letter.

But adverse Polish reaction to the virtual ultimatum for tightening up never got into *Pravda*, which reported the full support of other ruling Communist parties. TASS summaries of editorials from Party dailies in Hungary (June 17), Czechoslovakia (June 19), Bulgaria (June 26), Outer Mongolia (June 29) and Vietnam (July 1) were published. A recurrent theme was that de-stabilization in Poland had raised a threat to the security of the entire socialist community, but Polish leaders were still doing little more than making compromises with internal foes. Only the Hungarians agreed to the necessity of starting reforms in Poland, and the inclusion of that view in *Pravda* denoted the approval of some high officials in the Soviet Union.

A feeling of pessimism was conveyed by Zamyatin in a Moscow television commentary on June 20. He stated that "the situation in Poland is not only not improving, not only not stabilizing, but the crisis has encompassed the economic field and now the political sphere in the country is experiencing a crisis as is the ideological sphere." Zamyatin was waiting for "energetic actions" in order to "really lead Poland out of a catastrophic situation."

A counterpoint to Zamyatin was the article by Yu. Tikhonov, an unidentified critic of Polish liberalizers, in the journal of the Secretariat's Propaganda Department. Without giving details, Tikhonov asserted that "The specific actions of the leadership of the PUWP and PPR Government in fulfilling this resolution [of the June 9–10 PUWP Plenum] are already yielding positive results, which have been met with a feeling of joy by friends of the PUWP and people's Poland in all countries" (*Agitator*, No. 14, cleared for printing June 25, 1981). It will be seen that at least one regressive action was taken in Warsaw between June 20 and 25 insofar as Party management of the media was concerned; but the impact could scarcely have been so immediate as to have caused elation in Moscow. Tikhonov was varnishing a grim reality for some ulterior purpose.

Diversity of attitude in the Soviet elite was suggested too by press accounts of a ceremony at the Russian town where Polish Army units were formed in World War II. *Pravda* on June 25 gloomily cited a Polish officer on the "dangerous situation," "deep crisis," and "very grave threat" in his homeland, along with a Stalin-era reference to the concern of "the socialist camp." *Red Star*, however, in its treatment of the event on the same day was much calmer, noting only "the difficult political and economic situation" in Poland.

The media variations are suggestive of debate among Soviet leaders over what to do next about Poland. Some may have shared the downcast view of *Pravda* and Zamyatin, and urged armed intervention. Others could have taken the less pessimistic stance on display in *Agitator* and *Red Star*, and advised more patience. A cautious majority's lack of taste for dispute beyond the Politburo may have caused the decision not to hold the usual Central Committee plenum on the eve of the two-day Supreme Soviet session that ended June 24.

Yugoslav officials heard from a Polish Central Committee member that "the Soviet generals oppose intervention for purely military reasons after any invasion. They would lose the contribution of Poland's 16 Army divisions, as well as its Navy and Air Force. They reportedly estimate that a further 30 Soviet and other Warsaw Pact divisions to the Warsaw Pact would be tied down in subduing the resistance of the Polish Army and saboteurs. The Soviet generals are therefore said to regard nonintervention as the lesser of two evils as long as the Poles themselves do not leave the Warsaw Pact. . . . The Polish Central Committee member . . . further views the pro-intervention faction in the Soviet Politburo as being led by Mikhail Suslov. Suslov, in this view, fears erosion of Soviet-style authoritarian communist rule elsewhere in Eastern Europe if Poland succeeds in its pronounced shift to pluralism."[1]

The non-interventionists in Moscow seem to have counted on Premier and Defense Mininster Jaruzelski eventually to restore order in Poland. In contrast to its recent practice of snubbing Kania, *Pravda* repeatedly gave a positive image of Jaruzelski and his apparatus. The General's deprecation of political "arsonists" in a speech to his national assembly was welcomed (June 14). His presence was noted at a Party conference of the Warsaw military district which acclaimed the Kremlin letter (June 17). The Government cabinet was approvingly said to have directed State organs to curb lawbreakers (June 20). A review of pre-Congress meetings in the PUWP stressed the will of Communists in the military to fight counterrevolution as demanded in the Kremlin letter (June 23).

Kania had become anathema to Soviet leaders. An emigre reports that at the end of June 1981 a public lecturer in the USSR vilified Kania as a capitulator who made deals with antisocialist elements at any price. The speaker praised Grabski as a Polish Politburo member heedful of the Kremlin letter, and he told a questioner that direct Soviet intervention was not yet necessary (private source).

But Kania was still unable to gamble on the chance of Soviet indecision persisting. After receipt of the Kremlin letter he retreated on media and personnel issues. The liberalizing head of information services in the main Party office, Jozef Klasa, was replaced by Leslaw Tokarski, reputed client of the moderate conservative Politburo member Olszowski (*Gazeta Robotnicza*, June 19–21, 1981). Kania personally agitated for the re-election of hardline first secretary Zabinski at a Party meeting in Katowice, and he did the same to ensure Olszowski's election as a delegate to the Party Congress (Warsaw Radio, June 25 and 28).

Kania's appeasement of Moscow on the public information issue would inject more venom into regime-Solidarity relations. The union had demanded that popular control be ensured over radio and television programs so that community rights be honored. Solidarity soon affirmed that television programs were constantly directing a stream of spiteful, hostile and often slanderous propaganda against it (Warsaw. *Solidarnosc.* Special Supplement. September 11, 1981).

The fallback of Kania did have a certain moderating effect on the state of Soviet-Polish relations. Speaking at the Party conference in Katowice on June 26, Jaruzelski said that "the sharpness of the climate" which was caused by the Kremlin letter and June 9–10 Plenum had "in a sense, abated" (Warsaw Radio. June 27, 1981).

Nevertheless, the Soviet Politburo obviously wanted a promise of restraint at the Polish Party Congress and *Pravda* announced on June 29 that Gromyko would pay a "short friendly visit" to Poland in early July. Augmenting the foreign minister's powers of persuasion were measures suggesting that the option of invasion was left open. The world learned from June 25 until Gromyko's arrival in Warsaw on July 3 that joint Polish-Soviet military exercises were held in Silesia; a brigade-size force of Hungarian troops was being activated for possible representation in any Warsaw Pact operation against Poland; Polish-Soviet maneuvers were extended to the northwestern province of Pomerania; war games had started in East Germany; and Soviet troops in the western Ukraine had resumed intensive training for full mobilization.[2]

The Soviet-Polish communique issued on July 5 indicated that Gromyko was not entirely satisfied with what he heard from Kania and Jaruzelski, but did get pledges of resolve to avert a landslide of democracy at the PUWP Congress.

Moscow had drawn lessons from the backlash to its anti-Kania intrigue in June and the communique dwelt on foreign policy rather than Polish internal affairs. The Polish leaders, it was said, told Gromyko about preparations for their Congress, and that was the only direct mention of the obvious reason for the Soviet leader's visit. Indirectly, the Poles assured that they would bridle the radical democratizers, resisting Western attempts to "use the events in Poland" so as "to discredit the socialist system, the ideals and principles of socialism." Defense of governing institutions in Poland was jointly recognized to be a question of vital importance for the Soviet bloc at large—a restatement of the limited sovereignty doctrine. The two sides may have argued over the acuteness of a domestic threat in Poland or related matters since the atmosphere at the talks was described as only "businesslike and comradely."

A hint at the still-modest character of Soviet intentions was *Pravda's* selective editing of an open letter by CPUSA Secretary General Gus Hall. The letter, called "U.S. Imperialism and Poland: Strategy and Tactics of Counterrevolution," was summarized in the July 7 *Pravda* and a fuller version carried in the July 9 *Neues Deutschland*. Soviet editors softened the text by omitting two references to past Soviet military interventions in eastern Europe: "'Destabilization' was also the main factor in the [CIA] tactics of subversion and interference applied in 1956 vis-à-vis Hungary and in 1968 vis-à-vis Czechoslovakia"; "In all countries in which the CIA operated—among them Hungary, Czechoslovakia, Chile, Iran and Guatemala, where it has done enormous damage—the forces of counterrevolution penetrated and took possession of the mass media—television, radio and press." (Coincidentally, the flexible chairman of the Polish Government's Radio and Television Committee, Zdislaw Balicki, was replaced by the conservative Wladyslaw Loranc on July 7.) If the Kremlin was planning a military blow at Poland, the allusions to similar actions in the past might have been included in the *Pravda* version of the Gus Hall letter.

Moscow's barest tolerance of the Polish experiment, however, is clear from its disdainful press coverage of the PUWP Plenum held on July 10, 1981. The July 8 *Pravda* tersely noted that the Polish Politburo had called the Plenum to discuss Party Congress issues, and on July 11 *Pravda* just as briefly recorded that this business was concluded. The brief TASS cables without names or details amounted to further slighting of Kania, who chaired the Plenum and made a closing speech, as well as moderate PUWP Secretary (for Party organization) Barcikowski, who keynoted the session. Authoritarian Soviet officials were no doubt contemptuous of the Plenum resolution, which affirmed the supremacy of the PUWP Central Committee over the Party Politburo, Secretariat and first secretary.[3]

A heavier volume of publicity was given to a four-hour strike of about 6,000 Polish airlines employees over the issue of self-management. Solidarity leader Walesa had opposed the strike action, which was a failure insofar as the Government installed its own general manager rather than the candidate elected by the airline workers (*New York Times*, July 10, 1981). TASS obfuscated the dispute and muted the conciliatoriness of Walesa. It blamed Solidarity leaders inside the airline for making "demands of a political nature that were knowingly unacceptable" and instigating a strike that inflicted "great material harm" on the state (*Pravda*, July 11, 1981).

Soviet coolness towards the Polish developments was reflected in the choice of Viktor Grishin to head the CPSU delegation to the PUWP Congress. A Politburo member and Party leader of Moscow city, the colorless Grishin had long identified with the suppression of dissident intellectuals and was equally hostile to economic reformers. The sending of Grishin to Warsaw was evidently designed to inspirit the Polish conservatives without stirring the emotions of their antagonists.

Kremlin thinking about Kania was not easily discernible from the full-page summary of the Central Committee Report he delivered to the Party Congress which *Pravda* ran on July 15. The reader could infer Soviet displeasure from *Pravda's* lack of specificity about democratic reforms in Party administration ("the rapporteur described proposed changes in the PUWP statutes"). But a Soviet perception of Kania as judicious rebuilder loyal to the USSR—not unlike the Hungarian Kadar —might have been adduced from the *Pravda* text alone.

Over a dozen substantive cuts in the *Pravda* version of Kania's report indicated a basic distrust of the Polish leader for his integrity and nationalism. The omissions included forceful recommitments to such ideas as Solidarity's legitimacy as a worker lobby; speedier enlistment of younger and better-educated people into all levels of Government; truthful journalism; bureaucratic austerity and narrowing of the range of employee incomes; and increased educational opportunities for the offspring of workers and farmers. Also missing from the *Pravda* text of Kania's speech were tributes to the Catholic Church and Polish socialist thought (Warsaw Radio. July 14, 1981).

A narrow intolerance marked the speech of Grishin on the opening day of the Congress. It ruled out any "improvement" of socialism that was not based on the Party's guiding role and public ownership as these concepts were understood in the USSR. If the Soviet model of governance ("general objective laws of Marxism-Leninism") was rejected, agents of imperialism would pose as refurbishers of socialism and steer matters to a restoration of capitalism. Grishin made a veiled threat of Soviet economic sanctions in the event of drift on the production front in Poland: "We consider it useful to continue to develop economic cooperation to general benefit. But this naturally requires efficient fulfillment of the commitments assumed, a clear realization of the fact that the breaching of cooperative ties harms painfully the national economy and interests of fraternal countries." (This utterance may well have created a stir in the hall since Jaruzelski in his Katowice speech of June 26 had referred to Soviet economic ties as "that great lifebelt which is keeping us on the surface.") As though reflecting the presumed crosscurrents inside Soviet leadership, Grishin alternated between expressions of "hope" and "conviction" that the Party Congress would take the right decisions for normalization (*Pravda*, July 15, 1981).

The summaries of delegate speeches in *Pravda* July 16 execrated the idea of worker self-management. Bydgoszcz Party secretary Henryk

Bedarski was said to have called the issue one of "key importance" and to have attacked the nationwide Solidarity leaders for taking a view of self-management that endangered public ownership of firms. Gen. Josef Baryla, head of army political training, reportedly voiced "alarm" over "attempts to disorganize the administration of state enterprises under the guise of the radical conception of self-management." (The safe notion was outlined in the Government's "Draft Law on Work Force Self-Management in State Enterprises," protective of Party/State authority, published in the Warsaw *Glos Pracy* on July 2.)

Pravda muffled the indignation of Congress delegates against the senior bureaucrats who were thwarting economic reform and refusing to come to terms with past injustice. The Soviet version of Prof. Jozef Kaleta's speech did not mention his charge that the central economic administration was responsible for the present troubles, delayed the introduction of reform and fiercely defended its positions (PAP. July 16, 1981). Jan Labecki, Party secretary at the Lenin shipyard in Gdansk, had asked for the establishment of a commission to investigate the causes of violent squelching of worker unrest in his area in 1970, but *Pravda*'s account of his remarks glossed over the plea (*Ibid.*).

Entirely concealed from Soviet audiences was the speech that had gotten the warmest ovation in the discussion period. Deputy Premier Mieczyslaw Rakowski hit at every ordinary apparatchik from the Elbe to the Pacific. "Until now," he complained, "we have been unable to initiate, I emphasize the word initiate, daring, profound and wise reforms for the system of governing which would anticipate social demands." Rakowski used the Gierek period as an example of how "the conservative forces of the Party, not numerous but sometimes occupying strategic positions in the Party, in the power apparatus . . . in a sterile way opposed every change, keeping a grip on their leadership, acting as a brake." The Soviet codeword for reforms was disparaged in the further course of Rakowski's attack on Communist diehards: "They did not permit the Party to anticipate events, initiate social changes and to be the vanguard of changes. Their reaction caused all agreements and reforms to be called *concessions"* (emphasis supplied). Rakowski said that a vacuum was created by elimination from the Party of ideas and of thinking people. He argued that the only means to offset misguided schemes that came from outside the Party was for it to "sketch out a vision—attractive enough for the majority of the nation" and bring to the fore "a leadership bold in thinking and in action" (Warsaw Domestic Television. July 15, 1981). These bitter words apparently caused the correspondent of *Izvestiya* (July 17, 1981) to grouse that "some speeches of a revisionist nature have sounded a clearly discordant note."

Soviet abhorrence of reform at the doorstep was noticeable too from *Pravda*'s suppression of other statements by Congress delegates. Jozef Kurdzielewics, a physician and secretary of the town PUWP committee in Rabka, dismissed the Congress program assumptions as "mere noble intention" rather than "the right prescription" for national recovery (PAP. July 17, 1981). The lack of a genuine program to overcome the crisis was also protested by Fiszbach, first secretary of the Gdansk regional Party committee. He observed that the authorities had not even articulated the principles of an economic reform and without taking that step quickly there could be no basis from which to launch actions aimed at reversal of the debacle. Fiszbach seemed to be arguing for a dramatic statement of the regime's intent to divert any or all funds at its disposal to supply to the population at once basic foodstuffs, medical supplies and articles required for personal hygiene (Warsaw Domestic Television. July 18, 1981). Even the Polish media accounts of the Congress fail to show discussion of a proposal that was interesting to Solidarity advisers and editors: a two-chamber parliament, one responsible for problems of state and controlled by the Party, another comprised of representatives elected by enterprises and concerning itself with socio-economic problems.[4] That sort of proposal, however, would have been unacceptable to the Soviet Union, where ideologues attributed to "bourgeois propaganda" the thought that "settlement of the [Polish] internal crisis is possible only if the political authority structure is changed, in other words if the PUWP repudiates its leading role in society" (*Kommunist*, No. 11, cleared for printing July 23, 1981).

Grishin blessed the Congress's unventuresome guideline documents in a speech he made at a Warsaw factory on July 16. He showed no sympathy for Polish changes and harped on the danger of an imperialist plot against Poland. A barrier to counterrevolution would be raised, he said, if the PUWP's leading role was strengthened and Congress resolutions put into effect (*Pravda*, July 17, 1981).

Keeping silent about the ongoing debate at the Congress, *Pravda* that same day offered "evidence" of Western subversion against Poland. A Czechoslovak intelligence agent who had spent three and a half years abroad in emigre circles surfaced at a press conference in Prague. Especially sinister was the allegation that Polish emigres in Paris had collected a large sum of money to buy arms that would be sent to counterrevolutionary forces in Poland under the cover of a food shipment (*Pravda*, July 17, 1981). This assertion was close to one made during the stage-setting for intervention in Czechoslovakia: A secret cache of American weapons was supposedly found in Czechoslovakia near the West German border and the arms were to be used by anticommunist groups (*Pravda*, July 19, 1968).

Congress debate was again eclipsed in *Pravda* on the following day with the summaries of speeches by Soviet bloc guests and one that Grishin made at the Polish-Soviet Friendship Society. The Hungarian orator alone came out for the conduct of "reforms" in Poland. Grishin reassured that he had no quarrel with the non-program that the Congress was about to adopt. He insinuated that Western penetration had gone a long way in Poland, it being awash with illegal literature from Western agencies that incited antisocialist, nationalistic and anti-Soviet moods (*Pravda*, July 18, 1981).

One of the last, fleeting mentions of debate at the Congress was in the July 19 *Pravda*. "Sharp discussions" with "contradictory assessments and opinions" was all that the censors would let through for Soviet citizens. By then, Poland's bureaucratic class had revealed itself to be hopelessly divided into essentially Social-Democratic and pro-Soviet factions.

The cleavage was typified by such *de facto* exchanges as one between Zbigniew Ciechan, PUWP committee secretary at a plant in Torun, and Stefan Zawodzinski, first secretary of the Bialystok regional Party committee. "Our own Polish model of socialism" was demanded by Ciechan, who wanted no domination of the Party rank and file or State officeholders by the Party machine; democratic and law-abiding government; Catholics allowed to serve in any public job; guaranteed individual landownership; intellectual freedom; and unhindered foreign contacts (*Trybuna Ludu*, July 16, 1981). Zawodzinski retaliated with an attack on "some people" who were "fascinated by achievements in the democratization of life, by the Party's renewal, by the freedom of speech, by the variety of appraisals, by the far-reaching concessions to the church." He belonged to the group of "other people" who looked upon the last 11 months as a period in which "social discipline slumped, crime increased, respect for the laws diminished and the market was thrown into disorder." Zawodzinski refused to accept a reduced status of partnership for the Party apparatus. "We must stress here most strongly," he said in defense of the Party's supremacy over the State, "that political power is impossible without economic power" (*Trybuna Ludu*, July 18–19, 1981).

The Soviet media tactic of concealing democratic procedure was extended to handling of Kania's election to the post of leading Party secretary by secret ballot from the floor of the Congress, something unheard of in the Eastern bloc. *Pravda* on July 19 went so far as to admit that "candidates" for the first secretaryship were examined at a meeting of the newly-elected Central Committee. But it said only that "The Congress elected S. Kania as First secretary of the CC PUWP," ignoring the fact that Party Secretary Barcikowski if only nominally had run against Kania, who won by a vote of 1,311 to 568 (Warsaw Television

Service. July 18, 1981). *Pravda* also ignored Kania's re-election speech, in which he reiterated his un-Bolshevik view that a Communist Party first secretary should be "organizer of the collective wisdom of the Central Committee" instead of "something called leader" (Warsaw Radio. July 18, 1981). Observing the niceties of protocol, Brezhnev sent to Kania a message of congratulations, but it omitted the usual personal compliments and expressions of confidence (*Pravda*, July 20, 1981).

Disesteem was exhibited towards the reshuffled Politburo and Secretariat elected by the new Polish Central Committee. *No names of the Politburo and Secretariat members were listed in the July 21 Pravda, which reported the election.* This unusual occurrence suggested Kremlin refusal to accept the ouster from the PUWP leadership of Soviet loyalists Grabski and Zabinski, though some conservatives were named to the Politiburo and given portfolios in the Secretariat for ideology (Olszowski) and security (Milewski). Soviet leaders probably felt that Kania had become so strong that he could easily impose his centrist line on the many neophytes brought into the highest Party echelons during backstage politicking.

At the same time as it withheld recognition from new members of the Polish ruling team, *Pravda* (July 21) devoted over five columns to the Congress speech of Gen. Jaruzelski. His statement of readiness to declare a state of emergency if that was required went into the Soviet text with only minor stylistic change: "There are boundaries which must not be overstepped. . . . It would be disastrous for the nation, for the state. We must not allow this to happen. This is the patriotic duty of every citizen and, above all, the duty of the people's authorities. In the name of superior reason, when the situation justifies it, the authorities will be forced to carry out with determination their constitutional duties in order to save the country from disintegration and the nation from catastrophe" (Warsaw Radio. July 19, 1981). One of Jaruzelski's associates, Gen. Florian Siwicki, chief of the General Staff, evidently gained no less credit in Moscow for a speech deposited with the Congress records that lamented a weakening of the material-technical base and sense of social responsibility for the country's defense (Warsaw. *Zolnierz Wolnosci*, July 21–22, 1981).

A new sign of Kremlin uncertainty about the Polish leadership cropped up on July 22. Brezhnev, Premier Tikhonov and Defense Minister Ustinov were more hopeful about Polish prospects than was Grishin in Warsaw. The Soviet President and head of government in their cable of congratulations to Polish rulers on the anniversary of the PPR noted that the Polish Party "doubtless is capable of rallying all the working people, to inspire them to resolutely rebuff anarchy and counterrevolution" (*Pravda*, July 22, 1981). Ustinov's message to Jaruzelski for the same holiday avowed "confidence" that Polish working people and servicemen "will give the necessary rebuff to counterrevolutionary forces" (*Red Star*, July 22, 1981). Grishin, however, in his speech to a meeting of Polish Central Committee members hesitantly said that "life and practice will show to what extent" the "important tasks" that had faced the Congress would be solved. Grishin added that "we hope" that Poland's new leaders would fight for bolstering their Party and state (*Pravda*, July 22, 1981).

At the same time, the cautious group of Soviet leaders to which Marshal Ustinov evidently belonged at that stage of events was by no means reconciled to the unsettled conditions within Poland. That is clear from a massive article devoted to the arms race and war danger which Ustinov wrote for *Pravda* July 25, 1981. Ustinov spoke of an "impression" that "circles" had ascended to power in Washington which were "pursuing a policy of destabilizing the social-political situation which took shape in Europe after the Second World War." This policy entailed *"a direct threat to the security of the USSR and its allies"* (emphasis supplied). Ustinov's illustration of this immediate peril to Soviet safety was fateful for the cause of Polish liberty: "One example of this threat are the events in Poland where, along with the action of internal counter-revolutionary forces, one has poorly camouflaged interference by imperialism." A special group on Poland at the U.S. State Department, Ustinov alleged, was working out proposals for maintaining "controlled tension" in Poland—an absurd invention but good description of the consequence that was bound to result from the stubborn resistance to domestic reforms that pro-Soviet elements were mounting in Poland. Although Ustinov restated the view that Poles would be able to resist U.S. subversion, he made a point of their ability to rely on the Soviet Union for unspecified kinds of support. The author's professional duties may have reassured staunch Communists that if everything else failed in the battle with Poland's Solidarity movement the Soviet Army was ready to protect its country's vital interests.

A standoff of the Kremlin power groups may have caused one more break with decorum in Soviet press treatment of the Polish Party Congress, a landmark event on the political calendar. *Pravda did not run a lead article devoted to the Congress after it ended.* The politically interested were accordingly left to make up their own minds if the Congress was a cause for relief that the Polish Party's self-destruction had been averted or a reason for distress that Kania's mandate was extended.

There was no vagueness about Soviet handling of the main resolution of the PUWP Congress that was published by *Trybuna Ludu* on July 29. A TASS summary in the July 31 *Pravda* stiffly avoided even mention of the resolution's title, "Program for *the Development of Socialist Democracy*, for the Strengthening of the Leading Role of the PUWP in Socialist Reconstruction and for the Socioeconomic Stabilization of the Country" (emphasis supplied). The digest highlighted orthodox warnings against "attempts to rehabilitate right-wing groupings and their reactionary conceptions," "nationalism, cosmopolitanism and anti-Soviet tendencies," "conceptions of 'dual power'" and "antisocialist activity." The Soviet version of the program theses obscured a diagnosis of the crisis that might have been read as criticism of internal-political aspects of the Brezhnev regime. Under fire in the document and ignored by *Pravda* were Gierek-era vices such as "lack of a coherent conception of a solution of the conflicts in socioeconomic relations"; "limiting of the people's power and self-management and the seizure of real power by the executive apparatus"; "disparity between the authorities and society"; and "negative phenomena in the economy" resulting from "the defective functioning of the authorities." Remedies for certain ills were also shrouded in *Pravda*: "measures to ensure the actual supremacy of the legislative authorities over the executive authorities"; "partnership with the whole trade union movement"; "systematic and honest informing of society"; and "all-round strengthening of the principles of the rule of law."

A backhanded slap was taken at Kania, it seems, in the same July 31 *Pravda* by the chief editor of *Kommunist*, Richard Kosolapov. His theory article alleged that class enemies had pondered the collapse of their models of counterrevolution in Hungary (1956) and Czechoslovakia (1968). "Not all Communists," however, had come to understand the new subversive ploy of infiltrating the worker ranks in a socialist country and weaning the masses away from sound beliefs. Enemies of socialism in Poland, Kosolapov held, were pretending to be defenders of labor's interests in order to use labor against the Communist Party and pro-letarian-dictatorship system as a whole. Kosolapov hinted broadly that Lech Walesa, whom he named, was a real or potential dupe of Western anticommunists, who were inducing him to work for the return of private ownership of Polish industry. The former leadership in Warsaw was berated for having pursued a Western-oriented economic policy that helped to cause among workers a sense of alienation from State goals that was typical of a part of Solidarity and whipped up by right-wingers in the union. A single reference to the PUWP Congress in Kosolapov's article was innocuous, citing a Congress document extolling the socialists of old Russia and Poland as exemplars of political steadfastness.

The PUWP Congress had come and gone without mitigating the harsh Soviet view of those who personified the thrusts for dialogue in

Polish politics and society. That view and the military power behind it can be interpreted as the root cause of a subsequent, widely-shared complaint in the Polish national assembly that Party Congress speeches often expressed nothing new and some even threw into question the hopeful idea of reaching a durable accord between the authorities and the populace (Deputy Janusz Zablocki, Warsaw Radio, July 30, 1981).

Meanwhile, decisions were taken in Polish ruling circles and "below" that would send the country further along the road of misfortune. Solidarity leaders announced on July 17 that the union's national congress would be held in Gdansk in two stages, September 5–16 and October 1–3. Almost a week later discontent increased suddenly after the Government ordered meat ration cuts of 20 percent for August and September. Solidarity decided to forestall wildcat actions and organized protests marches that were held in many provincial cities from July 25 through 30 (Warsaw. *Solidarnosc.* Special Supplement. Sept. 11, 1981). What the headline writers of TASS alarmingly called "Situation in Poland" was about to be discussed anew for the first time in many weeks.

NOTES

1. "Yugoslav view: Poland not safe yet." By Elizabeth Pond. *The Christian Science Monitor*, July 27, 1981.

2. *Soviet and Soviet-proxy Involvement in Poland*, p. 3.

3. Plenum materials were reported by Warsaw Radio/Television and PAP July 10 and 11, 1981. The resolution stated *inter alia*: "The most important strategic problems, intentions and decisions of the Politburo must be submitted to the Central Committee for deliberation. . . . Politburo members and members of the Central Committee Secretariat have a duty to disclose their stands as regards most important problems of the socioeconomic and political life of the country. . . . The Politburo must present the Central Committee with periodical and systematic reports on its activity. The protocols of the meetings should contain the motives of the decisions taken and should show the opinions and attitudes of the Politiburo members on every issue."

4. This corporatist proposal was favored by Solidarity's Bronislaw Geremek and Janusz Onyszkiewicz during interviews published in: Paris. *Le Nouvel Observateur*, July 11–17, 1981 and Amsterdam. *De Volkskrant*, July 21, 1981, respectively.

EIGHT

Stake on Generals
and *Apparatchiki*

(AUG. 1–OCT. 15, 1981)

The Warsaw street demonstrations which Solidarity militants staged in early August to protest food shortages are likely to have convinced Soviet leaders that Poland's Communist Party structure had become completely ineffectual. Jaruzelski and his security aides were increasingly brought to the fore in Soviet media, as if representing the best hope for creating strong stable government. USSR Defense Ministry leaders met with Jaruzelski on a frequent basis and almost certainly restated the openly expressed view of Polish generals that Solidarity actions were undermining national military power. The Kremlin was visibly angered over Solidarity's national convention, which demanded extensive political-economic changes, and it unleashed a torrent of hostile propaganda unmatched since the eve of the Czechoslovak invasion. Solidarity's congress may be regarded as a stimulus to more vigorous anti-Kania intrigue by Moscow: *Pravda* then began to flatter the discipline-minded PUWP Secretary for ideology Olszowski, who might have been seen as a candidate for strongman in Warsaw or lever to pry Jaruzelski away from Kania and towards a hardline stand.

The first confrontation between the regime and Solidarity involving large numbers of people in Warsaw occurred on August 3. Despite an appeal from the Politburo against further street demonstrations over the worsening food situation, a column of buses and trucks bedecked with flags and placards noisily drove through the main streets of the capital. The cavalcade's progress was stopped by ordinary police to prevent its reaching the Party headquarters building, and a vast traffic standstill was created. The angry mood of protestors came through in the reply of one to the question of whether he thought the police might order the demonstration to disperse: "They don't dare. This business of giving orders finished a year ago. Now we will finish them off." The protest vehicles were not dispersed and a two-day blockage ended after a brief strike shut down the entire region (*New York Times*, Aug. 3–6, 1981).

Soviet shock over the popular unrest in Warsaw was such that details of it were withheld in press reporting. Warsaw like the rest of Poland was said to be experiencing a "wave of tension" that included "attempts to shift discontent from the grounds of enterprises to the streets," according to a resolution of the local PUWP committee cited in the August 5 *Pravda*. This item hinted too at the impotence of the Kania-led Politburo: *Pravda* a day before had informed readers that the Politburo met and warned of the "grave threat" inherent in "planned strikes, especially street demonstrations."

A more far-reaching conclusion than the incapacity of Kania's team was apparently drawn in Soviet ruling circles. The entire Polish Party network for social control was thought to be in disrepair, to judge from the fact that *Pravda*'s correspondent in Warsaw had his last reportage from a Party unit in the August 7 issue till after the imposition of martial law. From August 7, newsman O. Losoto wrote largely on marginal themes such as a Lenin book publication, Auschwitz museum opening, and an international violin competition. This unusual blackout of news about PUWP cells also makes it appear that Kremlin leaders saw as a reality what *Trybuna Ludu* soon claimed was the aim of right-wing groups in Poland: "weakening of the power apparatus to such a degree that it will become only a screen behind which various political centers outside the Party and people's government bodies will operate" (*Pravda*, Aug. 9, 1981).

The Soviet factor may have added to the onset of new disarray in Polish leadership. A Central Committee plenary meeting was convened by the PUWP Politburo for August 8 (*Pravda*, Aug. 5, 1981). But the Politburo a few days later decided to postpone the session until August 11 (*Pravda*, Aug. 8, 1981). According to a Polish source, letters from the leaders of the USSR, East Germany and Czechoslovakia were received by Polish chiefs on August 7. The messages were said to call for a reassertion of Government authority and to have expressed readiness to provide technical or material assistance (*Washington Post*, Aug. 12, 1981). On the surface, Soviet Marshal Kulikov paid another visit to Warsaw on August 8 and spoke with Jaruzelski about "combat readiness of the Polish People's Army" (*Pravda*, Aug. 10, 1981). Kulikov may have told Jaruzelski that major land and sea maneuvers would be held under the direction of Soviet Defense Minister Ustinov in the western USSR on September 4–12, or during the first stage of the Solidarity congress (*Pravda*, Aug. 14, 1981).

Soviet interest in Polish affairs was clearly running high and the August 11 Plenum of the Polish Central Committee was given rather broad coverage in *Pravda*. A TASS cable of about 1300 words was published on August 13 and informed that a briefing on measures for tackling social-economic hardships was offered by new Deputy Premier Janusz Obodowski, who headed a new joint civilian-military crisis staff; a report on Party activities was delivered by Party Secretary Barcikowski; Kania had made a concluding speech and a resolution was adopted. A resume of Barcikowski's report was printed immediately while Kania's speech and the resolution were summarized in a TASS dispatch of about 600 words on the following day.

The forces of restraint in Moscow assuredly shaped *Pravda*'s account of the Polish Plenum. Generalities were used to indicate that Polish leaders were aware of a need to close Party ranks; mobilize the public to satisfy basic wants; and convince Solidarity members to repudiate extremists who were jeopardizing civil peace. The prospect of a review of the social accord policy if Solidarity radicals did not mend their ways was held out.

The selective editing of Plenum materials was at the same time suggestive of Soviet disgust with the squabbling and wavering of the political hierarchy in Warsaw.[1] Only the Plenum texts as carried by Polish media revealed that the moderate Obodowski and Barcikowski had clashed with the archconservative worker member of the Politburo Albin Siwak. The dispute was over whether to revive the old practice of compelling farmers to deliver most of their products to the State at below-market prices. *Pravda* concealed too the growing battle of authoritarians and democratizers inside the Party, muffling Barcikowski's reference to "various kinds of forums on the one hand and structures on the other, [that] are still conducting, even intensifying, their organizational activity." Barcikowski's tentativeness on the question of how much influence the radicals had gained inside Solidarity was unacceptable in Moscow, and his words were twisted into a blanket condemnation of the union:

> The nature of recent action and of the statements by numerous leaders show that *at least large parts of* Solidarity are taking the road of adventurism. (Warsaw Radio. Aug. 11, 1981) (emphasis supplied)

> The nature of recent actions and statements by numerous leaders of the trade association are evidence that Solidarity is sliding onto the path of adventures. (*Pravda*. Aug. 13, 1981)

Pravda censored out of Kania's speech a mild overture to non-Party social activists: "We shall continue to create conditions of agreement.

Perhaps we shall have to consider whether institutional embodiment should be imparted in a symbolic form to this concept, this catchword. We shall discuss this problem at the Politburo and we shall consider it together with all those whom it interests." Thus, the Soviet position seems to have been that even nominal change of the governmental pyramid was out of the question.

The hawks of the CPSU would probably have wanted *Pravda* to run extracts from the closing speech of Barcikowski, who disclosed a scandalous anti-Soviet incident at the Katowice steelworks. Earlier, the authorities had taken out of circulation there a cartoon that mocked the Soviet Union as a helpless bear with the countenance of Brezhnev. But the sketch was now said to be appearing in a Solidarity newsletter printed in the steelworks' press shop. Soviet specialists at the works, Barcikowski said, had lodged a protest and announced that the matter would be presented to the USSR Consulate. Barcikowski warned that if Soviet ore shipments to the works were halted the whole enterprise would close down since it could not smelt any ore apart from the Soviet one. This commotion, like the wind-up speech of Barcikowski as a whole, was ignored by *Pravda*, maybe to keep ammunition away from the pro-intervention faction of Soviet bureaucracy.

All of the Kremlin groups could draw satisfaction from new evidence of Polish military rumblings at the August Plenum. Deputy Defense Minister Gen. Tadeusz Tuczapski gave decidedly qualified support to the idea of holding more talks with Solidarity. He argued that "undisputed proofs" existed that in Solidarity's local and regional branches the forces abjuring constructive cooperation with the Government had "gained the upper hand." Speaking for the Armed Forces, Tuczapski anguished:

> I wish to stress most strongly at this point that our defense system is at present exposed to great danger and perturbations. It is with serious concern that we are watching some trade union activists' attempts to interfere in the internal operational and mobilizational affairs of the Armed Forces and in the systems of command and defense structures and to organize strikes in the armament factories.

The disfavor of Soviet superiors in the Warsaw Pact command, Tuczapski hinted, was galling to senior Polish officers: "Our membership and place in the socialist community indicate that we must be an authoritative partner who is worthy of trust, is politically strong and has a defense force that corresponds to our economic potential and the jointly agreed pledges. We have still not regained that trust."

Alert to these sensibilities of the Polish generals, the Soviet leaders apparently tried to exploit them to the hilt for the purpose of getting the generals to do Moscow's bidding. One aspect of the Kremlin's seeming effort to drive a wedge between the Army and Kania was the granting of a sizable amount of favorable publicity to Jaruzelski and his retinue in *Pravda*.

A session of the Defense Ministry's Military Council chaired by Jaruzelski was reported to have examined defense/security issues and charted tasks of the military in economic development and fight on profiteering (Aug. 4). The Government's inner cabinet led by Jaruzelski was identified as creator of the crisis staff and a special commission to thwart the profiteers (Aug. 6). Jaruzelski's presence at a meeting of the Government's economic reform commission was recounted and he was ominously quoted to the effect that social protests were compelling the authorities to "think about more far-reaching means" to get out of the economic quagmire (Aug. 7). When Jaruzelski accompanied Kania on a short visit to Brezhnev's estate at Oreanda in the Crimea he received equal protocol treatment from Soviet hosts.[2] The joint communique had to sadden those among Jaruzelski's military associates who were eager to regain Soviet trust. Brezhnev said merely that the Soviet Union "wishes" that the positions of socialism be consolidated in Poland, eschewing a statement of confidence in Polish rulers' ability to repel internal challenges. The less than fully amicable atmosphere of the talks ("fraternal friendship and comradely mutual understanding") was also likely to be vexing to pro-Soviets at the Polish Defense Ministry (*Pravda*, Aug. 16, 1981).

But the Soviet Party paper continued to compliment the police set around Jaruzelski and the General himself. Politburo member and Party Secretary for internal security Milewski was cited as telling an interviewer from *Trybuna Ludu* that consistency was necessary in taking steps to "bring order" to Poland (Aug. 21). During another press interview, Deputy Interior Minister Pozoga was said to have complained about a steep rise of Western covert activity in Poland, with Solidarity a primary target group (Aug. 25). The Jaruzelski-chaired Government cabinet won acclaim for bracketing Solidarity leaders with a decline of social discipline and rise of crime (Aug. 28). At a military school ceremony, Jaruzelski was heard to warn that the policy of agreement could not long be tested further and to assert: "Enough of this disintegration!" (Sept. 1).

A Soviet appeal to Jaruzelski's sense of discipline in order to further his suspicion of Solidarity was perhaps made during his new meetings with high politico-military officials from Moscow. Gen. Aleksey Yepishev, chief of the Main Political Directorate of the Soviet Army and Navy, a branch of the CPSU Secretariat, visited Poland in late August and early September. Yepishev held talks with Kania and Jaruzelski on ensuring closer cooperation between their respective forces, and he inspected military installations (PAP. Aug. 31 and Sept. 3, 1981). A surprise announcement by TASS on September 8 listed Jaruzelski as being among the allied military leaders at the war-games headquarters of Marshal Ustinov somewhere in Belorussia. It seems a fair conjecture that Jaruzelski at such moments listened to negative remarks about Polish defense preparedness not remote from those included in the recently-published trip report of a Soviet journalist who had attended a documentary film festival in Krakow:

> I climbed along the narrow little streets of the old town to Jagelonian University. I looked at the leaflet that was done splendidly from the standpoint of the printer's art. It contained a demand to release from confinement a certain Malenczuk, who had burned his military induction notice and refused to serve in the Polish Army. The leaflet's authors asked "And wouldn't Christ have done the same?" There was a dangerous political thought behind this supposedly naive rhetoric. It was a desire to push youth towards an antipatriotic cult of distrust of the Polish nation's armed forces, to rouse a lack of desire to defend the country's borders, to compel youth to forget about the numerous emigre societies that are dreaming of expropriating ancient Polish lands with the help of NATO military forces.[3]

Unlike the partiality shown towards Jaruzelski and his security lieutenants, *Pravda* gave short shrift to Kania and his followers in its coverage of the PUWP Central Committee plenum held on September 2 and 3. The agenda item itself—worker self-management and economic reform—was distasteful enough for Soviet absolutists to take a decision to allot only half as much newspaper space as to the last such meeting: a TASS cable of about 950 words in the September 5 *Pravda*.[4] A small fraction of the text dealt with the keynote report by Jan Glowczyk, Politburo candidate and editor-in-chief of the weekly *Zycie Gospodarcze* (Economic Life). The Soviet opinion-molders clearly had little use for anyone who cautioned that the majority of Solidarity's members should not be blamed for the wrongful views and actions of some union activists. Glowczyk must have further irked Moscow by praising the many workforces that had agreed to work on some free Saturdays, in conformity with a Solidarity leadership appeal, and enthusing that this was a good start for widening the constructive activity of the whole union. *Pravda* ignored too Glowczyk's anti-bureaucratic and pro-reformist statement that headway was being made toward reducing the size of the central economic administration and introducing genuine profit-loss accounting at the enterprise level.

Pravda simply mentioned the resolution adopted at the Plenum. The editors accordingly refused to admit the propriety of seeing virtue, as the resolution did, in aiming at the elusive goals of worker self-management, limited market relations, and respect for expertise as the primary criterion in the selection of industrial managers.

The text of Kania's closing speech at the plenary meeting was sharply abbreviated in Soviet editorial offices. TASS put emphasis on the calls for keeping State job appointments in Party hands; raising labor productivity; and defending socialism. The joint Polish-Soviet communique issued after the Oreanda summit was hailed as a document of bilateral amity.

Soviet loathing of Kania for his relative magnanimity in dealings with Solidarity is perhaps the best explanation for the heavy censorship of his speech in *Pravda*. He had said much that harmonized with the Soviet outlook on politics and economics. The agreement with those urging prudence in starting up management reform; warning against firms getting carried away by the profit motive; demand for managers to enjoy wide powers and great prestige; threat to regime control of radio/television—all were inoffensive to good Communists in Russia. But Kania evidently could not be forgiven his past losses of nerve nor the following words of hesitation about the imminent Solidarity congress:

> It is an event of importance for that organization and for the country. Indeed, it makes a difference which trend will prevail at the congress and which program, which line of action will be mapped out, and who will be elected to the leading bodies. To a considerable extent it will depend on the congress whether that organization will develop as a constructive force of socialism or as a destructive factor of our economic and social life, as a tool of combat against People's Poland, against our Party, against our alliances which constitute the basis for our national security, of our independence. . . . We will judge Solidarity and draw conclusions after the facts.

Some of the 21 lower-ranking members of the Central Committee who spoke at the Plenum refused to give any benefit of doubt to Solidarity and the bulk of *Pravda*'s item on the September Plenum was devoted to summaries of their harsh rhetoric. In all, eight speeches were cited and almost all attacked the Solidarity leaders or the union for going on a virtually unchecked rampage against the governing bureaucracy. The speakers who disagreed with the opinion of this conservative group were criticized by *Pravda* for "truckling to the attitudes of the extremist circles of 'Solidarity'" and "spreading tenets alien to the principles of the socialist mode of production."

The most intriguing silences in *Pravda*'s treatment of the September Plenum relate to Kania's startling mention of the contingency of martial law, and the high profile of security officials who would be involved in the planning for a showdown with Solidarity.

Kania had affirmed: "Our enemies say that the authorities will certainly not introduce *a state of emergency* in Poland. I would like to state with full emphasis and calm that in order to defend socialism the authorities will resort to all means necessary. We do not want this and do not threaten use of this weapon. Our declaration aimed at agreement signifies an offer of alliance with all those who are not against socialism. This also signifies that a barrier shall be erected against all those striving for confrontation, who wish to strike against socialism, who are striving to topple it and who for all intents and purposes are leading things to national catastrophe" (emphasis supplied). *Pravda* limited itself to paraphrasing Kania: "He stressed that in order to defend socialism the government will resort to all means necessary. At the same time he spoke in favor of agreement with all forces standing in defense of the gains of socialism."

Kania's warning of martial law as a last resort may have been too spectacular a development for inclusion in the *Pravda* summary of his speech at the September Plenum. Despite the severe tone of the Kremlin letter in June and the general gloominess of Soviet commentary on Polish affairs, *Pravda* since March 30 had not run for more than two days in succession its high-tension headline "Situation in Poland" or "Events in Poland." The sudden appearance of a martial law threat against that background might have opened the Soviet leadership majority to a charge of complacency or even cover-up.

A wish to avoid excitement in broad circles of the CPSU may likewise explain *Pravda*'s concealment of disturbing statements at the Plenum by Deputy Defense Minister Gen. Zbigniew Nowak. Referring to "the country's complicated situation," he said it was "characterized by the ideological and political disorientation of some communities, whose temperature is being raised by recurring tensions, and which the enemies of our socialist fatherland continue to create in various regions of our country." Gen Nowak concluded that "All this is having a *highly negative impact on the country's defense capability, especially on the performance of special industry,*" i.e., defense production factories (emphasis supplied).

Baffling, however, was *Pravda*'s neglect of a speech at the September Plenum by Lt. Gen. Czeslaw Kiszczak, onetime head of military intelligence who became interior (police) minister after Milewski joined the Party Secretariat in July. Kiszczak polemicized with those who claimed that hostile and criminal actions were not checked firmly enough. He revealed that tens of thousands of noxious publications were seized in recent months, along with copying machines, paper, and type bits. Criminal proceedings were opened against persons engaged in producing or circulating such materials; others suspected of despoliating the graves of Soviet soldiers, private farmers who tried to seize State land; and people involved in cases of violence against policemen. Kiszczak cited among other instances of police firmness the foiling of attempts to organize a protest march on behalf of political prisoners and to close every official newspaper during a recent printers' strike. The police leader finally assured that his agency "is capable of counteracting and paralyzing manifestations of destructive activity, infringing upon social order."

Pravda's silence about the fighting speech of Kiszczak was not exactly in tune with the Soviet paper's recent kudos for the security corps nor with a current article by CPSU Secretariat official Rakhmanin which expressed confidence that Polish Communists were able to recoup their losses (*Voprosy Istorii KPSS* No. 9, cleared for printing Sept. 7, 1981).

In view of the rumor of an offer of technical assistance for restoring order from Soviet bloc leaders to Polish leaders in early August, a hypothesis might be ventured. It is that serious discussion of a martial law scenario had begun in Moscow by early September and *Pravda's* editors were instructed to avoid the publication of anything connected with the subject. Hence, Kania's "state of emergency" remark may have been thought too sensitive for citation, and Kiszczak as one of the chief actors in organizing a coup de main against Solidarity was looked upon as someone to be kept in the shadows. This, of course, is sheer speculation and evidence is necessary before a conclusion is reached. (President Reagan stated on December 23, 1981 that the Polish martial law proclamation issued 10 days before was printed in Moscow in September, but details are not available.)

A roar of indignation went up in the USSR over the first phase of Solidarity's congress, September 5–10. The meeting in Gdansk adopted a resolution expressing support for free trade union activists in other Warsaw Pact countries. It issued too a program declaration calling for free national and local elections, public control of mass media, economic reform through authentic workers' self-management, elimination of the Party's right to make appointments, and Westernization of the legal system (Paris. AFP. Sept. 8, 1981 and Warsaw Radio. Sept. 10, 1981).

Factory meetings were held throughout the Soviet Union for the transmittal of irate letters to Polish workers. The letters published in *Pravda* came from rallies in Moscow (Sept. 12 and 22), Leningrad (Sept. 13), Kiev (Sept. 19) and Magnitogorsk (Sept. 24). Solidarity leaders were pilloried as reactionaries and handmaidens of counterrevolutionaries seeking the return of capitalist bosses. Polish workers were reproached for having let matters go so far and exhorted to vanquish the regime's critics: "Stop the class enemy," deal a "resolute rebuff to enemies of socialism," take "resolute and immediate action against insolent, pro-imperialistic reactionary elements," "throw the self-proclaimed 'friends of the people' onto the refuse heap of history," "tear the mask off these 'friends of the people' and give them their due." Those who orchestrated this campaign of hatred against Solidarity no doubt wanted the Polish authorities to arrest the union's leaders.

The alternative of Soviet intervention was implied by the fact that meetings of Soviet worker protest against antisocialist elements in Czechoslovakia were organized about six weeks prior to the occupation of that country (*Pravda,* July 7, 1968).

A week after the first session of the Solidarity congress had ended, Soviet ambassador Aristov delivered to Kania and Jaruzelski a "Statement of the CPSU Central Committee and USSR Government." A summary of the text was broadcast on Warsaw Radio September 18 and carried in *Pravda* on September 19. In effect, the Statement demanded a return to pre-August 1980 censorship practices, which the Polish regime could accomplish only by outlawing Solidarity. The Statement requested a halt to an "anti-Soviet campaign" that was "penetrating increasingly deeply into different spheres of the country's social life, including ideology, culture and the system of education and upbringing." It asserted that "further tolerance of any kinds of phenomena of anti-Sovietism" was "in direct contradiction with the commitments based on alliance taken on by Poland," and concluded that Polish leaders were expected to take "resolute and radical steps" without delay.

The die-hard Siwak was the lone member of the Polish Politburo daring enough to favor a collision course in broad daylight. "I do not believe in the line of agreement and no one is going to change my mind," Siwak told a press conference in Warsaw, and that blast at Kania got into *Pravda* on September 16. Siwak's high Party title was not given in the Soviet daily, as it was in printing of the same story by the Prague *Rude Pravo* on September 15. Whatever the reason for that protocol oddity, *Pravda*'s editors sniped again at Kania with their September 18 version of a Statement of the Polish Politburo. The Soviet rendition omitted some key words: "The Party continues to affirm the program of socialist renewal. . . . Despite the tense situation the PUWP Central Committee Politburo still stresses the readiness and the necessity to build an alliance of all and agreement with everyone who is not against socialism and to whom the cause of the homeland and its rescue is dear" (Warsaw Radio. Sept. 16, 1981).

The screws on Polish leaders were further tightened by the descent of still more senior Soviet officials upon Warsaw. Gen. Gribkov, Chief of Staff of the Warsaw Pact Joint Armed Forces, conferred with Jaruzelski on September 22, ostensibly to discuss "problems of training and combat

readiness of the detached [Polish] troops which form part of the Joint
Armed Forces" (Warsaw Radio. Sept. 22, 1981). Soviet economic planning
head Nikolay Baybakov that same day met with Jaruzelski at the start
of a five-day visit to review joint economic relations amid rumors that
Moscow would sharply curtail raw material exports to Poland as a
means of bringing its Government to heel.[5] A Soviet commentator on
Polish energy shortfalls would soon complain that due largely to Solidarity
sabotage of Government plans, Poland's contract commitments to supply
the Soviet Union with coal were not being met month after month
(*Ekonomicheskaya Gazeta* No. 42, cleared for printing Oct. 12, 1981).

But the Soviet elite was defied if it wanted the Polish leaders to
prevent the second phase of Solidarity's congress. Jaruzelski addressed
the national assembly on September 24 and like Kania three weeks
earlier he cautioned against a rush to judgement about the union. The
sense of Jaruzelski's careful message was accurately conveyed in the
September 26 *Pravda*: "Now is really the moment of decision. Preserving
the readiness to defend the socialist state, we are waiting for an answer
from the leadership of Solidarity, and a change in the line decided by
the first round of the congress. The future course of the country and
the people depends on whether Solidarity honors its commitments
contained in the agreements of 1980" (Cf. Warsaw Radio. Sept. 24,
1981). It should be added that Jaruzelski does not seem to have been
playing sly: The parliamentary session enacted legislation amounting to
a compromise between the Government and Solidarity drafts on the
basic issue of worker self-management. Under the compromise, the
Government ministries would name the plant mangers in strategic
industries and public utilities, with the appointments submitted to
workers' councils for approval; in other cases, the workers' councils
would propose the appointments and the Government have the right
of veto (PAP. Sept. 25, 1981).

The Kremlin was certainly averse to the temporizing of Polish authorities. On the eve of the second phase of Solidarity's congress, held
September 27–October 8, *Pravda* made a hue and cry about the Polish
ferment. The boiling-point headline "Situation in Poland" was used
from September 22 through 25, or as often as during the Bydgoszcz
strike, when Soviet leaders were credibly rumored to be pressing for
martial law. The gist of these items was that Solidarity was a Nazi-
type organization in league with the Catholic Church and on the verge
of taking full power from Communist rulers who unaccountably tarried.

Given this Soviet antipathy toward Solidarity, nothing that the union's
leaders might have done at the second stage of their convention could
pacify the Kremlin. Walesa and his nonradical colleagues did succeed
in persuading the congress to endorse a resolution that stopped short

of rejecting in its entirety the compromise law on worker self-management that the national assembly had passed. Just as soberly, if grudgingly, the program adopted by the congress upheld Poland's alliance relationship with the Soviet Union. But the goals of Solidarity remained those of a social movement based on Christian ethics. They included un-Leninist notions such as separating economic from political power, ending the Party's monopoly of mass media, and establishing an independent judiciary, as well as reducing defense spending (Warsaw. *Solidarnosc.* Supplement. Oct. 16, 1981).

Without waiting for the close of debate, *Pravda* resumed its alarmist din. The caption signifying inner tumult, "Situation in Poland," returned on September 29 and was featured through October 4—a record high of six consecutive days. The same extraordinary action was taken from October 6 through October 11. Solidarity leaders were portrayed in these articles as eager to remove Poland from the Soviet alliance system and to demolish the country's social-political structure. Unlike its earlier tirades against Solidarity, however, *Pravda* on October 2 directly mentioned the fateful outcome that Soviet bloc hardliners were craving for some time: "Calls were sounded at the congress to take 'precautionary measures' in case a 'Solidarity' dictatorship was established in Poland, and to prepare for *'the introduction of martial law and outside intervention'* and for the implementation of the aims of the counterrevolution, if necessary by force" (emphasis supplied). This sort of talk about regime intent at the union convention was not groundless since keen observers report that in late September 1981 the Polish security forces were alerted to stand ready for a national state of emergency.[6] Was *Pravda* intimating as much via circumlocution?

The whole thrust of Soviet propaganda at the time suggests that the question which then headed the Kremlin's Polish agenda was who in Warsaw could be relied upon to lead a crackdown on Solidarity. Jaruzelski, to be sure, was still courted. His attendance at an Army Day rally in the Polish capital was noted in the October 11 *Pravda*, while Kania's name had by then dropped out of the paper. But it could not be excluded that Jaruzelski might continue to prop up Kania, especially in view of the moderate Walesa's ascendance at the Solidarity congress. Moscow needed another iron in the fire.

The top-level *apparatchik* Olszowski had flaunted his loyalty to the Soviet Union and personal ambition in a somber article on the PUWP Congress that he wrote for the October issue of the international communist journal *Problems of Peace and Socialism*. The essay quoted from the congress speech of Soviet Politburo member Grishin, and ignored both Kania and Jaruzelski. It was orthodox and combative insofar as the author deplored "tendencies of ideological capitulationism" and argued that "Contrary to soothing statements which one hears at times, antisocialist forces diverse in character and political origin do exist in Poland." Olszowski gave to understand that those forces were scheming for a bloodless anticommunist coup (*Problemy mira i sotsializma* No. 10, cleared for printing Sept. 9, 1981).

There is reason to believe that powerful figures in Moscow deemed Olszowski a good candidate for the role of Polish dictator. Around the time that Party Secretariat official Rakhmanin published his above-mentioned article dealing *inter alia* with Polish affairs, another devoted entirely to the subject was carried by the CPSU organizational journal. In contrast to the Rakhmanin piece, this one ignored Kania and Jaruzelski, voiced no confidence in the Poles to put their own house in order, and harked back to the bogey of NATO plans to grab Polish lands (V. Chernyshev in *Partiynaya Zhizn*, No. 18, cleared for printing Sept. 8, 1981). Olszowski may have struck the inspirers of this article as the Polish leader most likely to collaborate with a Soviet intervention force if one had to be deployed.

A Kremlin endeavor to incite rivalry between Olszowski and Jaruzelski may have lurked behind the Soviet media build-up of Olszowski just prior to the second phase of the Solidarity congress, or when Jaruzelski was still playing for time.

Olszowski spoke over Warsaw Radio on September 22 and some of his anxious remarks were repeated in the September 24 *Pravda*. "The state," Olszowski said to Soviet delight, "will use any and all means as will be required by the situation for the defense of socialism." Olszowski's talk with foreign communist journalists that *Pravda* reported on September 30 centered on the necessity of smashing enemies in the leading echelons of Solidarity. A weekly that Olszowski had helped to found was repeatedly cited in *Pravda* (September 29, October 6 and 10), which echoed its anti-Kania philippic that weakness, mistakes and inconsistency of the Polish regime was the source of the brazenness of Solidarity leaders. Parenthetically, Olszowski's unqualified support of these factional sallies and his readiness to order police assaults against Solidarity were to be seen from his interview with the Hungarian Party daily in which he encouraged the use of "administrative means" in struggle with the trade union (Budapest. *Nepszabadsag*, Oct. 4, 1981).

The Soviet leaders, it seems, expected Jaruzelski or Olszowski to impeach Kania at the Polish Central Committee meeting that TASS on October 13 announced would open in three days time. A massive article by "Aleksey Petrov" in the October 13 *Pravda* was agitatedly entitled "Solidarity Makes a Grab for Power." Kania's posture was derided: "The socialist foundations of Polish society are being eroded under the flag of the so-called 'renewal.'" Sympathy was envinced for the "many

Polish Communists" who were aware of the "special responsibility" of their nation's supreme leadership to ensure "preservation of the revolutionary gains of the Polish people" and believed that such awareness "should be translated into an effective rebuff to counterrevolution." A threat of Soviet intervention in the event of further inaction was inherent in the assertion that guarding socialist institutions in Poland was "a question that touches directly on the vital interests of all peoples and states that have chosen the path of socialism."

Olszowski's enmity for Kania was paraded in the next day's TASS item from Warsaw relating the main points of a keynote speech to a meeting of the regional Party committee. Solidarity was said to be using the regime's errors and swings of policy in its lunge for political dominance. A direct call for tough measures was coupled with a tacit one for even the highest leaders to stand up and be counted: "Each Party member *regardless of rank* must define his position in a clear-cut manner" (*Pravda*, October 15, 1981. Emphasis supplied). Suslov effectively promised Soviet support for those lining up with Kania's foes at the imminent plenary meeting in Warsaw. During a speech to an ideological conference on October 14, Suslov hit a note of exasperation, declaring that "for a long time now" the Western powers had endeavored to spur on the counterrevolutionary forces in Poland and "one needs to be reminded" that Polish Communists "can firmly count on" the support of the Soviet Union, along with allied states (*Ibid.*). It is also not difficult to imagine Suslov blessing the plans then reportedly being prepared in local headquarters of the PUWP to form a secret armed workers' militia loyal to the Party apparatus across the country with a view towards mounting a coup and arresting hundreds of regime enemies.[7]

In analysis, the form and content of Soviet propaganda had come to resemble most closely that prefiguring the 1968 clampdown in Czechoslovakia. As before, there was a rough coincidence of Soviet factory meetings to protest anti-regime activities in a neighboring socialist state and *Pravda*'s most authoritative commentator demanding the repression of internationally-backed subversives, with saber-rattling going on in the wings. Even the military pressure tactics were not too dissimilar: Czechoslovak Party leader Dubcek was invited to the site of Warsaw Pact war games in early summer and Polish premier Jaruzelski attended the Soviet Army's autumn exercise. One gets an impression that Soviet leaders had taken a decision to embark on a course of Solidarity's destruction by one means or another.

NOTES

1. Speeches and resolutions of the August Plenum were reported by Warsaw Radio, Aug. 11–13, 1981 and *Zolnierz Wolnosci*, Aug. 14, 1981.

2. The summit communique identified Jaruzelski as "PPR Chairman of the Council of Ministers and Defense Minister" instead of "PPR Chairman of the Council of Ministers and *National* Defense Minister," as usual. The shorter version could have been meant to signify the trans-national importance of the Polish military establishment.

3. "'Krakow-81': Impressions and Questions." by Igor Itskov. *Iskusstvo Kino*, No. 9, 1981.

4. September Plenum materials were publicized by Warsaw Radio, Sep. 2, 3 and 4, 1981, PAP. Sept. 3 and 4, 1981, PAP Maritime Service. Sept. 4, 1981 and *Trybuna Ludu*, Sept. 3 and 4, 1981.

5. John Darnton in the *New York Times*, Sept. 23, 1981 and Johnathan Steele in *The Guardian* (London), Oct. 3, 1981.

6. "Report on Poland. Solidarity's Tug-of-War." By Maxine Pollack and Janusz Bugajski. *Encounter* (London). Vol. LVIII. No. 1. Jan. 1982.

7. Mika Larsson report from Warsaw on Stockholm Radio, Oct. 15, 1981.

NINE

"This Crucial Historic Moment"

(OCT. 16–DEC. 13, 1981)

Polish events that were exceptional in the history of the Soviet bloc kindled a blaze of hardline sentiment in Moscow. Premier and Defense Minister Gen. Jaruzelski was suddenly named Communist Party head, which meant a concentration of personal power at odds with the democratic tendencies in evidence at the July Party Congress. Brezhnev greeted Jaruzelski's accession as if it created a golden opportunity for stifling the reform movement in Poland. Jaruzelski, however, attended a meeting with leaders of Solidarity and the Catholic Church which furnished hope of reconciliation among Poles. The Soviet response was unfavorable to prospects for bridging the rift between society and regime. Soviet disapproval of Jaruzelski's "summit" was likely to stiffen the resistance of Polish conservatives to the idea of building a national consensus. A new tone of impatience in Soviet commentary and signs of shifting influence around Brezhnev to the benefit of security leaders were further suggestive of Kremlin pressure on Jaruzelski to take firm action, which he made up his mind to do.

By October 17, TASS editors knew that a power conflict between Kania and Olszowski was raging at a session of the Polish Central Committee.[1] Warsaw media had informed a day before that Kania as Party first secretary was chairing the meeting and on behalf of the Politburo had proposed to include only two items in the agenda: an examination of the political situation, on which Kania himself would report, and problems of ideology, to be addressed by Olszowski. Unusually, a foundry worker in the Committee replied to Kania's invitation of comments on the agenda, and proposed inclusion of the item "assessment of the work of the Politburo and organizational matters," that is, top leadership posts. The same worker asked that only Committee members be allowed to be present during this discussion and the proposal was adopted unanimously.

The texts in Soviet hands showed that Kania was still trying to avoid bloodshed by reconciling the diverse interests of the Polish regime, Solidarity movement and the Kremlin. Kania did propose a rollback of some of Solidarity's gains, obviously trying to deflect on to the union some of the fire which Party hardliners were aiming at him. But Kania stood by the position that dialogue should be the main method of resolving social conflicts and argued that all of the country's crises to date had proven the need for reforms. Olszowski rejected Kania's pleas for moderation. The gist of his remarks was that Poland's state system was being dismantled and that fatal process could not be halted by making new agreements with nonparty elements. Offensive action had to be taken against Solidarity, Olszowski said, and he stressed the internal defense function of the Polish army in conjunction with Soviet military power as defender of socialism.

The Soviet opinion makers were aware too that civilian and military speakers at the Polish Plenum were urging that a stop be put to allegedly rife anarchy, increasingly violent public scenes, and Solidarity propaganda striking at the heart of the Polish-Soviet alliance. The most important figures so far identified with this school of resolute thought at the Plenum were Politburo member Siwak, Warsaw Party leader Kociolek, and Maj. Gen. Wladyslaw Honkisz, deputy head of the Polish Army's Political Board.

Since Kania had adroitly dodged factional bullets in March and June, Soviet onlookers may have been doubtful about the outcome of this latest battle. It is also true that a policy-sensitive article in *Pravda* August 21 had cautioned that while tardiness was harmful to Soviet journalism, haste was even worse because "incorrect interpretation of an event is fraught with losses of important positions in the struggle of ideas." In any event, Olszowski was only hinted to be the favorite of Moscow in a remarkably uninformative TASS cable from Warsaw dated October 17 that *Pravda* ran the next day. Kania's chairmanship of the session and his Party title were ignored. Equal billing was given to the antagonists: "S. Kania and S. Olszowski delivered reports at the plenum." *Pravda* tersely added that "Nineteen persons took part in the discussion during the first day of the plenum's work."

As much as three-quarters of the TASS item on the showdown of Kania and Olszowski was devoted to anti-reformist signposts. The names of eleven worker Communists in ruling Party bodies who had quit Solidarity were given, along with their titles. Each was said to have explained the grounds of his or her decision. The remainder of this cautiously partisan dispatch notified that Bratkowski, chairman of the

Polish Journalists Association, was expelled from the Party for political misconduct. (It will be recalled that in March he had openly demanded the ouster of conservative Party leaders.)

The wariness of TASS and its political masters likewise kept out of *Pravda* on October 18 the anti-Kania vehemence in the summary of Plenum speeches released by the Polish news agency PAP. The tone of urgency in rhetoric of the pro-Olszowski forces had to be welcome to Soviet insiders. Kociolek, asserting that Solidarity had broken the Gdansk accords and a three-year ban on strikes was needed, warned that "Time is running out." Interior Minister Lt. Gen. Kiszczak ascribed an increase of Western subversion to the anti-Polish bearing of Solidarity activists and he gave a dire prognosis that implied the need for a pre-emptive blow at Solidarity: "Forecasts for the future, he stated, appear very menacing, even explosive." The possibility of declaring a state of emergency was raised by local Party militants in no uncertain terms. Although his written remarks were not aired till later, it may have been gossiped that number-two at the Defense Ministry had turned against Kania: "Time is pressing," said Chief of Staff Gen. Siwicki, "and we cannot afford leniency or compromises any longer." (Siwicki was the graduate of a Soviet military academy, led the Polish forces that invaded Czechoslovakia in 1968, and was reputed to be more influenced by Moscow than were many of his colleagues.)

The Kania-Olszowski fight ended on October 18, or when *Pravda* was only murmuring that it had just started. A compromise of hardliners and centrists was evidently behind the surprise election of Jaruzelski to the post of PUWP first secretary. In secret ballots, Kania's resignation was accepted by 104 votes, with 79 against, and Jaruzelski succeeded Kania by a vote of 180–4. The avoidance of a sharp break with the policy of self-control that Kania had pursued for over 13 months was underscored in several ways. Party Secretary Barcikowski, Kania's alter ego, presided over the reshuffle and recommended Jaruzelski for the post of Party head. Jaruzelski in his closing speech at the Plenum eulogized Kania as "my close, warm friend," with whom he had travelled "a single and joint" road along which there regretably were "stumblings and weaknesses." The new Party chief assured that he would continue "on the same general path" but "do everything to make it more and more effective." Jaruzelski also justified a verdict not to oust Kania from the Politburo.

Jaruzelski's mandate to combine prudence with firmness was so solid that Soviet leaders could not reveal any regret that Olszowski had failed to secure Kania's key job. The best face possible was put on the less than clear-cut result of the Polish Plenum in the TASS item of October 18 datelined Warsaw that *Pravda* carried on October 19. Unlike the case with Kania's elections in September 1980 and July 1981, Jaruzelski's was marked by a warm reference to him as "comrade." Brezhnev's message of congratulations to Jaruzelski which TASS issued on October 19 suggested how the general might earn that advance payment of Soviet trust. Jaruzelski was told that he was in charge of Polish destinies at nothing less than "this historic moment" and enjoyed Soviet confidence that he would use his "great prestige" to protect socialist achievements from "the encroachments of counterrevolution."

The Soviet desire for Jaruzelski to display toughness was implied too by the editing of his inaugural speech to the Central Committee in the October 20 *Pravda*. A lone substantive change was the paraphrase that "W. Jaruzelski expressed recognition to S. Kania for his work in the PUWP Central Committee in recent times." The omission of Jaruzelski's exact words about Kania indicated that Moscow wanted Jaruzelski to renounce Kania as man and politician. (The Czechoslovak ideologue Bilak soon insinuated that Kania was a "traitor" to the cause of socialism.[2])

In particular, it seems that Jaruzelski was expected to define loosely the conditions which might require the imposition of martial law. *Pravda* on October 20 stiffened the harsh "programmatic resolution" of the Polish Plenum which appealed to the national assembly for a ban on strikes and revision of the Gdansk accords. It did so by deleting the underlined qualifier about the circumstances in which civil liberties should be suspended in Poland:

> In the situation of the current threat to the existence and safety of the state, the Central Committee considers it essential for the highest authorities of the Polish People's Republic, in the case of *supreme* necessity, to resort to constitutional powers in order to protect the most vital interests of the state and of the nation (Warsaw Radio. Oct. 18, 1981. Emphasis supplied).

The analyst can probably also deem meaningful that *Pravda*'s version of the resolution mentioned the regime's "line of accord and cooperation" with society rather than the "line of *dialogue*, accord and cooperation," as did the original text (emphasis supplied). Thus, the Kremlin's advice to Jaruzelski seemed to boil down to a change of his slogan "Enough of this disintegration!" to "Enough palaver!"

A good deal of skepticism about Jaruzelski's moral fiber appears to have existed among elites in the Soviet Union and eastern Europe. The Polish Plenum that brought Jaruzelski to controlling power was disregarded in the weekly "International Survey" which *Pravda* featured on October 19 and 25. Hardliner Siwak was the only Polish Politburo member cited in an article by Yuriy Kornilov, "Who Is Behind the Polish Counterrevolution?," which *Sovetskaya Rossiya* published on October 23 and Radio Moscow sent in Polish to Poland on the same day. Nor was notice of Jaruzelski taken in an October 21 panel discussion of Polish affairs on Prague television which welcomed the recent Warsaw Plenum and "cadre changes" if they were directed at heightening Party unity and effectiveness. If Jaruzelski was little more than a henchman of Moscow it is unlikely that such glaring anomalies would have surfaced at the time.

An anxiety in orthodox Communist quarters over how Jaruzelski would cope with a rising number of strikes and hunger marches in Poland was warranted. The general met with Primate Glemp on October 21 and they agreed to cooperate to ensure internal calm, the renewal program, and the creation of "a broad plane of national accord" (Interpress. Oct. 22, 1981). Informed sources reported that Jaruzelski seemed favorably disposed towards a compromise program which the Primate submitted to him. Under the compromise, according to these sources,

> The Party's leadership role and the alliances would be formally guaranteed, the Party would keep the "strategic portfolios" in the government (foreign affairs, interior, Armed Forces, transportation, communications) and its leadership role would be additionally stressed by Gen. Jaruzelski's presence as government and Party chief. On the other hand, the cabinet would be mainly formed by prominent independent people, technocrats, many of whom would be Catholics and Solidarity members although they would not belong to the government in that capacity. Above all the policy of the government, which would have general support, would be drawn up by it in complete independence and no longer by the Party leadership. In addition a socioeconomic council, requested by Solidarity, would be formed but—another compromise—it would comprise all the trade unions and not just Solidarity and would merely have a consultative and monitoring role.[3]

What lends plausibility to the claim that Jaruzelski was genuinely interested in the compromise proposals is the fact that hardliner Olszowski repeatedly attacked in public the idea of forming a coalition government.[4]

Soviet and East German leaders appear to have developed a strategy for bringing Jaruzelski around to a view that martial law was imperative in Poland. The plan seems to have been to initiate detailed preparations for the mass arrest of Solidarity leaders and sympathizers by Polish authorities. If the scheme was rejected in Warsaw, Soviet and East German forces would move into Poland and conduct their own police sweep of disloyal elements, with all the brutality and high risk of violence that might entail. As a longtime "team player" in the Warsaw Pact establishment, Jaruzelski would be expected to go along with the plan once it was set into motion, and as a Polish nationalist he could be expected to shrink from the prospect of foreign intervention. An additional calculation of Moscow and East Berlin could have been that no Communist ruler can govern for long in isolation but needs the broad based cooperation of the political governing class. If the October 16–18 Plenum in Warsaw had proven anything it was that Polish bureaucracy was more torn than ever between the partisans of repression and accommodation. Unity of the power elite was likelier to be achieved on a platform of confrontation with Solidarity, as it would mark a burning of bridges.

The evidence for an assumption of Soviet-East Germany collusion to inveigle Jaruzelski into taking a decision for martial law and in general a decided stiffening of Kremlin policy rests on a number of signs that cropped up from October 20 through November 14 which altogether were no less suggestive than original.

1. East German Party leader Honecker, as seen, had menaced the Polish liberalizers as early as October 1980 by asserting that "together with our friends" his country would "make sure" that Poland remained in the communist fold. Very soon after Kania's fall and Jaruzelski's advent, Honecker met with Soviet military and police leaders. On October 20, he received Marshal Kulikov, Supreme Commander of the Warsaw Pact Joint Forces. The two discussed "current questions of the international military-political situation" and "drew conclusions for the further cooperation of the GDR National People's Army with the Soviet Army and the other allied forces of the Warsaw Pact states" (ADN. Oct. 20, 1981). On October 22, Honecker received Army Gen. Nikolay Shchelokov, USSR Minister for Internal Affairs. The "exchange of views" included full agreement that "deepening of fraternal and friendly cooperation" of the two states' security organs "acquires increasing importance" in view of the "the exacerbation of the international situation and the threat to peace" (ADN. Oct. 22, 1981).

2. A survey of Soviet bloc press comment on Poland in the CPSU Secretariat journal *Partiynaya Zhizn* No. 21, cleared for printing on October 27, 1981, cited *Neues Deutschland*'s strident charge that Solidarity was tied to "committees for the release of prisoners" and veterans of the anticommunist "Home Army" resistance group of World War II; the writer himself virtually shrieked that "ransackings of the premises of State bodies" had lately occurred in most Polish regions.

3. *Red Star*'s review of letters from readers on October 30 echoed the line of Polish diehards that a race against the clock had begun: "Counterrevolutionaries are clearly seeking to seize power. Socialism's enemies are not dozing. They spare no means to accomplish their foul, vile deeds. Their actions must be suppressed *in time*" (Emphasis supplied).

4. USSR Defense Minister Ustinov was far less complacent about Poland in his leadership report for the November 7 holiday than

Chernenko had been during a similar exercise for Lenin Day in April. Ustinov drew up to 15 seconds of applause from his listeners with a prediction that effort by internal and foreign counterrevolutionaries to liquidate socialism in Poland would never succeed. Ustinov got more applause for a claim that resolve was swelling in Poland to repel the antisocialist forces that were openly grabbing for power (*Pravda*, Nov. 7, 1981).

5. A coup by Solidarity and the Polish regime's capacity to forestall it by using extraordinary powers was a thought expressed by indirection in *Pravda*'s "Situation in Poland" article on November 11. The Polish military daily was cited to the effect that Solidarity leaders had deployed "storm units" and were acting out a "scenario of counterrevolution." The Party, however, would not allow itself to be "caught by surprise" and the State would take "appropriate security measures" on the basis of its "constitutional rights."

6. Exasperation was registered anew in *Pravda*'s November 14 review of readers' letters on events in Poland. Soviet citizens were said to be declaring: *"It is time* for Poland's true patriots to ascertain exactly who is the country's friend and who its enemy"; *"Is it not time* for the Polish workers headed by the PUWP to deal a resolute rebuff to the 'Solidarity' adventurists and to prove *once and for all* that power in the country belongs to the working class and its vanguard—the Communist Party?"; *"There must be an end* to any connivance at the intrigues of Poland's enemies—that is what Soviet workers think" (emphasis supplied).

During this same period, Jaruzelski does not appear to have assented to Soviet prompting that he crack down on Solidarity. The general stated his intent to broaden the coalition dimension of the Government's base in the course of his speech to the Polish Central Committee on October 28, and *Pravda* October 30 negatively deleted this statement from its account of the plenary meeting address (Cf. Warsaw Radio. Oct. 29, 1981). The knowledgeable observer Daniel Passent wrote on Primate Glemp's grand coalition concept in the Warsaw *Polityka* for October 31 as though it were very much alive and he was aware of Soviet opposition. "Everything possible should be done," Passent said, "to obtain the understanding of our allies, since the external factor plays a great part in events in Poland. That our allies should comprehend the nature and importance of the process taking place in Poland is an absolutely essential factor for the success of the renewal." A short time later, on November 4, Jaruzelski met with Primate Glemp and Solidarity chairman Walesa in an unprecedented summit. Warsaw Radio announced just after the meeting that the participants "exchanged views . . . on the possibilities of setting up a front of national agreement—a permanent platform for dialogue and consultations between political and social forces based on the constitutional precepts of the Polish People's Republic." *Pravda* suggested the Kremlin's disapproval of such tripartite peace talks by taking no notice of the Warsaw summit. It was equally silent about Jaruzelski's hopeful words about the summit to his Government Presidium: "The momentous meeting has created favorable premises for the creation of a front of national agreement, for an improvement in the social climate, for overcoming of the crisis, and for the consolidation of socialist renewal within the framework of the constitutional principles of a socialist state" (Warsaw Radio. Nov. 6, 1981).

Olszowski was in Moscow on November 3 and 4, attending a conference of ruling Communist Party secretaries for international and ideological questions. Evidently he agreed fully with Soviet leaders that Jaruzelski's gestures of approach to Solidarity and the Church were misguided undertakings. The outlook in vogue at *Pravda* was at any rate the definitely combative one in the Statement of the bloc ideology meeting which it published on November 5:

> The representatives of the fraternal Parties reaffirmed their solidarity with the Communists and all patriots of socialist Poland in their struggle against the antipeople forces of counterrevolution and anarchy, for overcoming the crisis and consolidating socialism, the leading role of the PUWP in society, for the sure development of the PPR as an inseparable link of the socialist community.

The temptation is strong to assume that Gen. Jaruzelski made his fateful decision to end the days of liberty in Poland sometime between mid and late November 1981.

A Soviet lecturer, speaking to a public audience in the USSR shortly after the Polish declaration of martial law on December 13, stated that martial law had been in preparation for a month and said that it had been "brilliantly conspired," that is, the closest secrecy surrounded the operation.[5]

U.S. journalists at the end of December 1981 cited Polish Government sources to the effect that "about a month ago" Jaruzelski "was given an ultimatum by the Kremlin." This version had it that, "Soviet representatives told him—and him alone—that the Polish party was no longer in control, that the Sejm (parliament) was running wild, and that if he did not act to restore order, the Warsaw Pact would do it for him."[6]

A meeting of Marshal Kulikov and Jaruzelski in Warsaw on November 25 that was noted in *Pravda* on the 26th was surrounded by signs of mounting Soviet concern over Polish events coupled with a thrusting forward of security chiefs in Moscow.

"Political power is impossible without economic power" was the credo of *apparatchiki* throughout the Soviet orbit that was voiced at the Polish Party Congress in July. It stood to reason, therefore, that one of the gravest allegations that could be made against the opponents of a communist power monopoly in Poland was that they were trying to eject Party officials from production units. The accusation was not a tissue of lies but founded on real occurrences stemming from the workers' refusal to keep as many as 30 fulltime Party officials on a firm's payroll.[7] What is important here is *Pravda's* ballooning treatment of this most sensitive theme in its coverage of Polish affairs from the third week of November:

1. "Counterrevolutionary forces in the Polish People's Republic are unleashing a campaign for the elimination of PUWP party committees at enterprises and in offices" (Nov. 20).

2. "Lately at a number of enterprises 'Solidarity' representatives have been intensifying a campaign against PUWP committees and members. Striving to attain the goals set by illegal antisocialist organizations, the extremist forces are demanding that the Party be driven from enterprises. There is persecution of and moral terror against PUWP members, foremost the activists of plant Party committees" (Nov. 26).

3. "The Party's status at enterprises is fixed by the Republic's constitution and legislation. All attempts to dislodge the Party from plants and other enterprises will fail. . . . Many echelons of the 'Solidarity' trade association, implementing the political concepts of illegal, antisocialist organizations, are exerting pressure on the *aktiv* of PUWP plant committees and undertaking to force the Party out of enterprises. A decisive end must be put to such actions" (Nov. 30).

4. "The foes of socialism have become active at this enterprise too. A campaign is being conducted for dissolution of the plant's Party organization" (Dec. 4).

5. "They will not succeed in driving the Party out of industrial enterprises, as attempted at some plants and mines. . . . The actions of persons or organizations which make difficult or impossible the activity of PUWP organizations at industrial enterprises will be dealt with in accordance with the criminal code" (Dec. 5).

6. "The extremist forces of 'Solidarity,' under demagogic slogans, are unleashing a campaign against Party organizations at enterprises. . . . Political campaigns were conducted, even going so far as attempting to exclude the PUWP from industrial enterprises" (Dec. 8).

In the midst of this highly inflammatory propaganda against Solidarity, the clout of Soviet military and police leaders was indicated to have expanded. Defense Minister Ustinov and KGB chairman Andropov suddenly outranked Party Secretary Chernenko in a photograph of

Politburo members bidding goodbye to Brezhnev, who was flying to Bonn, at a Moscow airport (*Pravda*, Nov. 23). Chernenko had once served a roundabout warning to Kania against caving-in to Solidarity, it seems, but had espoused a relatively soft line towards the Poles in his Lenin Day speech in April. Ustinov, on the other hand, took a harder stand in his keynote at the Bolshevik Revloution rally on November 6. Chernenko's mildness does not appear to have been merely situational. In a Soviet election speech of November 23, Chernenko went no further than to mention the "great difficulties"—not even "crisis"—in Poland, and he disregarded the counterrevolutionary or antisocialist forces that Soviet media were screaming themselves hoarse about.[8] The short TASS account of Chernenko's speech in *Pravda* November 24 did not contain any of his statements about Poland, thereby forbidding the observer to put into the context of policy his slippage of prestige among the Soviet leaders. But enough was known about the sternness of Ustinov and Andropov to give bite to the more alarmist handling of Poland by Soviet journalists and editors.

The use of official coercion against unruly social groups in a socialist country was urged in materials clearly related to the Polish situation that were inserted into the issue of *Kommunist* delivered to the compositor on November 27–December 2 and cleared for printing on December 7 (No. 18, 1981).

An editorial rolled into one the legendary abortive movements for national independence in Soviet Europe and that still extant. "In 1956 in Hungary and in 1968 in Czechoslovakia," the editorial states, "the antisocialist forces relied on assistance from outside, as is to be observed in our day too in the Polish People's Republic." The editorial continued with an allusion to the martial law threat raised at the October 16–18 Plenum in Warsaw:

> It must not be forgotten that victory of the socialist revolution does not yet mean that the exploiters and their myrmidons are immediately deprived of their power and influence. They rely on old views, customs and morals, which cling to the minds of people, and they try to draw over to their side the small property-holders—peasants, artisans, handicraftsmen—as well as representatives of the intelligentisia and especially mass information workers, bribe all and sundry rabble from the dregs of society, the declassed and criminal elements, hinder the economy's organization, etc. All this requires from the worker class and its communist vanguard the creation of *a strong and decisive governing authority which in the event of necessity, in the interest of the defense of socialism, is able to compel people to heed it and subordinate themselves to its demands* (emphasis supplied).

Directly, the editorial referred to Polish society as one in which there was "an acute class struggle, at certain times secretive and at others open, but invariably warmed up from outside by the forces of imperialistic reaction which display a high sense of class solidarity in their antisocialist actions." The Soviet reader of these lines was unquestionably assumed to know that violent resolution of class conflict in any society was a central theme of communist philosophy. Behind the editorialists at *Kommunist*, Party Secretary for ideology Suslov perhaps ordered up the same lines with full knowledge that they were meant to justify an imminent clampdown on the Polish scene.

The same issue of *Kommunist* had still other material which was likely to appeal to the deep springs of political conformity in the Soviet Party ranks. Czechoslovak Party Secretary Bilak, scourge of Polish reformers, wrote a short article for Brezhnev's 75th birthday fondly recalling the Soviet leader's "decisiveness" at bilateral and multilateral talks when Czechoslovakia experienced "severe crisis years" (1968–69) and "creeping counterrevolution" had emerged. "He stressed," Bilak said of Brezhnev, "that one must not retreat before counterrevolution, but smash and destroy it, because only in that way can the historic gains of the masses be saved." If this praise of the younger Brezhnev as staunch Communist was not followed soon by a ringing down of the curtain on the Polish drama, the Soviet reader to whom it was directed might easily have construed it as veiled criticism of the older Brezhnev for having lost his political nerve. Bilak might have suspected that if his message was commissioned by the editors of *Kommunist*; Suslov as the watchdog of the journal almost certainly knew it.

Kommunist No. 18 was not available to foreign subscribers and maybe even not in Soviet kiosks before martial law was imposed in Poland. So its highly suggestive contents would not have been helpful to the Western students of Kremlin policy. But the warning signs in *Pravda* during early December were clear enough to have surmised that Soviet official opinion was being readied for something new to happen on the Polish front.

As a rule, Solidarity chairman Walesa was not directly criticized in the Soviet Party newspaper. One of the rare mentions of Walesa by *Pravda* was on March 22, 1981, when his name arose in connection with the police beating of protestors in the town of Bydgoszcz. The original TASS item alleging that Walesa had made an "instigatory" statement on the affair was notably softened in *Pravda* to avoid hanging a label of firebrand on the labor leader. A second unusual occurrence was the criticism of Walesa in the March 27, 1981 *Pravda* for supposedly brandishing Solidarity's might. And then there was the ideologue Kosolapov's sniping at Walesa in *Pravda* just after the Polish Party Congress in July. The Soviet decision to give minimal publicity to the now world-famous electrician from Gdansk sharply distinguished *Pravda* from Party dailies in, say, Czechoslovakia, whose ultra-orthodox Communists were not averse to seeing Solidarity regularly blasted as "Walesa's trade unions."

It was, therefore, significant that Walesa was suddenly pilloried along with the most radical leaders of Solidarity in the December 4 *Pravda*. Olszowski was said to have told a Party meeting in a Warsaw factory that "Walesa, Bujak, Rulewski and others" would not be allowed to put into practice the "designs" underlying some kind of "demands" that were lately made in Solidarity branches. Walesa alone was impugned for having allegedly threatened the country's leadership after riot police on December 2 forcibly ended an eight-day occupation strike at a fireman's college in Warsaw.

Pravda was quick to echo the intensive attacks made on Walesa in Polish media after the Warsaw press published on December 7 alleged excerpts from speeches by Solidarity leaders at their closed-door meeting in Radom on December 3 calling for the overthrow of the communist system.

Anti-Walesa notes were sounded in the final block of reports excitedly captioned "Situation in Poland" which *Pravda* ran for six straight days from December 8 through December 13. The Radom taped speeches as distilled for Soviet audiences were highlighted by a charge that Walesa was guilty of the capital crime of State treason: "For example, L. Walesa admitted that 'Solidarity' was eroding the system of authority in Poland, and said that it was necessary to choose 'such a road as to make a lightning maneuver' (to seize power)" (*Pravda*, Dec. 9, 1981). A commentary from Prague on the next day said that Walesa at Radom had "thrown off the mask" and "openly proclaimed what 'Solidarity' was interested in from the very start, why it really arose and what its main goal is." The rest of this article spelled out Solidarity's aim as the capture of ruling authority in Poland by violent means (*Pravda*, Dec. 10, 1981). On the very eve of martial law, Walesa was steadily castigated in Moscow. During a press conference in Gdansk, Walesa was said to have dwelt on need for Solidarity to check up on the Government and to have lied by stating that his speech in Radom was misunderstood and the union did not exclude the conclusion of new accords with the regime (*Pravda*, Dec. 12, 1981). The report of a meeting of Solidarity's National Commission accused Walesa of duplicity for supposedly claiming that union members were asking him to be flexible and reach agreement with the Government while he actually sided with the counterrevolutionary Rulewski's view that power had to be torn away from the Communist Party (*Pravda*, Dec. 13, 1981).

The most extraordinary of *Pravda*'s last stories tracking the denouement in Poland was published on December 10. No dateline was given for this TASS item, which was based on "information coming in from Poland." The intelligence was concocted to foster an illusion that anticommunism and anti-Sovietism was in floodtide as never before. Solidarity was wildly alleged to be arming itself in order to stage a coup and public places were no longer safe for regime loyalists:

> The leaders of local "Solidarity" organizations have begun setting up "commando units" at enterprises. Every shock unit includes 250–300 members. Theft of weapons and explosives from state storehouses has been recorded. Thugs from the inglorious "Confederation of Independent Poland" have gone out into the streets of Polish cities. They are flaunting the insignia of the Home Army which is known to have fought, arms in hand, against the establishment of the people's democratic system in Poland.

The internal security theme was just as uniquely and fulsomely harped upon in other passages:

> Leaflets have been disseminated in the Szczecin, Radom and some other regions announcing December 20 to be "a Sunday of crushing the PUWP." Slogans are called out to do away with Communists. The "Solidarity" organization of the Mazowsze region is carrying out preparations for a mass-scale gathering in the center of Warsaw. Mazowsze's leader, Bujak, said that they were planning to take over the premises of the central television and radio of Poland on December 17. . . . The critical situation caused by the rampage of counterrevolution is compelling the authorities to take additional measures to protect the constitutional foundations of the state. In particular, patrols at the premises of government and Party offices are being reinforced.

Acute danger to the vital interests of the Soviet Union was professed: "At the same time, attacks on Poland's relations with its allies are being stepped up and demagogical demands are being made for Poland's withdrawal from the Warsaw Treaty and the Council for Mutual Economic Assistance and for using the lines of communications passing through Polish territory to pressure Poland's allies." The foremost intermediary between Solidarity and regime was maligned: "Clerical circles and organizations have become perceptibly more active. Far more sermons aimed at discrediting the Government's activities to defend socialism are being read in cathedrals." What to do? Party meetings in many regions of Poland were said to be passing resolutions stressing the need to "defend the achievements of People's Poland and to frustrate the designs of the enemies of socialism."

A seeming political allegory in the same day's copy of *Pravda* (December 10) hinted at the expediency of shutting down the free labor union in Poland, rather than arriving at an even temporary modus vivendi, as suggested by the presumed allegory of September 6, 1980. The 90th birthday of V. Volodarsky, active figure in the Petrograd Committee of the Bolshevik Party when assassinated in 1918, was marked by a lengthy article. He could be readily associated with Polish hardliners of the present day in light of strong objection to the proposal of non-Communists that a true coalition government be formed to replace the one dominated by the Leninists. Volodarsky was quoted to the effect that "in this matter there can be no concessions." In the same fighting spirit imputed to Polish Communists elsewhere in *Pravda*, Volodarsky was heard to declare through the mists of history: "We are besieged. The enemy mad with rage is striving to clutch by the throat the young socialist republic. We shall defend ourselves to the last! To the last man. But around us, vipers are crawling, hoping to take us from within. The internal enemies of the Republic are making a noose. We shall be merciless towards them!" Volodarsky, *Pravda* concluded, was a man of "decisive revolutionary action."

What *Pravda* did not say was that Marshal Kulikov was in Poland while martial law was being initiated and Solidarity leaders interned along with sympathizers on December 13, 1981.[9] The official revelation of that fact would have been discordant with Soviet acclaim of military repression in Poland as a "national decision taken by our Polish friends." That was Brezhnev's way of putting it in a speech of March 1, 1982 delivered at a Kremlin dinner for a Jaruzelski-led delegation.[10] The truth had to seem a good deal more variegated to anyone who was following coverage of Polish affairs in *Pravda* over the past 16 months or so.

NOTES

1. The proceedings of the October 16–18 session of the PUWP Central Committee were reported by Warsaw Radio and PAP, Oct. 16–19, 1981 and *Trybuna Ludu*, Oct. 17–18, 19, 20 and 21, 1981.

2. *Rude Pravo*, Oct. 30, 1981.

3. "Poland: The Church Proposes a Plan for National Union." By Bernard Margueritte. *Le Figaro*, Oct. 23, 1981.

4. PAP. Oct. 23 and Nov. 12, 1981 on Olszowski's speeches in Ostrowiec Swietokruzyski and Legnica, and his interview in *Sztandar Mlodych*, Nov. 13–15, 1981.

5. *Soviet and Soviet-proxy Involvement in Poland*, p. 4.

6. New York. *Time*, Dec. 28, 1981, p. 13.

7. See Bernard Margueritte's Poznan dispatch in *Le Figaro*, Dec. 3, 1981.

8. K.U. Chernenko, *Utverzhdat leninskiy stil v partiynoy rabote* (Moscow, 1983), p. 73.

9. *Soviet and Soviet-proxy Involvement in Poland*, p. 4.

10. Leonid Ilyich Brezhnev, *Leninskim kursom. Rechi, privetsviya, stati, vospominaniya* (Moscow, 1982), Vol. 9, p. 405.

TEN

Conclusions

A narrow intelligence study could not have thrown much interesting light on Soviet objectives during the Polish crisis of 1980–81. The memoir of President Carter's national-security adviser shows that conventional intelligence sources could be misleading about the likelihood of an outright Soviet invasion in December 1980. A few months later, April 1981, according to another public source, U.S. Government analysts were in disagreement about how to interpret data on a build-up of Soviet forces in and around Poland. Imposition of martial law in Poland was a bolt out of the blue for U.S. policymakers, as it was for the average Polish citizen, although in retrospect it is apparent that there were significant clues to be found through the interpretation of Soviet media texts.

There is every reason to believe that the Soviet press furnished our best clues to Kremlin thinking about Poland. The press items could not have given total assurance that it was time to ring the tocsin or keep it muted. But the items did indicate an intense concern in Moscow about Polish events and in so doing told the analyst not to be complacent. In the circumstances, a nudge against complacence might have been valuable for the collators of raw intelligence data and the diplomats who were especially prone to optimistic assessments.

The unworried attitude to be observed among many on the eve of martial law in Poland can be explained in a number of ways. Basic factors that seem to have accounted for it were: exaggeration of post-Stalin changes in Kremlin politics by some academic Sovietologists; preoccupation with statements of the Soviet leaders as distinct from TASS reportage or *Pravda* commentary; and too sharp a focus on the subject of policy (Soviet hammer) at the expense of the object (Polish anvil). There is no need to dwell on the reluctance of some to "cry wolf" once again after several invasion scares proved to be nothing more than overreactions to Soviet bluffing.

"What if the Poles get away with it?" was a question asked during the crisis by persons who viewed the Brezhnev regime as something far more benevolent than any of its forerunners in recent Soviet history. A source of this outlook was the writings of American political scientists which portrayed the Brezhnev leadership as dedicated to internal reform and under heavy pressure to enlarge the scope of its collaboration with the United States. The primary aim of Brezhnev and his colleagues was supposedly to raise domestic living standards as rapidly as possible and to avoid at all cost any worsening in Soviet-American relations. Underlying the Soviet rulers' quest for peace and prosperity, the theory went, was the emergence of "institutional pluralism" in the USSR. The leading political actors in this model included civil servants, scholars and educators, whose innovative opinions as shaped by the findings of modern sociology were publicly debated on a vast scale, with the Politburo mediating whatever conflicts arose. A threat to this salutary process of renovation, however, was seen in U.S. misconceptions which helped to produce such harmful actions as new American arms programs, tying of trade credits to the emigration of Jews, or campaigns on behalf of dissidents.[1] Clearly, the purveyors of this rosy picture of a grim reality were unable to distinguish between organic change and the mere perfection of existing institutions, or between genuine reformers and more or less clear-sighted conservatives. The result was a not uncommon impression of Soviet leaders as essentially benign old men who might afford to tolerate internal diversity at their Polish doorstep.

Others in the midst of the Polish upheaval were calmed by the thought that for some time Soviet leaders were avoiding direct mention of Poland in their public statements. It was indeed striking that Gus Hall, Ceausescu, Honecker and Castro were vocal about the Polish crisis in 1980 while Brezhnev, Kirilenko, Tikhonov and Chernenko in their remarks to Soviet and foreign communist audiences as carried by *Pravda* were passing it over. The ideologue-in-chief Suslov and Ukrainian Party boss Shcherbitskiy, both CPSU Politburo members, were equally silent in the first quarter of 1981. Only Defense Minister Ustinov had by then addressed himself to the problem in a personal speech to a Soviet gathering. Could this be taken as a sign of smug contentment in spite of the agitated tone of Soviet media? The record should have instructed that Communist leaders do not always ventilate their strong sentiments on policy issues. That was true of Marshal Tito and his reticence about Stalin's role in the Soviet-Yugoslav dispute when it burst forth in 1948; Khrushchev and Mao in 1959 did not air their bitterness about each other's willful concept of national interest. The Soviet leaders may have disregarded the Solidarity phenomenon in speeches and articles for a variety of reasons other than lack of anxiety. They were perhaps intent on keeping Polish leaders guessing about their next step, aware that Kania could decipher the most ambiguous of pronouncements from the Kremlin and trim his sails accordingly. The Kremlin chiefs may also have been unwilling to commit their personal prestige to one or another line of action out of fear that events could overtake them, as did the initial surprise of the Polish August itself. One such eventuality was an undoing of the seemingly shaky consensus to engage in a trial of nerves with the Warsaw regime and conduct intrigues against it rather than go for the military bludgeon. The charge of being "weak-kneed" or "adventuristic" in dealing with foreign adversaries can stick to a Soviet leader and even hasten his exit from political life, as Malenkov and Khrushchev were to learn in 1955 and 1964, respectively.

Still other witnesses of the Polish rebellion were heedless of the substantial influence which orthodox Communists inside the east Europan countries can bring to bear on the national leaderships. Even students of Polish politics who rightfully advised during the crisis that it was misleading to think of the outlook solely in terms of Soviet invasion were blind to the latent or actual power of the oldstyle *apparatchiki*, choosing to accent instead the "movement of more than 35 million" which "is not likely to succumb to intimidations."[2] The astute Poland-watchers realized that Kania's strength was illusory since the mere presence of hardliners in the Polish Politburo gave license to diehards high and low to embark on acts of economic sabotage and police violence that were meant to discredit and provoke Solidarity over the entire course of the internal tug-of-war.[3] The hidebound dogmatists of Polish Communism had an enormous influence on events, forcing the populace to grow still more distrustful of the regime and doubly convinced that it was incapable of self-reform. Given the Soviet factor which shielded the hardliners from ouster, an iron-fisted personality other than Jaruzelski might have come to power in Warsaw during 1981 and used the regime's awesome security forces to restore the Communist autocracy. It is worthwhile to ponder the reflections of imprisoned Polish dissident Adam Michnik about this crucial aspect of the problem, even if one takes a different slant on how Jaruzelski was induced to crush Solidarity:

Let us return for a moment to the events of 18 months ago. All the interpretations of that December night, including mine, placed the emphasis on the structural conflict between the government apparatus and Solidarity. In that view, the December coup d'etat was merely a desperate defense of the totalitarian system faced with an organized society demanding its right to take its own decisions. It was that, but not only that. It was also the desperate defense of the government team threatened by a coup d'etat by party "hardliners," by those who are customarily described as the "rearguard."

According to this interpretation the rearguard planned to overthrow the Jaruzelski team at the next party plenum, as it had previously overthrown Kania. The rearguard, victorious and backed with the Kremlin's blessing, would then have called Jaruzelski, Rakowski, or Barcikowski—I am only citing these names by way of example—to account for their mistakes, in other words the "liberal liquidation" (of socialism) for which they were blamed in the Soviet analysis of the Polish situation. Martial law would have been proclaimed by other men and the demoted PUWP leaders would have shared the fate of Nagy or Dubcek, becoming the codenamed symbols of an erroneous policy. Numerous facts show that the rearguard had the unqualified blessing of the Soviet comrades, ready to engage their divisions in order "not to abandon Poland in need." What happened was different. Jaruzelski preferred the fate of a Kadar (or a Red Pinochet) to that of a Nagy or a Maleter, and he followed Husak rather than Dubcek (Paris. *Le Point*, June 27–July 3, 1983).

The analyst had to isolate himself from punditry about "institutional pluralism" or invincible "movement of more than 35 million" and develop his own conceptual framework for evaluating the wealth of Poland-related media texts that were produced in Moscow from August 1980 through December 1981.

The general factors likely to shape a Soviet decision on Poland had to be delineated. Basic influences that would help to determine which trigger Moscow would finger included history, doctrine and current politics. It is true that each was subject to interpretation, but that had to be done if only to avoid the pitfall of snap judgement.

Since the 18th century it was traditional Russian policy to subjugate Poland in concert with the other great powers. The Russian emperor ultimately became Poland's king, a grand duke commanded the Polish army, and a high commissioner from St. Petersburg resided in Warsaw. Polish sovereignty was restored in 1918 thanks to the collapse of imperial Russia and military weakness of the Bolshevik successor regime. A revitalized Russian state under the Soviet flag occupied eastern Poland in 1939–41 as part of a deal with Nazi Germany. The basic features of the Soviet order were imposed throughout Poland not long after the Red Army had turned out the Nazis in World War II and the West at Yalta had granted legitimacy to a Soviet-controlled Polish provisional government. Stalin's virtual imitation of the tsarist practice of exercising direct command over Polish affairs did not long survive him. Poland's Communist leaders were allowed a measure of autonomy from Moscow in 1956, but are known to have later resented deeply the Soviet impositions that no genuinely sovereign rulers would have tolerated. In effect, Poland was again harnessed to the eastern colossus and one could imagine that deadweight of the past was weighing on the brains of Soviet leaders if not like an alp then at least to more than a negligible extent.

Doctrine was important for the Kremlin in 1980–81 insofar as it served to maintain the internal stability and international position of the Soviet Union. The central theme of political philosophy was about a really practical problem: insuring the "leading role" of the CPSU in society, that is, a power monopoly for the Party at large and the right of its fulltime workers to have the last word in day-to-day management of almost every phase of national life. This basic principle of Party supremacy was held to be valid for each of the Warsaw Pact member-states, which had subscribed to it in documents signed at the highest level during the Czechoslovak crisis of 1968. "Party documents" have the force of law for Communists, who in this instance agreed to recognize as a threat to their own vital interests the erosion of *apparat* power in any other country of the alliance system. The unspoken presumption was that either Communists exclusively would direct the east European states and honor the treaty commitments of those states to Moscow or the scepter of rule would pass to nationalist forces destined to work against the USSR. This morbid orthodoxy was transmitted to large numbers of Soviet officials via the press and political training schools, creating a climate of opinion within the governing class inhospitable to a diffusion of political power anywhere in the Eastern bloc.

The current politics of the Soviet Politburo are assuredly devised without constant surveys of opinion in the lower Party echelons. That much can be safely assumed from the infrequent and brief nature of CPSU Central Committee sessions. But the Moscow chiefs and province bosses do meet at local receptions and central seminars. Demands from above cross with petitions from below, and the supreme leaders are doubtless aware that they must have the cooperation of their subordinates in order to rule effectively. Although the mind-set of Party administrators is hardly an open book, there is reason to believe that most are decidely conservative. In particular, the *apparatchiki* are likely to share with their masters a dislike and maybe even fear of so-called liberal Soviet Communists. These reportedly include Party intellectuals, some military officers, writers, critics, Party workers and a few KGB men. The Polish events may have given fresh enthusiasm to some in this radical wing of the CPSU rank and file who held "Neo-Shlyapnikovian" views.[4] Aleksandr G. Shlyapnikov (1885–1937) was formerly a metal-worker and People's Commissar for labor in the first Soviet Government. He was a founder of the Worker Opposition in 1920, a faction of the Bolshevik Party which demanded for the trade unions a vast increase of power in the management of State industries and freedom from the control of the Party center. The Worker Opposition also stood for open election to all Party posts and free discussions within the Party with facilities for the dissemination of special opinions.[5] In 1980–81, the

Politburo elite and its local clients had cause enough to abort the Polish reform movement if they suspected that such an old heresy as the Worker Opposition was still attractive to some CPSU members. That such was the case can be deduced from Soviet sources which tend to support the validity of the *samizdat* document cited above. In addition to the 1981 polemic among Soviet ideologues over the relevance of old heresies there is the following passage in a *Pravda* (Jan. 12, 1982) review of the Lenin play "Thus We Shall Triumph," which had scenes devoted to the Russian political occurrences of 1921:

> "Vladimir Ilyich, why such vehemence?," asks a perplexed interlocutor who espouses the views of the "Worker Opposition." And then Lenin proposes that she and her like-thinkers ponder over why their idle talk about the independence of trade unions from the Party and State, and the transfer of management of the economy to them, is going on "to the accompaniment of a roar of ovation from the White Guards abroad." Is it necessary to say that any fetid regurgitation of the "Worker Opposition" conception is dear to the present-day bourgeois weepers over the destinies of the workers in the lands of socialism? Lenin saw in that conception "a negation of the very need for the Party." Practical actions along the lines urged by the "Worker Opposition," even if the recipes are updated, would lead straight into the swamp of counterrevolution and to the restoration of capitalism. Doesn't the foreign witches' sabbath around the current-day Polish events, for example, testify to that?

The second dimension of Politburo politics, alongside the innerparty regime, is the Party-people relationship. A picture of boundless popular loyalty is painted in the official slogan of "monolithic unity of Party and people." But it is belied by information that aside from large border-guard formations the Soviet leaders maintain about 260,000 MVD security troops, equipped with tanks and armored fighting vehicles.[6] The labor force inside the USSR was becoming somewhat more restive at the time of the Polish troubles, as testified to by the exiling of free trade-unionist Borisov, rumors of strikes in provincial cities, and materials in Soviet publications suggestive of poor worker morale. Brezhnev's "food program," too, was being developed as a "political" measure, or a strategem to promote harmony among the diverse social groups in the Soviet Union. Chernenko in an obvious bid for Party support of the food program even raised the specter of Polish-type unrest developing within the Soviet Union if basic human wants were not satisfied, asserting that "an incomplete or belated analysis of social interests, scorning of the interests of any class or group, and inability to find the socially necesary 'measure' of their combination is fraught with the danger of social tension, political and social-economic crisis."[7] Others in the Kremlin may have concluded that a Soviet citizenry so potentially restive as Chernenko intimated it to be would be less likely to challenge the authorities if the Polish mutineers were finally beaten down. Moreover, the relatively frequent attacks on Solidarity in Party media of the western borderlands (Ukraine, Belorussia and Baltics) during the crisis hinted at bureaucratic fear of political contagion from Poland in those areas which was bound to have been noticed in Moscow. Only after the demise of Solidarity were these anxieties starkly indicated by the remarks of Yefrem Sokolov, first secretary of the Brest regional CPSU committee in Belorussia:

> Additional measures to increase the class sharpness of the educational process were taken by Party organizations in connection with the aggravation of the situation in the Polish People's Republic. Not a single inhabitant of the region was indifferent to those events. . . . As the situation changed in the PPR a new task arose: to analyze and explain to people the objective and subjective reasons for the situation that had crystallized there, to expose the slanderous inventions of Western radio centers that were directed against Poland and our country. Many Brest residents have family ties with citizens of the Polish People's Republic. It must be taken into account that a large part of the region's inhabitants can watch the transmissions of Polish television. Until the introduction of martial law in that country there were transmissions of an anticommunist nature. They paralyzed the will of Poles in struggle for the ideals of the working class and did not give a class evaluation of the activities of the right-wing leaders of the "Solidarity" trade association and their KOS-KOR advisors. Historical facts were often distorted and there were unfriendly attacks on our country.
>
> The political carelessness and placidity which sounded from the lips of certain Polish leaders could not fail to trouble the region's inhabitants. In such conditions the regional Party organization conducted constant and efficient work to explain the situation that had taken shape (*Kommunist*, No. 4, 1984).

Lastly, Kremlin politics involves the art of conducting foreign affairs. The CPSU Central Committee session held in June 1980 adopted a resolution on foreign policy which was the gloomiest of its kind in almost 20 years. A wish to keep afloat the rickety ship of East-West detente was manifest, but great play was given to the danger of general war, need to strengthen defense capability and importance of vigilance (*Pravda*, June 24, 1980). In conjunction with the readiness to carry on with the battle for Afghanistan, this indicated an absence of felt urgency to reduce the number of outside enemies of the Soviet state. Any security-linked constraint on Moscow's freedom of action in Poland lay more in the timehonored aversion to a possible two-front war than a pressing requirement to avoid irritating the United States. Besides, the West had accepted every highhanded Soviet action in eastern Europe since 1945 and returned to business as usual with Moscow after it salved its conscience with the delivery of a diplomatic note.

In all, the conditioning factors of a Soviet decision on Poland—history, doctrine and current politics—gave small reason to believe that Moscow would allow the Polish revolt to run its course. The credibility of Brezhnev and his innermost circle was on the line in all major areas of governance. Allowance for an independent and democratic Poland would have been a renouncement of Russian state tradition and Soviet hegemonic ambition. The ruling groups inside the USSR would have deemed noninterference an exposure of Soviet power and prestige to menace from internal democrats, West German and Polish irredentists, and American psychological warriors. A hands-off-policy such as the Italian Communists urged upon their Soviet friends in 1981 was apt to have ignited a factional struggle within the CPSU that would have shaken it to the foundations. For at stake was not merely a question of the funds and functions of one or another bureaucratic department in Moscow, but the survival of the system of modified totalitarianism in Soviet Europe.

The only feasible alternatives of Soviet rulers in 1980–81 were to invade Poland and install an obedient Communist leadership there, or to conduct a political-military siege aimed at exhausting the aroused populace and changing the guard at Warsaw from the inside. Analysts had to weigh up the costs and benefits of each option for the Kremlin. The disadvantages of military assault were more apparent than the possible immediate gains. A flooding of Poland with Soviet and East German troops might have incensed the many patriots to commit acts of sabotage and terrorism that could have escalated in the wake of harsh counter-measures. Soviet soldiers would have been put in jeopardy of demoralization if compelled to perform police duties in a hostile-worker environment that was physically similar to that at home. Above all, direct intervention would have raised the prospect of Soviet strategists waging two unconventional wars at the same time, one in the mountains of Afghanistan and the other in Poland's forests. History may not repeat itself, but it was conceivable that a Soviet invasion would be followed by a guerrilla struggle like the one that tied down many Russian divisions after the 1905 Revolution. On the other hand, what if the East Germans were right and Polish authorities were so enfeebled that they could not be expected to check on their own the onset of Solidarity?

Unreliable as precedent is in a changing world, it had to be kept in mind because of the past preparation campaigns of Soviet leaders who were bent on taking major actions. A pattern of action preparation was to be found in materials predating the invasion of Czechoslovakia in 1968. The pattern was a definite cluster of signs that Kremlin leaders were: unusually stirred up; intent upon hitting at the source of their vexation; and eager to enlist the approval of broad circles for a knockout blow against the main enemy of the hour.

In 1968 one could observe in the columns of *Pravda* from July 7 through August 20 a series of developments in treatment of the Czecho-slovak crisis which, taken in their entirety, amounted to something new under the Russian sun. The fresh wrinkles were: (1) reports of public meetings within the USSR expressing wrathful indignation over attacks on the socialist system and leading role of the Communist Party in Dubcek's realm; (2) feature articles by the stellar commentator of *Pravda* which denounced slippage towards political pluralism as the herald of capitalist restoration; (3) allegations of a threat to official life and property from anti-Communists; and (4) notice of Warsaw Pact military exercises and conferences involving high-level defense and political figures.

This distinctive cluster of facts was not visible on the eve of the invasion-of-Poland scares in December 1980 and April 1981. It evolved from early in September 1981 and became clear-cut after Jaruzelski's advent to the key Party job in Warsaw. This time, the network of signs did not point to the likelihood of Soviet invasion. So much was evident from the absence of military deployments of the kind that aroused high concern in winter 1980 and spring 1981. The speeches of Jaruzelski and PUWP resolutions gave one to understand that martial law was the weapon most likely to be used if a decision was made to chastise the contumacy in Poland.

It may have been objected that the coincidence of Soviet political-propaganda behavior in 1968 and 1981 could legitimately be dismissed as nothing more than that. Analogy, the argument may have gone, could not be drawn on the basis of a single example. A theory of happenstance, however, would have been at odds with the generally recognized mechanical nature of Soviet character. The spontaneity and individuality which often marks the deportment of a politician or military man in the Western democracies is a rarity in the official conduct of his Soviet opposite number. The same is true of Moscow's propagandists and their directors. Hence, a tone of "crossing the Rubicon" was conveyed by the anti-Solidarity rallies held at factories throughout the Soviet Union in September 1981. Such well-staged displays of popular anger had ac-companied historic purges of Moscow luminaries with most of the victims accused of seeking to resurrect the old regime. The very same charge of striving to restore capitalism was leveled against Poland's Solidarity leaders at the Soviet mass meetings and in the "A. Petrov" commentary which followed in *Pravda*. It was reasonable to draw a tentative inference that Kremlin chiefs had become unafraid of embarrassment over the future chain of circumstances in Poland, and were confident that a basic situational change was in the works. The same certainty that Jaruzelski unlike Kania before him would "turn the course of events" enabled the Soviet opinion-manipulators to give free rein to their imagination and to paint lurid images of anticommunist excesses in Poland. Against this background of a pulling of the stops on the propaganda scene, one could further hypothesize that new parleys of Soviet and allied security officials were devoted to the operational details of a great decision to re-bind Polish society.

Significantly, that verdict was coupled with a sign of realignment inside the Soviet leadership. Party Secretary Chernenko, a non-risktaker on the Polish question, to judge from his statements, was upstaged by Defense Minister Ustinov, whose comparable rhetoric grew progressively shriller, and by KGB chairman Andropov, whose staff had shown a strong authoritarian bent. This was the last in a long string of political anomalies that were relatable to Poland as Moscow's top priority issue, and it served to underscore the analytical necessity of keeping track of Soviet dynastics along with propaganda fluctuations.

The failure of most analysts of Soviet affairs to anticipate Kremlin behavior in episodes such as the fall of Khrushchev, invasion of Czechoslovakia and Polish martial law-declaration has not helped to inspire confidence in them as a group. If the present study has any practical usefulness it may be to suggest to colleagues that more of our energies must be invested in reading the Soviet press along the rigorous lines that Alexander L. George once recommended to investigators of politics around the world. If that were done, the volume of foreign "surprises" for U.S. policymakers might be diminished in the years ahead.

NOTES

1. See, e.g., Jerry F. Hough, "The Soviet System, Petrification or Pluralism?," *Problems of Communism* (March–April 1972), pp. 25–45; George W. Breslauer, "Political Succession and the Soviet Policy Agenda," *Problems of Communism* (May–June 1980), pp. 34–52; and "Hard-Line Fallacies." By Stephen F. Cohen. *New York Times*, Aug. 22, 1980.

2. "Poland and the Worst-Case Scenario." By Abraham Brumberg. *New York Times*, Feb. 19, 1981.

3. The cited article by Pollack and Bugajski in *Encounter*, Jan. 1981 is persuasive on the topic of bureaucratic obstructionism, even though necessarily inconclusive.

4. "The Distribution of Political Forces in the Communist Party of the Soviet Union." By S. Razumny. No date or place of origin; possible: Moscow, mid-1969. Radio Liberty *samizdat* document RLR No. 570. Munich: 1971, p. 7.

5. Edward Hallett Carr, *A History of Soviet Russia. The Bolshevik Revolution 1917–1923* (The Macmillan Company, NY, 1951), Vol. One, pp. 196–197.

6. *The Military Balance*, p. 12.

7. *Kommunist*, No. 13, 1981.

Appendix 1

HIGH-CRISIS HEADINGS IN *PRAVDA*
("SITUATION IN POLAND" OR "EVENTS IN POLAND")

1980

AUGUST: 28, 29
SEPTEMBER: 2, 3, 4, 5
OCTOBER: ----------
NOVEMBER: 19, 25, 26, 27, 28, 29
DECEMBER: ----------

1981

JANUARY: 10, 11, 21, 30
FEBRUARY: 1, 2, 3, 6, 7, 8
MARCH: 22, 27, 28, 29, 30
APRIL: 3, 4, 8, 19, 26, 29
MAY: ----------
JUNE: 2, 5, 6, 17, 19, 20, 26, 29, 30
JULY: 1
AUGUST: 4, 6, 7, 21, 25, 28, 29
SEPTEMBER: 1, 3, 4, 12, 15, 16, 17, 20, 22, 23, 24, 25, 27, 29, 30
OCTOBER: 1, 2, 3, 4, 6, 7, 8, 9, 10, 11, 26, 28
NOVEMBER: 11, 12, 20, 26
DECEMBER: 3, 4, 5, 8, 9, 10, 11, 12, 13

Appendix 2

1980

2 July– 14 August	Polish workers went on strike to protest increased meat prices.
1–2 August	Communique of Brezhnev-Gierek meeting in Crimea ignored the Polish strikes.
15 August	TASS announced Warsaw Pact maneuvers in the Baltic region and G.D.R. Soviet reservists were called up during the month.
20 August	*Pravda* summary of a Gierek speech broke Soviet media silence on Polish labor unrest and stressed the resolve of Polish rulers.
26 August	Gierek's self-criticism omitted from *Pravda* version of his speech on Polish TV.
28 August	Soviet media reported Polish Government-labor talks on Baltic coast.
31 August	Gus Hall in *Pravda* blamed Polish strikes on leadership "weaknesses."
1 September	*Pravda* article by "A. Petrov" tacitly criticized the Gdansk accords.
2 September	Lech Walesa assailed by Moscow TV as "one of the members of an opposition group."
6 September	*Pravda* rejected use of "fist in a dispute over principle," urged "caution and prudence . . . ability to . . . keep cool in the most critical situations."

8 September	40,000 Warsaw Pact troops began 4-day maneuvers in the G.D.R.
8 September	Kania inaugural in *Pravda* omitted his criticism of Fuehrerprinzip. Also toned down was his readiness for political debate and reform.
10–11 September	Polish Politburo member and Deputy Premier Jagielski visited Moscow, met Suslov and Brezhnev. Soviet economic aid committed to Poland.
18 September	Western intelligence reportedly detected signs of unusual military activity in the G.D.R. and USSR.
20 September	"A. Petrov" in *Pravda* warned that anticommunist subversion would increase in Poland as the situation there became more stable.
23 September	Radio Free Europe was sending orders to antisocialist elements in Poland, according to V. Bolshakov in *Pravda*.
25 September	Lenin's attack on advocates of free trade unions under socialism was stressed by Prof. G. Alekseyev in *Pravda*.
27 September	"A. Petrov" of *Pravda* saw a division of "patriots" and "enemies" among Poles.
7 October	*Pravda* version of Kania's report to the Polish Central Committee detailed internal failings like those in USSR but muted the reformist policy proposals.
19 October	Romanian Party head Ceausescu's confidence in the PUWP reported by *Pravda*.
21 October	Brezhnev addressed the CPSU Central Committee Plenum. A full text was not released and the summary ignored Poland.
30 October	TASS Statement on Soviet-Polish summit in Kremlin. Brezhnev voiced confidence in Poles and Kania joined him in attack on Western meddling.
5, 21, 23 November	Gen. Moczar, Polish symbol of law and order, given favorable publicity in *Pravda*.
6 November	Soviet Premier Tikhonov disregarded Poland in his leadership report for Bolshevik Revolution day.
7 November	Kania was disdainfully referred to as Party *"first"* rather than *"First"* secretary in *Pravda*.
10 November	Joint Soviet-Polish army maneuvers noted by *Pravda*

as Solidarity deadline of November 12 for general strike approaches. Signs of high-level meetings at Soviet Embassy in Warsaw, probably over Solidarity legalization dispute.

19 November *Pravda* reported that PUWP meetings were calling for "urgent measures" to ensure the "full restoration" of the Party's "leading role and authority."

21 November CPSU Politburo member and Secretary Chernenko attacked "capitulationists" and quoted Lenin against free trade unions under socialism, in *Kommunist* article.

24 November TASS warned that a general strike on Polish railways could disrupt land communications through Poland.

26 November Solidarity's theft of official secrets hinted in muted *Pravda* account of the union's demand for curbing the State security service. Another item hit at the Polish Government for neglecting pro-regime unions.

28 November *Pravda* cited Polish war veterans' demand for "a halt to anarchy." In the paper's theory article, a "timely response" was urged to actions of "anti-socialist forces."

28 November Dissident leader Kuron in Warsaw warned strikers of the danger of Soviet military intervention.

30 November *Pravda* softened a Czechoslovak press commentary on Poland.

1–5 December Soviet troop activity in western military districts was reportedly stepped up and some reserves mobilized.

1 December Warsaw Radio announced a Soviet promise of $1.3 billion aid package.

2 December Romanian Foreign Minister Andrei flew to Moscow for an unscheduled meeting with Brezhnev.

3 December *Pravda* summarized at length Kania's report to the Polish Central Committee. The tough passages were reprinted and innovative ones bowdlerized.

5 December Warsaw Pact emergency summit in Moscow. Statement hinted that Polish leaders should be given more time to reassert their authority.

5 December	Alarmist lines in the Polish Central Committee's appeal to the nation were not in the *Pravda* version. But a "grave threat" to internal stability was claimed in the communique of the Polish Defense Ministry's Military Council, also cited in *Pravda*.
5–7 December	White House vigil on Poland after intelligence reports warned of impending Soviet armed intervention in Poland.
8 December	Moscow Radio broadcast a TASS cable from Warsaw stating that Solidarity had begun to move against Party and management officials. The Soviet press did not run this item, later denied by Polish officials and Solidarity sources.
10 December	Soviet Politburo member and Defense Minister Ustinov told military Communists that reactionaries were trying to hurt Poland.
12 December	*Pravda*'s brief text of a CPSU Politburo resolution on results of the 5 December Warsaw Pact summit lacked a "political evaluation," suggesting leadership dissension.
18 December	"A. Petrov" told *Pravda* readers that NATO was eager to launch military intervention in Poland.
18 and 28 December	*Kommunist* and *Pravda* commentaries on Poland diverged on whether the social conflicts there were both "antagonistic and nonantagonistic," that is, if regime-Solidarity clash was inexorable.
19 December	Fidel Castro cited by *Pravda* on the "explosively dangerous situation around Poland" and need to avoid "concessions" to "the class enemy."
26 December	Polish Foreign Minister Czyrek visited Moscow and met with Brezhnev, who voiced confidence in the PUWP.
26 December	*Pravda* theory article on trade unions held that strikes in Poland benefited antisocialist elements.
30 December	*Pravda* and *Izvestiya*'s weekly magazine *Nedelya* differed on the socio-political climate in Poland.

1981

| 9 January | Gromyko in the CPSU journal *Kommunist* seconded Brezhnev's confidence-in-Poland line. |

13 January	Marshal Kulikov was received by Kania and Premier Pinkowski. Gen. Jaruzelski took part in the talks.
13–20 January	Zamyatin-led delegation visited Poland and discussed Party control of media.
29 January	*Pravda* neutrally cited the French President on the wisdom of non-intervention by all powers vis-à-vis Poland.
7 February	Solidarity was instigating anti-Party violence and harassment, according to *Pravda*.
8, 10 February	U.S. intelligence sources said Soviet troops alerted for crisis in December (26 divisions) remained in a high state of readiness on Poland's border.
11 February	*Oktyabr* ran an article by old ideologue Bugayev linking Polish events with those in Hungary 1956 and Czechoslovakia 1968.
12 February	*Pravda Ukrainy* reported a harsh indirect criticism of Solidarity at the Ukraine Party Congress.
17 February	New Polish Premier Gen. Jaruzelski met with Warsaw Pact ambassadors to Poland.
23 February	Brezhnev Report at 26th CPSU Congress ignored Kania's "line of agreement" formula and vowed support of the weakened Polish regime.
24 February	Kania reassured the Soviet Party Congress that Polish leaders had both patience and resolve.
February	Soviet Army divisions along the Polish borders were reportedly put on a much lower state of alert.
4 March	Soviet-Polish summit held in Moscow. PUWP was to "turn the course of events" and the doctrine of limited sovereignty was reaffirmed.
8, 13, 14 March	*Pravda* hit at Solidarity for creating armed bands, sheltering renegades, taking C.I.A. funds, and backing the legal defense of right-wing dissident Mosczulski.
9 March	Soviet trade union chairman Shibayev stated in *Kommunist* that trade unions under socialism must recognize the Communist Party's leading role.
11 March	Warsaw Pact command-staff exercise in Poland and elsewhere scheduled for second half of March, *Pravda* announced.

19 March	PAP reported Warsaw Pact "Soyuz-81" maneuvers in Poland, G.D.R., USSR and Czechoslovakia.
20 March	One day after Polish police attacked protestors in Bydgoszcz, a *Pravda* editorial cited Brezhnev's harsh rhetoric about Poland at the CPSU Congress.
22 March	Soviet press disarray on whether Walesa made an "instigatory" statement in Bydgoszcz.
22 March	*Pravda* cited without criticism the West German Foreign Minister's praise of the Polish leader's nonviolent internal course.
23 March	CPSU Secretary Ponomarev in *Kommunist* deplored the idea of power-sharing in a socialist society.
26–29 March	*Pravda* criticized Solidarity and Polish media for gravely disrupting public order. A rare personal criticism of Walesa surfaced on the 27th.
26 March	USSR Defense Ministry journal *Voyennyy Vestnik* compared the Polish events to those in Czechoslovakia 1968.
29 March	U.S. State Department reported signs of Soviet military moves for possible armed intervention in Poland.
30 March	Unsuccessful challenge to Kania by hardliners Grabski and Olszowski concealed in TASS report of Polish Central Committee session.
2 April	*Pravda* alleged PUWP tolerance of anti-Soviet seminar at Warsaw University.
3 April	Bydgoszcz Solidarity leader Rulewski accused of a criminal past and pro-Nazi family ties in *Pravda*.
3 and 4 April	U.S. media cited intelligence sources to effect that Soviet military was upgrading its capability for rapid action against Poland.
4 April	Soviet press discordance on the chances of a Polish solution to Poland's crisis.
5 April	*Izvestiya* claimed Solidarity "terror" and lack of effective regime resistance to "creeping counter-revolution."
7 April	Brezhnev voiced qualified confidence in Polish leaders during a speech to the Czechoslovak Party Congress.
7 April	TASS announced the end of Warsaw Pact exercises.

7 April	U.S. State Department reported unusual levels of Warsaw Pact military activity, increases in Soviet troops near Poland, the establishment of a Soviet communications and command network, and supply stockpiles in Poland.
13 and 16 April	*Pravda* informed that at the East German Party Congress Suslov ignored Poland while Bulgarian guest speaker Doynov gave the confidence-in-Poland line.
15 April	Speakers at a meeting in Warsaw cemetery, *Pravda* claimed, accused the Soviets of massacre of Polish officers during World War II.
22 April	Chernenko in Lenin Day report hit at Western meddling in Poland and aired trust in PUWP to defend socialism.
23 April	Suslov made a surprise visit to Warsaw and reportedly clashed with Polish leaders over their internal policies.
24 April	CPSU Secretary Rusakov made a highly nuanced speech on Polish events at a Moscow ideology conference.
26 April	*Pravda* attacked efforts from below to democratize the Polish Party.
30 April	Kania's report to Polish Central Committee meeting as summarized in *Pravda* omitted pro-democracy and pro-Solidarity statements.
4 May	*Pravda* ran letters from war veterans expressing concern about preparations for the special PUWP Congress due in July.
4 May	Western military sources reported that Soviet troops in southeast Poland were building-up military communications.
12–16 May	Delegation of USSR State Committee for Television and Radio Broadcasting led by Committee chairman Lapin visited Poland.
13 May	*Pravda* and *Literaturnaya Gazeta* complained about liberalism on the Polish cultural scene.
18–23 May	CPSU Secretariat delegation led by Petrovichev visited Poland and met with Kania.
30 May	Marshal Kulikov met with Kania and Jaruzelski in Warsaw.

2 June	*Pravda* favorably cited an attack on Polish Politburo guidelines for the special Party Congress by the hardline Katowice Party Forum.
5 June	CPSU Central Committee Letter to Polish Central Committee criticized Kania and Jaruzelski by name for pursuing a "policy of concession and compromise." Polish leadership needed "revolutionary will" to "reverse the course of events."
11 June	Marshal Bagramyan in *Znamya* recalled the Red Army's low-damage campaign to liberate Poland in 1944.
12 June	*Pravda* ran the Kremlin Letter to Warsaw and failed to summarize Kania's essentially moderate speech to the Polish Central Committee session held 9–10 June.
20 June	Zamyatin on Moscow TV saw the Polish situation as worsening and urged vigorous corrective measures.
22 June	Marshal Kulikov in *Red Star* assailed "counterrevolutionary forces" in Poland.
23–24 June	USSR Supreme Soviet met without the usual preliminary meeting of the CPSU Central Committee.
25 June	*Pravda* and *Red Star* differed on the gravity of Polish events in comment on a World War II anniversary.
25 June	In contrast to Zamyatin on 20 June, *Agitator* claimed that Polish leaders were implementing resolution of their 9–10 June Plenum and positive results were a cause for rejoicing.
25, 29, 30 June	Polish media reported Polish-Soviet military exercises and the East German press reported military maneuvers in G.D.R.
3–5 July	Gromyko met with Polish leaders in Warsaw and heard about the PUWP Congress preparations. The limited sovereignty doctrine was restated in communique.
11 July	*Pravda* gave far more coverage to a four-hour strike of Polish airlines workers than a Polish Central Committee session recommiting PUWP to democratize itself.

15 July	*Pravda* ran Kania's report and Soviet Politburo member Grishin's speech to the Polish Party Congress. Reformist and nationalist lines omitted from Kania text. Grishin warned against rejection of the Soviet model of governance.
19 July	Brezhnev's congratulatory message to Kania on occasion of his re-election as Party head did not laud him.
19 July	Western subversion against Poland was "proven" by a Czechoslovak intelligence officer at a press conference in Prague reported by *Pravda*.
21 July	*Pravda* did not list the names of Polish Politburo and Secretariat members elected by the new Polish Central Committee.
22 July	*Pravda* showed Grishin in his Warsaw speech more uncertain about Polish leaders' competence than were colleagues who greeted the same leaders in connection with their national day.
25 July	Defense Minister Ustinov in a *Pravda* article cited the Polish events as an example of "direct threat to the security of the USSR and its allies."
31 July	*Pravda* version of PUWP Congress resolution edited to accent orthodoxy, disregarding criticism of systemic ills and remedial formulas.
31 July	*Pravda* theory article by *Kommunist* editor Kosolapov rebuked Communists blind to danger in Poland and portrayed Walesa as a great hope of anti-Communists in the West.
5 August	*Pravda* reported anti-regime street demonstrations in Warsaw.
7 August	The last article by *Pravda*'s Warsaw correspondent about PUWP cell activities until imposition of martial law in December.
7 August	Polish leaders reportedly got letters from Soviet, East German and Czechoslovak leaders urging reassertion of authority and offering technical assistance for that purpose.
8 August	Marshal Kulikov met with Jaruzelski in Warsaw.

13–14 August	*Pravda* coverage of Polish Central Committee meeting held on August 11. Kania's readiness to discuss change of the constitution toward democracy was ignored.
14 August	*Pravda* announced Soviet military maneuvers led by Defense Minister Ustinov for 4–12 September, or during Solidarity Congress's first stage.
16 August	Communique of Soviet-Polish summit in Crimea featured by *Pravda*. Brezhnev withheld an expression of confidence in Polish leaders.
31 August– 3 September	Gen. Yepishev, chief of the Soviet Armed Forces' Main Political Directorate, visited Poland, met with Kania and Jaruzelski.
1 September	*Pravda* quoted Jaruzelski's irritation over social unrest during speech at military college: "Enough of this disintegration!"
4–12 September	USSR hosted "Zapad-81" military exercises.
5 September	TASS reported Jaruzelski among allied military leaders at Ustinov's war-games headquarters in Belorussia.
7 September	CPSU Secretariat official Rakhmanin in *Voprosy Istorii KPSS* voiced confidence that PUWP leaders could solve their internal problems.
8 September	Unlike *Voprosy Istorii KPSS* article by Rakhmanin, one by V. Chernyshev in *Partiynaya Zhizn* ignored Kania and Jaruzelski, as well as the confidence-in-Poles line, and warned of NATO plans to seize Polish territory.
12, 13, 19, 22, 24 September	*Pravda* reported factory meetings in USSR voiced extreme anger over Solidarity Congress (5–10 September). Polish workers were exhorted to throw false friends onto "the refuse heap of history."
19 September	*Pravda* summarized a CPSU Central Committee and USSR Government Statement given to Kania and Jaruzelski by Soviet ambassador Aristov. An immediate halt to anti-Sovietism in Poland was demanded.
22 September	Jaruzelski received Gen. Gribkov, Chief of Staff of the Warsaw Pact Joint Armed Forces.

22 September	Soviet Gosplan chief Baybakov began a 5-day visit to Poland and reportedly threatened to curtail raw material exports to Poland if its economic slump continued.
22–25 September	*Pravda* denounced Solidarity as a facist-style body with close Church ties and nearing a takeover of State power.
29 September– 11 October	*Pravda* comment on Solidarity Congress (27 September–8 October). Union activists were said to be anticipating "martial law and outside intervention."
13 October	TASS announced that a Polish Central Committee meeting would open on 16 October.
13 October	"A. Petrov" in *Pravda* ridiculed the Kania-linked slogan of "socialist renewal" and urged "effective rebuff to counterrevolution" in Poland. The limited sovereignty (Brezhnev) doctrine was reiterated.
14 October	TASS reported a Warsaw regional PUWP plenum which accused Solidarity of seeking confrontation and political dominance, using regime mistakes; Polish authorities were hit for lack of consistency and effectiveness. Decisive steps were needed to guard socialism.
15 October	*Pravda* text of Suslov speech at ideology conference in Moscow assured that Polish Communists could rely on Soviet support in struggle with counter-revolutionary forces.
18–20 October	*Pravda* coverage of 16–18 October Polish Central Committee session. Kania's resignation was accepted and Jaruzelski elected to head the PUWP. Jaruzelski's speech was the only one reported at length in *Pravda*, along with the plenum's stiff resolution.
19 October	Brezhnev's cable of congratulations to Jaruzelski expressed trust that at "this historic moment" he would use his "great prestige" to roll back "encroachments of counterrevolution."
10 October	Marshal Kulikov met with G.D.R. Party leader Honecker in East Berlin.
22 October	USSR Interior Minister Army Gen. Shchelokov met with Honecker in East Berlin.

27 October	*Partiynaya Zhizn* alleged "ransackings of the premises of State bodies" throughout Poland.
30 October	*Pravda* omitted from its version of Jaruzelski's speech to the Polish Central Committee his professed intent to broaden the Government's coalition dimension.
4 November	Jaruzelski, Walesa and Primate Glemp held an unprecedented summit. *Pravda* ignored the event.
5 November	*Pravda* ran the Statement of a Soviet bloc ideology conference, which backed PUWP's "struggle against the antipeople forces of counterrevolution and anarchy."
6 November	Ustinov stressed in his report for Bolshevik Revolution day that counterrevolutionaries would not win in Poland and resolve was growing there to rebuff antisocialist forces.
14 November	*Pravda* review of readers' letters hinted impatience with toleration of Solidarity by the Polish regime.
16 November	Brezhnev spoke to the CPSU Central Committee Plenum. A summary ignored Poland.
20 November	*Pravda* began a series of attacks on Solidarity for campaigning to evict Party committees from industrial works.
23 November	Ustinov and Andropov outranked Chernenko in a *Pravda* photograph with top leadership line-up. Chernenko that same day made a Soviet election speech and referred to Poland without mentioning "crisis," "counterrevolutionaries" or "antisocialist forces."
25 November	Marshal Kulikov met with Jaruzelski in Warsaw.
4, 7, 9, 10, 12, 13 December	*Pravda* directly attacked Walesa as a political extremist.
7 December	*Kommunist* editorial linked events in Hungary 1956 and Czechoslovakia 1968 with those in Poland. "Acute class struggle" was said to be raging among Poles. Czechoslovak Party Secretary Bilak in an article for Brezhnev's 75th birthday quoted him on the need to "smash and destroy" counterrevolution.
10 December	*Pravda* ran a TASS item without dateline accusing Solidarity of arming itself for a coup and giving specific dates on which anti-regime actions would be undertaken (17 and 20 Dec.). Soviet commu-

nication lines through Poland were allegedly tar-getted by "counterrevolutionaries." Also, a *Pravda* "historical" article asserted the necessity of re-pressing internal foes of socialism.

13 December   Radio Moscow reported a state of emergency was invoked in Poland. Soviet media were silent on Marshal Kulikov's reported presence in Poland.

Index